D0758726

Quaker Experiences in International Conciliation

Quaker Experiences
in International Conciliation

C. H. Mike Yarrow

New Haven and London   Yale University Press   1978

Published with assistance from the Louis Stern Memorial
Fund.

Designed by Thos. Whitridge and set in
IBM Baskerville type.
Printed in the United States of America by
The Murray Printing Co., Westford, Mass.

Published in Great Britain, Europe, Africa, and
Asia (except Japan) by Yale University Press, Ltd.,
London. Distributed in Australia and New Zealand by
Book & Film Services, Artarmon, N.S.W., Australia;
and in Japan by Harper & Row, Publishers,
Tokyo Office.

Library of Congress Cataloging in Publication Data

Yarrow, C. H. Mike.
    Quaker experiences in international conciliation.

    Includes bibliographical references and index.
    1. Peace.   2. Friends, Society of, and world
politics.   3. Mediation, International.   4. Peace—
Research.   5. International relief.
I. Title.
JX1952.Y36   327'.172'0904   78-7415
ISBN 0-300-02260-3

To Margarethe Lachmund,
    Embodiment of Quaker Conciliation

Contents

Foreword

In the early 1920s Lewis Fry Richardson embarked on a program of research that occupied him until his death in 1953. The central theme of his investigations was the causes of wars. A Quaker and a pacifist, Richardson pursued this inquiry for somewhat the same motives as someone appalled by physical suffering might search for the causes of disease.

Besides being a pacifist, Richardson was also a scientist. He had a commitment to truth and the specific conception of truth that characterizes the scientist's philosophical outlook. The scientist is concerned not so much with Truth in the abstract as with the truth of specific assertions. The scientist always asks two questions of anyone who makes an assertion: "What do you mean?" and "How do you know?" To answer these questions to the satisfaction of the scientist, one must be able to say *what to observe* and what the *results* of the observations must be to corroborate the truth of the assertion in question.

This criterion of truth—the verifiability criterion—is generally understood to be the basis of the scientific outlook. Less widely understood is the falsifiability criterion. That is, one must be able to say what the results of observations should be to refute the assertion.

Take the assertion "Wars are caused by wickedness." To make sense of the assertion the scientist must first ascertain whether the implied "cause" is a necessary condition of war, a sufficient condition, or both. If it is meant as a necessary condition, the assertion can be paraphrased, "If people were not wicked, wars would not occur." If it is meant as a sufficient condition, it implies that wars will always occur as long as men are wicked. The two assertions are quite different. Once this point is clarified, however, the assertion is not yet scientifically meaningful. One must specify observable criteria of wickedness and also what should be observed to either refute or support the assertion. Since it would be practically impossible to satisfy all these criteria in the above judgment about the causes of wars, a scientist qua scientist would not be interested in the assertion.

Corroboration of a scientific assertion involves the realization of predictions implied by it. For this reason, scientific assertions are expected to conform to a conditional format: "If so . . . then so . . ." or else "Not so . . . unless so. . . ." When a scientist speaks of sufficient causes, he means the "if so" part; when he speaks of necessary causes, he means the "unless so" part; when he speaks of effects, he speaks of the "then so" part.

If the conditions comprising the causes of an event were completely known and exactly realizable, the event in question would be completely predictable. Precise predictability, however, is achieved only in narrow sectors of the exact sciences. In situations involving human behavior, complete predictability cannot be expected and, in the opinion of many scientists and perhaps most laymen, such predictability is in principle impossible. Human beings are often said to be endowed with "free will," and for this reason their actions cannot be assumed to be causally determined in the way physical events are determined.

Richardson thought otherwise. His special field of competence was meteorology. In his day, before electronic computers, prediction of weather was notoriously difficult. Like any physical scientist, however, Richardson was convinced that the erratic "behavior" of weather is only apparent. The impression stems from the crudeness of our observations and the inadequacy of existing mathematical methods to deal with the complexities of atmospheric phenomena. Ultimately, these phenomena, like any other physical phenomena, are governed by known physical laws, and their predictability can be a matter of degree. It can be improved as our techniques of observation and our mathematical skills increase. In fact, weather prediction has become much more reliable as the density of weather stations has increased and as rapid computations by electronic computers has become possible.

It is not necessary to assume strictly physical determinants of human behavior to believe that it is at least to some degree predictable. In attempting to predict events generated by human behavior, we often resort to statistical predictability. While the actions of the individual may appear erratic, events generated by masses of people often exhibit regularities. If they did not, insurance companies could not operate and, in general, no social planning would be possible. For all such planning, from economic policies to traffic engineering, is predicated on at least statistical predictability of the massive effects generated by the actions of many individuals.

It was in this spirit that Richardson undertook his studies on the causes of wars. Most of his work was published posthumously in two books, *Statistics of Deadly Quarrels* and *Arms and Insecurity*.[1] In the first, Richardson searches for the statistical correlates of wars and other outbursts of violence; in the second, he attempts to develop a mathematical theory of arms races, which he supposed to be propelled by escalating mutual stimulation.

These approaches established what is sometimes called the

---

1. Lewis F. Richardson, *Statistics of Deadly Quarrels* (London: Stevens and Sons, 1960) and *Arms and Insecurity* (London: Stevens and Sons, 1960).

Richardsonian tradition in peace research. To assess the contribution of this tradition to the cause of peace, it is less important to evaluate it on purely scientific grounds than to examine the fundamental assumptions upon which its justification rests.

Of his mathematical theories of arms races, Richardson wrote, "The equations are merely descriptions of what people would do if they did not stop to think." In other words, no claim is made that the equations predict the inevitable course of an arms race. They only specify what will occur *unless* some corrective action is taken. The rationale of the Richardsonian tradition in peace research is based on this distinction between what is bound to happen and what is likely to happen unless. . . . There is ample room for human intervention, for "free will," as it were. In fact, the entire philosophy of applied science rests on this amalgam of determinism and free choice. As Engels wrote, "Freedom is the recognition of necessity." Knowledge of causes of physical events enables us to utilize the forces of nature to satisfy our needs. Knowledge of the causes of diseases enables man to control, avoid, cure, or eradicate them.

It is tempting to conclude that reliable knowledge about the causes of wars will enable man to avoid them or stop them or to eradicate war altogether. Thus, the Richardsonian tradition is embodied in the assumption that most global misfortunes, including wars, stem largely, perhaps even mainly, from ignorance. The "international weather," being the result of policies, perceptions, and interactions of people, could be controlled if its determinants were sufficiently well known. Peace research based on this assumption is concerned with revealing the determinants (or, at least, the statistical correlates) of war. Peace action, in this view, consists of modifying policies, perceptions, and interactions in ways calculated to make the incidence of wars less likely and the establishment of a peaceful global community more likely.

In a way, the often drawn analogy between peace research and medical research is defensible. If war is conceived as a "disease," endemic in the international system, which frequently explodes into an acute stage or an epidemic, there is a good case for directing all-out effort toward learning its etiology and epidemiology in the hope of eventually learning to control or eliminate this disease.

The analogy fails, however, on the level of applying knowledge to organized action. In applying knowledge produced by medical research, there are no insuperable problems. Institutions empowered to translate such knowledge into action already exist: the medical profession, hospitals, a pharmaceutical industry, departments of public health, etc. Let a new drug demonstrably effective against leukemia be discovered, and within months this knowledge will be put to work to save thousands of lives. But where are the institutions ready, willing, and (most important) *empowered* to translate new findings about the causes of wars into appropriate action, no matter how strongly these findings may be supported by scientific evidence?

With regard to some presumed (but by no means scientifically demonstrated) causes of wars, some such institutions may be said to exist. Some United Nations agencies, international nongovernment and government organizations, and even some governmental agencies have been engaged in building an "infrastructure" for peace: cultural exchanges, worldwide aid to impoverished countries, arms control and disarmament agencies, etc. In one important respect, however, the existing organizations and agencies are all but powerless to attack what may be the central source of war: the war-making institutions, that is, the military establishments and *their* infrastructure, the arms industry, the world armament trade, the war research institutes, and so on. The dominant conception of war within the war profession and its entourage is not that of a disease to be controlled or eradicated but that of a means to an end. In Clausewitz's immortal definition, "War is the continuation of politics by other means."

Even if this definition can be shown to be entirely inappropriate in the age of megadeath technology (what defensible ends can be served by a global nuclear war?), the war-making institutions do not immediately appear obsolete. For the professions created by these institutions are no longer committed to the traditional *goals* of war making. They are committed to the *process* of preparing, organizing, and conducting war. And this professional commitment is as absorbing and ego-building as the commitment of the dedicated physician or medical researcher, who takes pride in contributing to advances in the "state of the art." General William C. Westmoreland expressed this pride in his glowing picture of the future:

> On the battlefield of the future, enemy forces will be located, tracked and targeted almost instantaneously through the use of data links, computer assisted intelligence evaluation, and automated fire control. With first round kill probabilities approaching certainty, and with surveillance devices that can continually track the enemy, the need for large forces to fix the opposition physically will be less important. . . .
>
> Hundreds of years were required to achieve the mobility of the armored division. A little over two decades later we had the airmobile division. With cooperative effort, no more than 10 years separate us from the automated battlefield.[2]

"Wars begin in the minds of men," says the Preamble to the UNESCO Charter. In their peace action projects, such as those described in this book, the Quakers are guided

_____

2. Quoted in Paul Dickson, *Think Tanks* (New York: Atheneum, 1971), p. 169.

by this assumption. The "diagnosis" is indisputable, but there are at least two ways of interpreting it. The prevalent interpretation is that the minds of men are vulnerable to "infections" in the form of prejudices, race hatred, xenophobia, destructive impulses generated by frustrations, and so on; and that these feelings produce the pressures that erupt in the massive violence of war. Another way of seeing war as beginning "in the minds of men" is by examining the now prevalent attitudes within the war making institutions. There fear and hatred are no longer necessary components of warmaking mentality. In bygone ages, wars were fought by warriors, men endowed with great courage and often with the brutal disposition required for killing fellow men. Neither courage nor cruelty nor even the instinct of self-preservation are required to motivate organized efforts to "improve" megadeath weapons, to plan effective ways of utilizing them, or to design the "automated battlefield," the utopian dream of the contemporary technology-worshipping military professional and his scientist-aides. The mass exterminations carried out by the Nazis were predicated on dehumanizing the victims, but the victims of modern war need not even be dehumanized. Their existence can be simply ignored. The chain of organized action from the typing of an order to the pressing of the Button can be completely disengaged from the envisaged effects of these actions on human beings. The links in that chain of action can be performed by "normal" people, gentle, reasonable, and kind in their personal lives.

In their peace actions, the Quakers are guided by the first interpretation of the principle "Wars begin in the minds of men." To assess their work fairly, the limitation of this orientation must be recognized at the outset. Inducing people on one side of a conflict to perceive the people on the other side as human may to some extent constrain the pressures for war generated by fear, hatred, and prejudices; but it is difficult to see the relevance of these distortions of human per-

ceptions to the other fountainheads of war, namely global
politics conceived and conducted as a game of strategy and
the self-propelling dynamics of war technology. It seems that
Richardson's equations can describe what happens when
people do stop to think, as long as they think in strategic
rather than in human terms.

Once this limitation is kept in mind, the solid positive
contributions of the peace actions undertaken by the Quakers
can be evaluated from a proper perspective. To begin with,
the situations they select (at least the three described in this
book) are those where personal orientations of the decision
makers, predicated on internalized or rationalized images,
presuppositions, and ideological commitments were clearly
integral components of the conflicts. Moreover, in all three
situations described, barriers to direct communication erected
by political-strategic aspects of conflicts were a formidable
obstacle to conflict resolution. In these specific situations, the
Quakers' conception of conflict resolution—with its emphasis
on providing an outlet for pent-up grievances by attentive
listening, on bridging the communication chasm, and on
avoiding the harsh glare of reaction-triggering publicity, as
well as their centuries of experience in peacemaking—have
made their efforts appear as significant inputs to the cause of
peace.

Nevertheless, in each case, two questions arise that are un-
avoidable in our age, when enlightened thought is at least to
some extent guided by respect for scientific criteria of truth:
How can the actual effectiveness of this work be objectively
assessed? And have the concomitant experiences generated
knowledge that satisfies scientific criteria of reliability and so
can guide the work to productive results in subsequent
efforts?

In the author's judgment, the Quakers themselves are keenly aware of the impact of these questions. One need not be a
scientist to be concerned with them. One needs only to be

"reality oriented," that is, aware that one's actions have "objective" consequences, and to seek justification of one's actions in those consequences and not only in a gratification of having done "what is right."

The Quakers' conception of their mission, which stems from their specific interpretation of Christianity, is certainly based on such reality orientation. Withdrawing from mundane affairs in search of personal salvation and so abandoning reality testing has no place in their religious commitment. So the author, himself a Quaker, raised the issue with me point blank. Is the account of the peace actions presented in this book a contribution to peace research? Can actions of this sort be made more effective by utilizing knowledge generated by peace research, and, if so, how? In a way, this foreword is an answer to these questions.

Although these questions reflect soul searching on the part of at least some Quakers, they could serve as stimuli for some soul searching on the part of the peace researchers. For the avowed goal of peace researchers is to produce knowledge useful in coping with the "problem" of war. Therefore, whatever division of labor is necessary or possible between peace research and peace action, each must nurture the other. The peacemaker looks to the peace researcher for knowledge to help design demonstrably effective peace actions. The peace researcher looks (or should look) to the peacemaker for assessment of the relevance of the knowledge he generates. The separation of the two functions is predicated on the supposed divergence between the modality of scientific thinking and that of value-oriented activity. The former must adhere to ideals of "objectivity" by following investigations to whatever conclusions might result; the latter is committed to specific prescribed goals and is based on a conviction that the goals can be achieved by the means chosen.

In my opinion, this categorical dichotomy stems from confusing "objectivity" with moral neutrality. By definition, a scientist must be objective, which means that he must not allow his preconceptions (which, incidentally, may be epistemological as well as moral) to prejudice his evaluation of evidence and thus his conclusions. But a scientist need not be morally neutral; nor can he be, in research involving human affairs, for the very selection of lines of inquiry is inevitably influenced by his moral commitments. And these provide also the driving force behind his efforts, without which no investigation can be effectively pursued.

Some researchers recognize the inseparability to commitment to truth and commitment to values in the mind of the investigator, but nevertheless insist on the separation of peace research and peace action in practice. To their way of thinking, then, the peacemaking actions of the Quakers, valuable as these may be in themselves, do not fall into the scope of peace *research,* since their design is not guided by experimental controls, statistical inference, mathematical models, and all the other accoutrements of scientific inquiry.

Some insights gleaned from the history of science suggest that this simple distinction between "pursuit of objective truth" and value-directed intervention may not be justified. In ancient times and through the Middle Ages, "science" was largely embodied in philosophy; knowledge regarded as important, such as knowledge pertaining to the structure of the universe, the nature of man and of the deity, was pursued by speculation and reasoning. Contact with physical reality, especially working with matter, was left to the artisans, whose job required know-how, not know-why.

The differentiation of function was associated, as is usual in human societies, with a differentiation of status, the higher status being ascribed to the thinker and the lower to the moulder of matter. During the Renaissance, however, when the artist emerged as an artisan who incorporated high spiritual values, a fusion of ideation and direct active contact with physical reality became respectable. So the experimental method, one of the pillars of modern science, was born.

Empirical verification of hypotheses, generated by speculation and cerebration, was not the only impetus to science.
When the thinker finally condescended to handle matter, his
whole outlook on the nature of reality changed. The new outlook stimulated questions and suggested ways of answering
them that had been completely outside the scope of human
consciousness. And this came about as a result of subjectively
appreciated *experience* no less than through objectively established results of *experiments*. In other words, science, as an
activity incorporated into human affairs, changed not only
the material conditions of human existence but also the range
of human concerns and aspirations.

It is with reference to these effects that the peacemaking
efforts of the Quakers must be evaluated when their relevance
to peace research is questioned. To begin with, the efforts
represent a fusion of thought and action, analogous to the
amalgam that gave birth to modern natural science.

Further, in the investigations of human behavior, problems
arise with which the natural scientist need not be concerned,
for the instruments of observation developed in natural
science are not adequate in the behavioral sciences. The behavioral scientist must frequently turn *himself* into an instrument of observation. So *as a scientist* he must be concerned
with the sensitivity and accuracy of this instrument. It is by
no means true that confining his attention to what is immediately observable and measurable, the behavioral scientist
makes the most effective use of his "instrument." In fact, in
doing so he may impair it. Here is where much of the criticism
leveled at "action research" as falling short of being "scientific" misses its mark.

The account of the three peace actions presented in this
book contains ample evidence that these undertakings certainly deserve to be regarded as research as well as efforts in
the cause of peace. Experiments are not reported here but a

rich treasury of experience. The results are not evaluated by statistical significance tests, but they are evaluated by profound analysis drawing on the experience, generated by action.

The central problem in the mainstream of peace research—uncovering the causes or correlates of war—is not posed. It need not be, for the actions are based not on scientifically formulated hypotheses but rather on a fundamental conviction, namely, that acute and violent conflicts are overt manifestations of internal aberrations—frustrations, misconceptions, delusions—and that consequently peace action ought to be a therapeutic enterprise aimed at eliciting the "true" nature of man, rational and compassionate. If this were an assumption, its general validity could be questioned, as I have pointed out above. As a *conviction,* it serves to guide peacemaking efforts to just those situations where it may be justified.

Not being a scientific hypothesis, this religiously inspired conviction of the Quakers is not subject to criticism on scientific grounds. But the specific methods and techniques of the Quakers can be subjected to careful scrutiny, and this is certainly done in this book. Moreover, this scrutiny is seen to be not far removed from the self-critical scrutiny of the scientist, once the vital role of the sensitized human being as an indispensable instrument of observation is recognized.

Anatol Rapoport

Preface

If I could use the custom of the seventeenth century when Robert Barclay, one of the first Quaker conciliators, wrote his *Epistle of Love and Friendly Advice to the Ambassadors of the several Princes of Europe*,[1] the title of this book would give a more complete account of the work, somewhat as follows:

> Some experiences of Quakers acting as unofficial, self-appointed, powerless intermediaries between national-state antagonists in crisis situations: to wit, the conflict of the two Germanies from 1961 to 1973; the war between India and Pakistan in 1965; and the Nigerian Civil War, from 1967 to 1970: with reference to the Quaker background of religious testimony and active work against war; described and analyzed in the light of contemporary studies of conflict analysis.

This does not leave much to add except a definition of some of the terms and an explanation of the way this book came about.

Conciliation has many different meanings. Quakers have used it interchangeably with reconciliation to cover a wide

1. The full title: "An Epistle of Love and Friendly Advice, To the Ambassadors of several Princes of *Europe*, met at *Nimeguen* to consult the Peace of *Christendom*, so far as they are concerned: Wherefore in the true Cause of the present War is discovered, and the right Remedy and Means for a firm and settled Peace is proposed."

range of activities intended to bring persons to a closer understanding and to make a more harmonious and constructive
climate for human fulfillment. The wellspring of these activities is described in a brief outline of Quaker faith and
practice in chapter 1. Conciliation in Quaker terms has taken
the form of major relief operations, such as the child-feeding
program in Germany after World War I; rehabilitation programs, such as the Rasulia Village Project in the Madhya
Pradesh province of India; lobbying at the United Nations for
better rules of international conduct; actions in a situation
many Quakers consider one of injustice, such as the British
rule in India or United States intervention in Vietnam; and
conciliation between hostile groups.

It is in this last aspect, the intervention of an outsider seeking a peaceful resolution between hostile parties, that the
term *conciliation* is used here, and in this study the parties
are nations. *Intervention* is used in the sense defined by
Oran Young in his book *The Intermediaries*: "any action
taken by an actor that is not a direct party to the crisis, that
is designed to reduce or remove one or more problems in the
bargaining relationship and, therefore, to facilitate the termi-
nation of the crisis itself."[2] *Conciliation, intervention, intermediaries* are all strong words used regularly for official activities with a great deal of public prestige and systems of
governmental sanctions. In using these same terms for the
Quaker role as an unofficial, nonpolitical, self-invited third
party, I am not implying that our work had the same kind of
influence or importance as more official efforts to mediate.
Since the hostile parties in these case studies were highly
organized national entities with claims of protocol and
hierarchies of power necessitating official channels for official action, the Quaker effort was necessarily subordinate

2. Oran R. Young, *The Intermediaries: Third Parties in International
Crises* (Princeton: Princeton University Press, 1967), p. 34.

and ancillary to conciliation or negotiation by official mediators between official parties. We found, however, in the course of this work that our quiet, off-the-record, go-between endeavors, by virtue of our lack of power and lack of official identity, could help the process of conciliation in a way that was appreciated and utilized by the main actors.

For the historian of these episodes the Quaker efforts would be such a small part of the total forces as to be hardly worth mentioning. In magnifying this small part in some detail, I do not want to overemphasize its importance, but I hope that the experience will be helpful to future unofficial conciliators, Quaker or non-Quaker, and give some concrete material for the growing study of conflict and peace research.

The term *conciliation* has many uses in international politics and law; the main usage in these case studies will be a socio-psychological one to signify the process of promoting better understanding and agreement between persons or groups in conflict by helping to change their perceptions and images. As Kenneth Boulding writes in his general theory of conflict, messages between hostile parties that pass through an intense emotional field are likely to be distorted:

> The conciliator has the advantage of being outside the emotional field that is created by the conflict. . . . By acting as a go-between therefore, the conciliator can transmit messages between the parties with greater accuracy than is possible with direct messages and so can achieve a certain reconciliation of images that would have been impossible without him.[3]

In a similar analysis, Adam Curle gives a definition of conciliation appropriate here: "Activity aimed at bringing about an alteration of perception (the other side is not as bad as we

3. Kenneth Boulding, *Conflict and Defense* (New York: Harper and Row, 1962), p. 316.

thought; we have misinterpreted their actions; etc.) that will
lead to an alteration of attitude and eventually to an alteration of behavior."[4] We should add that Quaker conciliators,
while "outside of the field," found it important to identify
as fully as possible with the aspirations and memories of the
parties in order to be able to understand the distortions and
to help promote better communication.

Conciliation, thus defined, is most appropriate for conflicts
such as the three looked at here, in which differences of perception are a major ingredient in the dispute. The concluding
chapter in part considers the relation of conciliation to conflicts that arise primarily from gross injustice between parties
of unequal power where the quarrel is not one based on perceptions, which are real enough, but over basic human rights.

The three case studies chosen are ones in which I was involved from 1963 to 1972 as secretary of the International
Affairs Division, at that time one of five program divisions of
the American Friends Service Committee. I did not engage in
the direct conciliatory work, but along with associates in the
home office of one of the two collaborating organizations, I
was in long-range contact with the actual work and handled
coordination with the other organization, the Friends Service
Council, London. The idea that these experiences should be
described occurred to me as I thought of the value to future
Quaker practitioners and to the developing field of conflict
analysis. I was greatly encouraged by Adam Curle, now holding the Chair of Peace Studies at Bradford University, who
first got interested in peacemaking on the international scale
from his participation in two of these efforts, and Sydney
Bailey, an important figure in the development of Quaker
international work who has made a lifetime study of the
United Nations.

4. Adam Curle, *Making Peace* (London: Tavistock Publications, 1971),
p. 173.

The staff of the American Friends Service Committee and Friends Service Council have given every assistance and encouragement, but, as is to be expected, they are so busy with ongoing work that they are glad to leave such leisurely history writing to retired personnel. I used the archives of the two organizations extensively for source materials; citations, when given, are to the Archives at Friends House, London, or the American Friends Service Committee, Philadelphia. I have not attempted to cite all the letters, reports, and memoranda used.

A fellowship for one year at Woodbrooke, the Quaker study center in Birmingham, England, enabled me to get started, and a grant from the Joseph Rowntree Charitable Trust of York, England, has helped with expenses. On trips to London I was privileged to use the facilities of the Richardson Institute for Conflict and Peace Research, and I have had valuable advice from its director, Michael Nicholson. The high point of this association was a seminar with researchers of the Institute in which I presented the outline of this work. Many challenging questions came up, such as the pertinence of conciliation to situations like those of southern Africa and a possible Quaker propensity to conciliate—meaning "to patch things up"—when fundamental human rights are involved. The questions have guided my writing, especially in the last chapter, though I cannot claim to have answered them to the satisfaction of all.

One difficult and fundamental question has to do with the problem of exposure of confidential material. It has been on my mind constantly; it was raised in the seminar and in conversations with the heads of the two Quaker organizations. A first solution has been to conceal wherever necessary the identity of official spokesmen. As time moves on this becomes less important. Conversations can be disguised and persons protected, but there remains an innate contradiction in writing about activity that was carried on with the under-

standing that the activity itself would not be revealed. I hope
the value to be derived from this exposure of the process will
be sufficient to make up for any impairment of confidence
which might be involved.

During the period from 1963 to 1972, I also had firsthand
knowledge of manifold Quaker activity in three other conflict
situations, but these have been ruled out of this work for differing reasons. The Quaker efforts in arranging numerous
dialogues between the West and the Soviet Union are a story
of quite a different kind. Quaker activity in the Vietnam
War, which involved visits to both sides, would be a better
case study of American Quaker confrontation with the
American government, rather than conciliation between opposing national forces. A more direct parallel case was
Quaker conciliation in the Arab-Israeli dispute, but both the
conflict and the conciliation continue, and the situation is
too close for study and evaluation.

My work on this book was interrupted by a year in Northern Ireland (1973–74), where my wife and I were asked to do
conciliatory work for the Friends Service Council in consultation with Irish Friends. Our efforts were a small part of a
series of Quaker undertakings in that lovely, strife-torn land.
The absorbing, exacting, saddening experience added to our
knowledge of conflict, but again does not lend itself to
evaluation at this time.

Through most of the period of these episodes I had the
expert support of Nora Booth and Irene Krueger, associates
in the International Affairs Division. Nora Booth was in on
the beginning and development of the seminars and conferences and has made some valuable corrections to my writing. Irene Krueger gave loving and devoted attention to the
Quaker international affairs representatives in Germany
throughout most of their period of work. She read early
drafts of the second chapter, but her failing health and un-

timely death did not allow for as much participation in the writing as I should have liked. I especially want to mention the office assistants who one after another gave eminently able and lovingly indulgent assistance and without whom the home office support for the work here described would have faltered lamentably.

In the writing stages I have submitted each chapter to the main protagonists and have received many suggestions, greatly improving both fact and interpretation. For overall screening of fuzzy statements and Quaker in-group terminology, I am greatly indebted to Maureen R. Berman, who has labored unendingly to make each draft a little clearer than the last. If there remain some muddy spots it is not her fault. A general thanks is due to all those people, from Birmingham, England to Honolulu, Hawaii, who have had a hand in typing over the last four years. My wife, Margaret, has been a sustaining and cheering companion as I labored painfully to get it all down in sensible sentences.

I am grateful to the Columbia University Press for permission to use part of my chapter, "Quaker Efforts toward Reconciliation in the India-Pakistan War of 1965" in *Unofficial Diplomats,* Maureen R. Berman and Joseph E. Johnson, eds., 1977.

Chapter One

The Background of Quaker Conciliation

Beliefs and Precedents

Quaker Faith

Quakerism grew out of the turmoil of the Reformation in seventeenth-century England. A new interpretation of the relation of man to God and man to man, it sought new light on Christian faith by looking directly to Christ as the first disciples had.[1] The concepts and methods of Quaker conciliation have their origins in the movement, which sought from the beginning to turn people toward peace and away from killing other sons and daughters of God.

Throughout seventeenth-century Britain, people fought and kings were deposed over the question of what human authority could rightly interpret God's truth and grant salvation. Was it the church, the priest, or the Bible? Was it the pope, the episcopacy, the presbytery, or the congregation? Mutually exclusive answers were voiced with conviction by the

---

1. Several good explanations of Quaker approaches are available: Robert O. Byrd, *Quaker Ways in Foreign Policy* (Toronto: University of Toronto Press, 1960), especially good for the political field of these case studies; A. Neave Brayshaw, *The Quakers: Their Story and Message* (London: George Allen and Unwin, 1921), paperback edition (York, England: William Sessions, 1969); Howard H. Brinton, *Friends for Three Hundred Years* (Wallingford, Pa.: Pendle Hill Publications, 1965).

1

Roman Catholic Church, the Established Church of England, the Presbyterians, the Baptists, and the Independents.

In 1647, George Fox, the twenty-three-year-old son of a Leicestershire weaver, after four years of prayer, Bible reading, and persistent discussion with clergy and theologians, found an answer to his personal search: "I heard a voice which said, 'There is one even Christ Jesus that can speak to thy condition,' and when I heard it my heart did leap for joy." Christ, Fox believed, is still present teaching us, if we will only listen. There is no earthly, human authority, but only Christ, "who enlightens and gives grace, and faith, and power. . . . And this I know experimentally."[2] On the mystical experience of direct communion with God in Christ, Fox founded his faith. With this radical and simple answer he preached to the people and confronted the authorities.

Christ or God was accessible to each person, Fox taught, because all were born with the potential for hearing Christ. "A light within, a seed" responded to the divine message, and this light was in all men in all stations of life, of all creeds and religions. George Fox experienced it and found a joyous and releasing power; others to whom he preached had similar experiences. Traveling to Westmoreland and Lancashire in 1652 he found several thousand people, the Seekers, who had become skeptical of the contradictory answers of religious authorities and were ripe for his message. They gathered about him, and many were inspired to go forth and preach. The Publishers of Truth, as the leaders were called, set out, not to start a new sect, but to spread throughout Christendom and beyond the word of Christ's continuing presence.

Fox called on all people to seek the experience of God's love in the worshiping group, waiting in silence, feeling the presence, and speaking when inspired by the Spirit. The

2. *The Journal of George Fox*, ed. John L. Nickalls (London: London Yearly Meeting, 1975), p. 11.

experience was more important than any words or forms of worship. Creedal formulations, outward ceremonies, elaborate edifices, formal readings, music, stained-glass windows were all shunned as "crutches" that might interfere with the direct experience. The Scriptures were important, "given forth by the Holy Spirit of God through the holy men of God."[3] but they were secondary: "a declaration of the fountain and not the fountain itself."[4] The Friends movement was a revival of first-century Christianity, which sought its inspiration directly in the words of Christ.

The growing company of Children of the Light,[5] as they frequently called themselves, and later Friends,[6] numbering around forty thousand by 1662, coming from all classes but mostly craftsmen and farmers, soon brought down the wrath of clerical and secular authorities, and over fifteen thousand Friends in the years from the beginning in 1650 until the Act of Toleration in 1689 were thrown into prison for holding meetings, for not doffing their hats to their betters, for not paying tithes, and for refusing to swear oaths. All of these practices stemmed from the initial root inspiration of the presence of Christ, teaching his Gospel equally to all. Since all had the seed of Christ within, Friends taught, man-made distinctions and prerogatives were false. Since the truth was available to all who would seek it, "hireling ministers" were only deceivers, and paying tithes to the established church was wrong. Since one should speak the truth at all times, it was wrong to swear to speak the truth; oaths of allegiance to worldly power were against God's will.

3. Ibid., p. 604.
4. Robert Barclay, *Apology for the True Christian Divinity* (Philadelphia: Friends Book Store, 1908), p. 72.
5. 1 Thess. 5:5, "Ye are the children of the light."
6. John 15:15, "I have called you friends." The term "Quaker," applied initially in derision by opponents of the movement, came to be accepted equally with "Friend."

Despite severe persecution, the Quakers persevered in their evangelism, gathering some one hundred thousand converts in England, Ireland, the American colonies, and to a lesser extent in the German states, Holland, and France. Toward the end of the first three decades, as conversions tapered off, it became evident that all of their efforts would not bring the kingdom of God on earth in the seventeenth century. The natural reaction was to withdraw from involvement in the evils and injustices of the world and carry out the Quaker way of life as closely as possible with each other, keeping the witness alive, so that at some time in the future the truth might prevail. While this tendency toward withdrawal lead to a period of so-called quietism, the Quakers did not set up separate communities like the Mennonites and other pacifist groups. There was always a strong testimony that the Lord's business was carried out in the world and Quakers had a mission to work in society, running their business honestly, establishing schools to educate the young, using their talents to develop labor-saving devices, extending the scientific knowledge of truth, working for reform of prisons, mental hospitals, and other institutions.

The central concept of Quakerism to this day is that each person has the capacity to respond to God. As a modern Quaker author puts it, Friends

> express this opinion variously, sometimes giving it a secular expression as the dignity, worth or preciousness of the individual personality. More often the expression is religious, "that of God in every man, the seed within, the Light within, or the Christ within." However expressed it means that there is something of infinite worth in every individual, and that there is an active or latent striving and capacity for creative and harmonious living in every personality.[7]

7. Byrd, *Quaker Ways in Foreign Policy*, pp. 3–4.

People also have the capacity for hatred, cruelty, and greed, but Friends believe that the power of love, being of God, is primary and ultimate.

From this core belief arose the practices and attitudes that led to persecution in the early days and still influence Quaker behavior both within their own circles and in relations with the outside world. The recognition of a God-seeking capacity in all men led to witness in words and deeds for equality, justice, peace, and simplicity: equality for women, for slaves, for rejected minorities, for all; justice for the oppressed and wronged, sought through nonviolent methods; peaceful relations in families, in communities, between nations; simplicity in living so as not to exploit people or nature. Through all these ethical derivations, which Quakers have called "testimonies," runs a thread of optimism regarding man's potential. Some of Fox's strongest accusations were against the Calvinist preachers, who, he said, were "pleading for sin."

Not long after the Quaker movement began, the leaders felt the need to organize in order to help members suffering from persecution and to deal with the excesses and aberrations of those who tended to carry the new doctrine to extremes of individual interpretation. George Fox led the way in organizing as well as in preaching. From an unstructured movement of the Children of the Light, an organization called the Friends was formed.[8]

As in earlier Congregational and Baptist practice, the local worshiping group constituted the most important governing unit. Since the members were rebelling against the formalism of church buildings and church authority, they called this basic unit simply a "meeting," not a "church." The local group or several in a small area met to transact business once a month at a "monthly meeting." Questions of acceptance

8. In the early nineteenth century the names Society of Friends or Religious Society of Friends came into currency.

and conduct of members, property matters, and general policy were talked over in a spirit of worship and decided by the group as a whole. The clerk selected by the meeting sought the "sense of the meeting" by gathering views of all the speakers, paying deference to the more cogent and earnest opinions, and formulating a minute, or record of action, on which all could agree. Since the truth of Christ under which they were guided was single, it was necessary for all to labor together to find this truth. No vote was taken and no division into majority and minority. Certain individuals who seemed to live closer to Christ's teaching were thought of as "weighty Friends" whose words had more influence, but on specific issues a young and untried member might be thought to hold views closer to the truth. Unanimity was not the aim, but unity in which all would go forward on a course of action, some enthusiastically and some less so, some even reluctantly, but not standing in the way.

Monthly meetings of a wider territory joined together in quarterly meetings. Once a year all the members of monthly meetings who could come gathered in a yearly meeting to report on programs, exchange important insights, and transact business affecting the whole group. As in the monthly meeting, a clerk was selected to moderate, along with assistants for reading and recording minutes of the proceedings. London Yearly Meeting was formally established in 1668.[9] In the yearly meetings the members sought God's guidance in establishing policies for the constituent bodies. Specific decisions reached or general testimonies and advice were usually followed in the monthly meetings, but the yearly meeting had no enforcement powers. Only the monthly meeting could disown individuals for departing too far from Quaker ways,

9. London was the acknowledged center of Quakerism for many years, and the London Yearly Meeting is still primus inter pares; but in point of time New England Yearly Meeting, established in 1661, was first, indicating the rapid spread of the movement.

a frequent practice in the first two centuries for such offenses as joining the army or marrying out of the faith, but one that has lapsed in this century.

It was in these meetings, monthly, quarterly and yearly, that the interplay between the individual and the group took place. The individual would submit his vision of what the Lord would have him do to the tempering influence of the group, or the group, concerned over some situation, would ask the individual to represent the group. In the meetings "concerns" were tested and developed. The word *concern* has a special significance in Quaker use; it means the religiously inspired impulse to put God's love into action in some concrete situation. Concerns sometimes arose out of the meeting as a whole. More often an individual would submit a concern and in the quiet of worship ask if he were following the right "leading." If the group found unity with the concern they might help it forward. If not, they might still stand behind the individual as he carried out his concern or "moved as the way opened." If definitely opposed, they might appoint a committee to wait upon an individual and try to point out the error of his or her ways, a process called "eldering."

Early in the organizing process committees took on an important role, frequently performing functions that in other religious groups fell to the pastor. Regular standing committees had a care for the spiritual health of the meeting and its members, making recommendations to the monthly meetings on acceptance of members, relations with other church bodies, or requirements of secular authorities. Committees functioned at monthly meetings, quarterly meetings, and yearly meetings. They were selected by nomination and approval in the business meeting. While Quakers have as many jokes about committees as others do, they also have a high regard for their potential.

The promise of the Holy Spirit was to a group. We need

one another to strengthen each other's will to goodness. The concern of an individual should be laid before the worshiping group, so that corporate guidance may be given by an expression of unity or disunity.[10]

The grandfather of all committees was the Meeting for Sufferings, a group of representatives from many monthly meetings. Originally organized for defense against persecution, the Meeting for Sufferings became, in effect, an executive committee for London Yearly Meeting, acting between annual sessions.

Quaker methods of achieving consensus were strained as the movement spread and became subject to many influences. To the yearly meetings formed on the basis of geography were added those formed on the basis of disagreements on faith and practice, but all considered themselves part of the Society of Friends. There are now over fifty yearly meetings in the world, with close to two hundred thousand members. While essentially independent units, the yearly meetings have cooperated and joined together in various coordinating groups. The most inclusive is the Friends World Committee for Consultation, formed in 1937. "Consultation" indicates the Quaker's premium on local initiative and their fear of hierarchical control. No one person or group can speak for the Society of Friends. There are many voices, more or less in tune, and most Quakers are careful to qualify their statements: "This is *a* Quaker point of view," not "*the* Quaker view."

Quaker Peace Testimony and Conciliation

The Quaker testimony against war and for conciliation arose from the basic religious assumptions. In 1650 when George

10. London Yearly Meeting, *Christian Faith and Practice in the Experience of the Society of Friends* (London Yearly Meeting, 1960, reprinted, Richmond, Ind.: Friends United Press, 1973), par. 359.

Fox was offered release from prison if he would join the army, he refused. "I told them I lived in the virtue of that life and power that took away the occasion of all wars."[11] The refusal to participate in wars was first given a public corporate expression in 1660 in a declaration to Charles II:

> We utterly deny all outward wars and strife and fighting with outward weapons for any order or under any pretence whatsoever. And this is our testimony to the whole world. The spirit of Christ, by which we are guided, is not changeable, so at once to command us from a thing as evil and again to move unto it; and we do certainly know, and so testify to the world, that the spirit of Christ which leads us into all Truth, will never lead us to fight and war against any man with outward weapons, neither for the kingdom of Christ nor for the kingdom of this world.[12]

The guidance of the inner light brought both the negative witness against war and the positive efforts for achieving the life that does away with war. Interpretations of the basic testimony have varied from century to century and many Quakers as individuals have not held to the testimony, but regularly constituted Quaker bodies have consistently upheld the position against war and in all periods have directed efforts toward human reconciliation.[13]

Within this basic consistency of Quaker views there have been two strands of thought on how to secure peace: some believed that peace would come through the conversion of leaders or masses to true Christian life or to pacifism; others

---

11. *The Journal of George Fox*, p. 65.

12. From "A Declaration from the Harmless and Innocent People of God, called Quakers," presented to Charles II in 1660, ibid., p. 399.

13. For a recent exposition of the history of the peace testimony, see Wolf Mendl, *Prophets and Reconcilers* (London: Friends Home Service Committee, 1974).

said peace would come through reform of society and by developing the institutions of peace. The two views became contradictory only when advocates espoused individual conversion or social reform as the only way. Usually the two views have coexisted, supplementing each other, since in their own way both are necessary and both can contribute to peaceful relations.

The first belief was characteristic of the first thirty years of the movement, when hopes were high for overcoming the evils of war, injustice, and cruelty, which arose, Quakers thought, from the alienation of man from God. Quaker leaders did not consider themselves as "pacifist" or as having a "peace testimony," but rather as preachers of the truth of Christ. Those who accepted Christ would naturally reject all warlike ways. An eloquent expression of this view and of oft-cited precedent for Quaker intervention in international disputes is the *Epistle of Love and Friendly Advice* addressed by Robert Barclay, the first systematizer of Quaker thought, to the *Ambassadors of the Several Princes of Europe, Met at Nimeguen to Consult the Peace of Christendom.*[14] Inspired by George Fox's revelation of Christ's teaching, Robert Barclay exhorted the rulers of Europe to give up their evil ways, to renounce greed, ambition, vanity, wantonness, and vainglory and to find a new birth in Christ and thereby bring peace to the Christian world.

Traveling among Friends in Holland and Germany, he saw the destruction and suffering that the futile dynastic wars of the period brought to the people. His solution, written with humanitarian passion, was a religious one: the conversion of the heads of state to a Christianity that they professed in

14. Written 2 November 1677, Latin version delivered at Nimeguen 23–24 February 1678. Published in English 1679. In Robert Barclay, *Truth Triumphant, through the Spiritual Warfare, Christian Labours, and Writings of the Able and Faithful Servant of Jesus Christ, Robert Barclay,* 3 vols. (Philadelphia: Benjamin C. Stanton, 1831) 2:557–68.

words but denied in deeds. To give the princes the benefit of his thinking, he sent them copies of his magnum opus, *Apology for the True Christian Divinity*. Thus began the Quaker tradition of "speaking truth to power."

The strand of thought that urged social reform led many Quakers toward practical, political peacemaking, which could also be a valid witness, they thought, through working toward compromises rather than the conversion of all individuals to the true Christian way or, in later terminology, to pacifism. William Penn was an outstanding spokesman for this point of view, and these words of his are an important part of the Quaker heritage: "True godliness don't [sic] turn men out of the world, but enables them to live better in it and excites their endeavors to mend it."[15] Like Barclay, one of the few members of the privileged classes who joined the movement, Penn labored to establish a commonwealth in America that would embody the social testimonies of his faith. His conciliatory approach to the Indians, whose customs and thought he studied in a way remarkable for the age, initiated an extended era of peace for Pennsylvania, not broken until the French and Indian Wars after 1756, when the Quakers withdrew from the legislature. Penn also proposed a Confederation of European Nations deliberating and adjudicating in an international parliament, thus providing the precedent for later Quaker activity in the League of Nations and the United Nations.

Precedents for Quaker Conciliation

While Barclay and Penn made general appeals for peace, the one emphasizing conversion and the other institutions for settling disputes, perhaps the earliest specific precedent for conciliation between opposing parties in international con-

15. William Penn, *No Cross, No Crown* (London: Society of Friends, 1930), p. 63.

flict was the effort of Rhode Island Quakers to stop the war between Indians and colonists in 1675. When the English first came to Plymouth Colony in 1620, they were welcomed and befriended by Massasoit, chief sachem of the Wampanoags. Before he died he made his two sons, Alexander and Philip, offer a pledge of peace to the settlers, but the clash of cultures and territorial demands could not be averted. Alexander died as he was forcibly being brought to court by the English. The Indians were sure he had been poisoned. Philip, who succeeded his brother as chief, became more and more embittered as he saw Indian lands taken over under one ruse or another and the Indian way of life increasingly subverted by the white men. An able leader skilled in both diplomacy and the military arts, Philip visited neighboring tribes throughout New England and drew them together in a confederation to drive out the English. Rumors of this activity reached the colonists from Indians who had been converted to Christianity and had thrown in their lot with the settlers.

In a last-minute effort to stave off full-scale war, John Easton, deputy governor of Rhode Island, rowed up Narragansett Bay with four associates to seek a conference with King Philip. They went unarmed and Philip met them graciously enough when he heard they were Quakers from Rhode Island. The Quakers, as they have through the years, began by denouncing the folly of arms for settling conflicts and by pleading that "the quarell might rightly be desided in the best way and not as dogs desided their quarells."[16]

The Indian chief acknowledged that fighting was the worst way to settle a dispute, but asked how else their grievances could be settled. The Quakers proposed arbitration, but the

16. John Easton, "A Relacion of the Indyan Warre, by Mr. Easton, of Roade Isld., 1675," in Charles H. Lincoln, *Narratives of the Indian Wars, 1675–1699* (New York: Scribner, 1913), p. 9; see also Rufus Jones, *The Quakers in the American Colonies* (London: Macmillan, 1923), pp. 181–83.

Indian experience with arbitration after the Treaty of Taunton in 1671 had been that "all English agred against them, and so by arbitration they had had much rong."[17] The peacemakers proposed impartial arbitration, in which each side would select an arbitrator known to be uninvolved in the dispute. Thus, the English might choose the governor of New York, they said, and the Indians, an Indian king from a distance. Philip was impressed with this proposal, and the delegates were persuaded that the Indians might accept arbitration of this kind.

At this point in the conference the concilators thought their work accomplished. They sought to cut off a long recital of Indian grievances by anticipating them in their own words, saying that the people of Rhode Island had improved the methods of justice for the Indians and had heeded Indian complaints about high-pressure proselytizing by Christian ministers. King Philip, however, reminded them of the importance of listening (which their own Friendly precepts might have told them) saying that it was improper for John Easton and his colleagues to give their statement without letting the Indians have their say. The king then proceeded to give an impressive, lengthy catalogue of complaints, covering the inequities of English justice, the corruption of land sales, the spoiling of Indian corn by English horses and cattle, and the sale of liquor, which made Indians drunk and quarrelsome. All this, the Indians said, after

> thay had bine the first in doing good to the English, and the English the first in doing rong. When the English first came, their king's father [Massasoit] was a great man and the English was a litell Child, he Constraened other indians for ronging the English and gave them Corcn and shewed them how to plant.[18]

---

17. Lincoln, *Narratives of the Indian Wars, 1675–1699*, p. 9.
18. Ibid., p. 10.

Toward the conclusion of the parley the Quakers referred again to the arbitration proposal and reported later that it would have been accepted if officially tendered. The weakness of the Quaker position, however, was revealed by the "if." Coming as they did under the semiofficial auspices of Rhode Island, they had no authority from the governments of Connecticut, Massachusetts, or Plymouth Colony—all of which had excluded Rhode Island from the New England Confederacy of 1643 because of the heretical beliefs and rival territorial claims of Roger Williams's colony. Unsure, then, that they could persuade the English to participate in arbitration, they used a practical argument to convince the Indian leaders: "We indivered that however they should lay doune ther arems for the English wear to strong for them." The answer came back in terms starkly reminiscent of Christ's teaching. "They saied then the English should do to them as thay did when they wear to strong for the English."[19]

John Easton was unable to pursue the possibility of arbitration with the leaders of the New England alliance. Incidents of violence brought retaliation, and within a week the conflict escalated into a full-scale war in which the Rhode Island leaders participated on the English side with great reluctance. The Quaker effort could not reverse the remorseless thrust of colonization. Theirs was an impossible mission, since the clash of Indians and white settlers seems in retrospect a clear case of what analysts call a "zero-sum" conflict, in which the only solution is the elimination of the claims of one party.

From the eighteenth century comes an important precedent for high-level intercession by Quakers. The English court physician, Dr. John Fothergill, and the merchant David Barclay, grandson of Robert Barclay, attempted to avert the impending rebellion of the American colonies against the mother country. Through travel and correspondence the two

19. Ibid., p. 11.

leading Quakers were familiar with opinion in the colonies. Dr. Fothergill had long been a warm friend of Benjamin Franklin, with whom he shared scientific interests. Franklin had been in London for eight years when the increasingly repressive measures of Lord North's government brought increasingly retaliatory words and actions from the American colonists. David Barclay and John Fothergill made repeated attempts from December 1774 to March 1775 to work out compromise proposals with Franklin. An outline was drawn up by Franklin with seventeen headings to cover points at issue under the title "Hints for Conversation, Upon the Subject of Terms That May Probably Produce a Durable Union Between Britain and the Colonies."[20] The two Englishmen worked to get Franklin to concede points that in their view were necessary to make a compromise acceptable to the king and his ministers. The two Quakers had excellent channels to the more moderate men in the cabinet, and the "Hints" were studied by several key ministers. Under pressure from the peace wing of the cabinet, Lord North, the prime minister, put forth a last-minute measure on January 21, 1775, which balanced conciliatory proposals with threats. It was the latter that were heard in Boston. The mood of the colonists was becoming more demanding, and the group in the cabinet closest to the king was all for strong measures to subdue what they saw as a minor riot of a few rebellious subjects. Both sides continued on a collision course.

Shuttling back and forth between Franklin and the cabinet members, Barclay and Fothergill made intense efforts to explore all realistic possibilities. The effort was in a way vindicated when in 1778 the king grudgingly assented to and Parliament passed an Act of Conciliation which conceded the

20. R. Hingston Fox, *Dr. John Fothergill and His Friends* (London: Macmillan, 1919), app. A. See also Amelia Mott Gummere, *The Quaker in the Forum* (Philadelphia: Winston, 1910), pp. 232–50.

main points contained in the "Hints" of 1775. By that time, however, nothing less than full independence would satisfy the Americans, and the war went on for five more years. Looking back at the years of devastation, suffering and brutality, Franklin wrote to Barclay in February 1781 on the occasion of Fothergill's death: "How much might have been done and how much mischief prevented, if his, your, and my joint endeavors in a certain melancholy affair had been attended to."[21]

In these instances the conciliators were to an extent identified with one of the parties to the dispute, although they attempted to assert their own neutrality. John Easton and the Rhode Island delegation were leading citizens of one of the colonies bound to be involved in any war with the Indians; Dr. Fothergill and David Barclay were loyal, though critical, subjects of the king of England. It was a further step for Quakers to presume to intercede in foreign quarrels in which they themselves were not directly involved as nationals of one side or the other. A precedent for this kind of involvement was the effort of Joseph Sturge and two colleagues to bring peace between Denmark and the Duchies of Schleswig-Holstein. The opportunity arose out of an incident at the privately organized Third International Peace Congress at Frankfurt in 1850. A group of influential men in Berlin sent a telegram to the Congress asking the assembly to receive their representative, Dr. Bodenstedt, a liberal politician and writer. The learned doctor made an impassioned plea to the Congress, which was discussing arbitration in the abstract, to appoint a commission of inquiry to promote arbitration of the Schleswig-Holstein dispute so that, as he put it, the iniquitous war being waged by Denmark against the German people in those provinces could be ended.

Although the Congress as a whole, without any delegated

21. Fox, *Dr. John Fothergill and His Friends,* p. 365.

power from component organizations and individuals, could not accept the proposal, three leaders of the conference, Joseph Sturge, Frederick Wheeler, and Elihu Burritt—the first two English Quakers, the third a peace leader from New England—decided to carry out a quiet mission to both sides. The team prepared for their task by listening to a number of people in Hamburg and Berlin who could tell them about the issues and give them introductions to top officials on the Schleswig side. In the midst of the activities they found time to "sit down in silence together."[22] With appropriate Quaker understatement Joseph Sturge wrote, "I feel little expectation of any benefit arising from the attempt, except the conviction that we have done what we can to prevent the continuance of war. I hope we shall do no harm."[23]

In a written statement the team stated the origins of their mission, disclaimed all intention of entering into the merits of the case or of acting as mediators, and entreated the contending parties to refer the question to impartial arbitrators. In making this appeal they referred to a treaty of alliance between Denmark and the Duchies dating back to 1533, which provided for arbitration of differences. The statement was also used to give a modest and factual account of their trip to the public press, for they found the secrecy of their mission breached on their first entrance to Berlin.

With strong support from Germans who had identified themselves with the cause of the Duchies, they found no difficulty in traveling through the military checkpoints to the embattled town of Rendsburg, where the officials greeted them cordially. The leaders of the provisional government did not want to make a public move toward negotiation, fearing it would be taken as a sign of weakness by the enemy and

22. Letter of Joseph Sturge in Henry Richard, *Memoirs of Joseph Sturge* (London: S. W. Partridge, 1864), p. 440.

23. Letter of Joseph Sturge in Stephen Hobhouse, *Joseph Sturge: His Life and Work* (London: J. M. Dent, 1919), p. 135.

by their people in the heat of a war they thought they could win, but they indicated confidentially their willingness to refer their claims to impartial arbitration provided that suitable signs came from Denmark.

Traveling then by boat to Copenhagen, the peacemakers secured an interview with the Danish prime minister. A major obstacle in the minds of the Danes was that they did not want to concede to the Schleswig-Holsteiner rebels the semblance of international status implied by seeking an outside arbitrator. Burritt's detailed knowledge of the previous treaty helped to make their case, though his account stresses the spiritual appeal of Joseph Sturge:

> The deputation addressed themselves to this difficulty with great earnestness and assiduity. There is no question that the simple eloquence of Joseph Sturge's goodness of heart, and the plea he made with tears moistening and illuminating the beautiful radiance of his benevolent face, impressed the Danish minister more deeply than any mere diplomatic communication could have done.[24]

The prime minister referred the Quakers to the minister of foreign affairs, who emphasized his own interest in bringing peace and recounted that on several occasions the Danish government had offered to settle the matter through direct negotiation with the "rebels." He could not give an answer that evening, he said, but he would take the matter up with his colleagues. The next day the team wrote the minister asking whether his answer was Yes or No, and saying they intended to publish the results of their mission, thus threatening to appeal to international public opinion. In Sturge's words, "We wished to do strict justice to all parties, we should be obliged by a reply whether the Danish Government took the responsibility of rejecting our proposition or not."

24. Richard, *Memoirs of Joseph Sturge*, p. 450.

Whether because of or in spite of this threat of publicity, a reply did come stating that the government could not give a written message but would be quite open to a proposal of arbitration from the provisional government of the Duchies. After further talks a distinguished citizen from each side was appointed to confer on the constitution and terms of reference of a court of arbitration. At this point the Quaker team went home feeling that it had achieved its aims.

Whether arbitration would have succeeded will never be known. Within a few weeks Prussia and Austria, intent on restoring the status quo after the vexing revolutions of 1848 and abetted by Britain, France and Russia, forced the submission of the duchies to Denmark. This settlement was very unpopular with the people of the territory in dispute and in 1864 served as excuse for the move by Bismarck—promoter of a new Prussian drive to unify the Germanics—to claim the Duchies and drive Denmark out.

The Quaker effort had been based on the hope that a just peace could be brought about by arbitration between the two parties at war, but the issue had been greatly complicated by the rivalries among the ruling groups of France, Russia, Britain, Austria, and Prussia, which were attempting to maintain stability in Europe by channeling or curbing, in their own interest, the emerging forces of liberalism and nationalism. The lesson for future conciliators was to study carefully the international entanglement as well as the merits of the case. The threat of using publicity to force the issue might be questioned in light of later experience, but this whole private undertaking had many of the elements used in later Quaker conciliation: an earnest desire for peace and the relief of suffering, a quiet, unpublicized carrying of messages between the disputants, and a carefully studied impartiality combined with sincere friendliness to both sides.

The better-known mission of Joseph Sturge and two others sent by the London Yearly Meeting to Czar Nicholas I of

Russia in January 1854 was an attempt to avert the Crimean War. Less pertinent to our study, it shows the kind of Quaker peace effort which, like that of Robert Barclay, is a spiritual appeal with little practical political thought or conciliation activity involved. It is also a good example of the way in which a Quaker "concern" arises in a time of crisis and produces an urge to "speak truth to power."

Friends had had contact with the czars of Russia on several previous occasions. At the end of the seventeenth century, Peter the Great, sojourning incognito in London, had attended a Quaker meeting. In the early nineteenth century, Daniel Wheeler, an English Quaker, had been called by Czar Alexander I to help drain the swamps around St. Petersburg.[25] In 1853, when war broke out between Russia and Turkey over the Russian claim of a protectorate over all the Christians in the Ottoman Empire, Britain and France were about to become involved, as allies of Turkey, to check Russian expansion. Inflamed by reports in the press of the annihilation of the Turkish fleet by the Russians at Sinope, British public opinion was aroused against the Autocrat of the Russias. British Quakers tried to combat the war fever. John Bright and Richard Cobden, Quaker members of the House of Commons, argued eloquently and cogently against the war. The yearly meeting decided to send a delegation to the Czar with a carefully worded statement emphasizing the Quaker's abiding testimony that war is against the precept of Christianity and saying they had repeatedly pressed this conviction on their own rulers in a "language of bold but respectful remonstrance." Declaring that the Society of Friends did not presume to offer any opinion on the question in dispute, the statement appealed to the czar as a great Christian ruler to "practically exhibit to the nations . . . the efficacy of the

---

25. For an expansion of this interesting history, see Richienda C. Scott, *Quakers in Russia* (London: Michael Joseph, 1964).

Gospel of Christ and the universal application of his command, 'love your enemies; bless them that curse you; do good to them that hate you; and pray for them that despitefully use you and persecute you.' "[26]

The Quaker team was warmly and hospitably received by the czar, but the Russian ruler answered their Christian admonition in their own terms by saying that although he abhorred war, held the English in high regard, and had no plans for the conquest of Turkey, he could not disregard the welfare of the Greek Church in Turkey, from which Russia had received the blessings of Christianity. Accepting for themselves the precept to "love your enemies," they left the czar, telling him that whatever happened "there were those in England who desired his temporal and spiritual welfare as sincerely as his own subjects."[27]

While the Quaker delegation was still in St. Petersburg news came of the opening of the British Parliament in February 1854. Along with many warlike speeches in the House of Commons came a vote to increase armaments. The Quakers, unsuccessful in stopping the move toward war at home, could hardly expect the czar to call off a war with Turkey in which Russia was already fully engaged. The personal appeal to the czar, though politically unrealistic, was a gesture of Christian love in a time of imminent war when he was pictured in the British press as an aggressive tyrant of the worst order. The Quakers did not regret their effort; in their view, they had borne their witness, and the results were in God's hands.

Their widely publicized effort brought on the Quakers a torrent of obloquy from press and public throughout the war, which they nevertheless steadfastly condemned. The *Times* excoriated the Quakers and enthusiastically supported the war. In 1861, four years after the war ended, the editorials

26. Richard, *Memoirs of Joseph Sturge*, pp. 474–75. See also the account in Hobhouse, *Joseph Sturge: His Life and Work*, chap. 10.

27. Richard, *Memoirs of Joseph Sturge*, p. 476.

changed and said of the "ill-starred" war, "Never was so great an effort made for so worthless an object."[28]

Recent International Programs

To find the immediate sources for the conciliatory activity of the 1960s we must look to the proliferation of Friends' international work in the period after the two world wars. Following the First World War, an "international centers" program was developed to provide an organized, geographical base for many activities intended to strike at the roots of war on a more sustained basis than the previous sporadic efforts in times of crisis. After the Second World War this trend was continued with programs specifically directed toward certain leadership groups that might influence nations to look for peaceful solutions to conflicts.

Intrinsic to this development was the increased reliance on committees for international affairs, with full-time staff. I have mentioned the regular committees dealing with internal affairs of Friends. Special committees had been established from time to time to carry out concerns for peace or for better social conditions in society as a whole, but usually they had been limited in duration and scope because of the Quaker aversion to permanent organizations and the personnel, buildings, and finances they entailed. As interest and experience in the problem of preventing wars developed, committees and staff became more enduring. As Robert Byrd relates, "By the 1920's most of the Monthly Meetings of Friends, as well as the Yearly Meetings, had their standing committees on international affairs."[29] Generally the committees had to raise their own budgets inside or outside the circle of Friends.

28. Ibid., p. 496.
29. Byrd, *Quaker Ways*, pp. 155–56.

While some argued against the increasing structure and organization, the convincing rebuttal was that there was a job to be done and the means must be supplied for doing it.

Friends International Centers

The interplay between individual concern and committee structure is well illustrated by the rise of the Friends international centers. The initial vision came from Carl Heath, who became a member of the Society of Friends in 1916 after twenty years of teaching on the Continent and eight years as secretary of the (British) National Peace Council. Dismayed by the collapse of the National Peace Council under wartime pressure when only a small band, mostly Quakers, remained true to pacifist tenets, Heath became convinced that peace work needed a firmer base in religious convictions if it was to withstand the fervor of patriotism. He had long been interested in the Society of Friends, feeling that the teachings of Quakerism were largely ones he had been seeking in his own spiritual pilgrimage. In April 1917 he brought to a Friends conference at Skipton, Yorkshire, his inspiring vision of a new dawn of peace after the darkness of war. The Quakers would earn special respect from those who came to see the futility and terror of war, Heath thought, and thus would have a special responsibility to work positively for peace. He proposed a series of "Quaker Embassies" in the capitals of the world "to carry the Quaker message of the direct inner light of the Christ, confirmed in experience, and of the transvaluation thereby of human purposes to every great city in Europe and to every people."[30] The Society of Friends would send out "ambassadors" for two years of service, and their homes would be the centers of all manner of activity: working out schemes of international social service and re-

30. Carl Heath, *Quaker Embassies* (2nd ed., Oxted, Surrey: privately printed, 1920), p. 10.

form, building international political institutions for peace, cross-fertilizing adult education movements across national lines, and bringing together children in holiday camps and students in studies and conferences of all kinds.

The "Quaker Embassies" would be coordinated through a joint organizing committee, or "Foreign Office," in London. Students between school and university could go out as "attachés." A major purpose of all the activity would be to

> bring the foreigner to us and learn from him as well as bring our message to them. The true relation of nations, as members of the family of God, can only be reached when we each understand with profound and affectionate sympathy the wonderful message which each nation and each national group has to bring to the service of common humanity.[31]

Heath's broad vision was anything but modest and might be considered contrary to Quaker humility, but just as Robert Barclay did not think his address to the princes of Europe presumptuous, twentieth-century Quakers also inclined to ambitious dreams. The Yearly Meeting accepted the general idea and in 1919 established a Committee for International Service alongside the Friends War Victims Relief Committee. The grandiose words of Heath, who was new to Quaker ways, were toned down. "Embassy" gave way to "center" and "ambassadors" to "Quaker representatives," except for allusions in Quaker circles, where Heath's initial speech continued to inspire staff and committees.

As Carl Heath had anticipated, the major concern of Quaker work immediately after the war was in relief and reconstruction, but this activity was imbued with the spirit and practice of reconciliation of former enemies. For example, the extensive work of the British Friends War Victims Relief Commit-

31. Ibid.

tee in providing care and comfort for the large numbers of enemy aliens interned in Britain during the war was a fitting prelude for relief work in Germany after the war. Similarly, the first project of the American Friends Service Committee, which came into existence in 1917, was the work of American conscientious objectors in France in getting German prisoners, waiting for repatriation, to rebuild French villages. The prisoners were not allowed by regulations to receive wages, but the Quakers arranged that in lieu of pay, money from relief funds would be saved in individual accounts and taken to their families in Germany at the beginning of the relief effort there.

As Quaker relief work expanded across Europe from France to Russia, a few of the offices established by the Friends War Victims Relief Committee and the American Friends Service Committee held potential as Quaker international centers. Carl Heath, the secretary of the Friends Committee on International Service, was not responsible for relief work but moved around bringing spiritual inspiration to the healing process. In Heath's broad terms, any witness of good-will at any level, from the cup of water to the lecture on disarmament, was reconciliation and part of the important work of Christ on earth. For Heath, Christ and his teaching were central, but he thought in terms of a new kind of evangelism which would not be trying to make Christians or bring members into the Society of Friends, but would be spreading Quaker ideas and ways of dealing with situations of conflict. He was wont to say that he was not trying to preach Quakerism but to find friends.

There was a latent confusion in Heath's words that aroused some misgivings on the other side of the Atlantic, and American support for the centers idea was slow in developing. To understand this it is necessary to clarify the difference in approach and background of the English and American organizations. The difference came to the fore in relief work, where there was a potential contradiction between impartiality in giving help and zeal in conveying a message.

Emphasis on the Word versus Emphasis on the Deed

All Quaker workers and organizations agreed that assistance should be granted each individual as a child of God in a manner to promote good-will and reinforce the dignity of the recipient. There were disagreements, however, on how much the implicit message of compassion in giving should be made explicit by engaging in conversation or handing out tracts about Quaker ways, pacifism, and Christian beliefs. In general, the direction from London emphasized, while the direction stemming from Philadelphia minimized, the overt message.

These varying emphases arose from differences both in structure and in practice. Strong influences in London came from the Quaker missionary movement of the nineteenth century, which established missions in China, India, the Near East, and Africa. While the Friends Foreign Mission Association, established in 1868, had always emphasized practical service in health, education, and agricultural improvement, it still had a strong Christianizing motive. The move toward turning over missions to local leadership and thus withdrawing from a paternalistic role had gained headway by the 1920s. Thus, by 1927 it was possible without too much strain to merge the Friends Foreign Mission Association with the Friends Committee on International Service to form the Friends Service Council, responsible to both London and Ireland yearly meetings with joint secretaries, Harry T. Silcock and Carl Heath, until 1932, when Heath became sole secretary.

While the committees in London were responsible to two yearly meetings, The American Friends Service Committee was set up as an independent agency relating to twenty-five separate and quite disparate yearly meetings. While the AFSC sought representation from all yearly meetings who wanted to cooperate, the closest and strongest influences came from the two Philadelphia yearly meetings, whose missionary work overseas had been minimal, rather than from the western bodies of Friends, whose practice on this score resembled more that of London Yearly Meeting. Moreover, from the days of the mass-feeding project in Germany in 1920–22, the largest financial support for the work came from non-Quakers. When Herbert Hoover, administrator of the American Relief Administration, turned over the feeding in Germany to the American Quakers, he did not impose limitations on Quaker propaganda, but the workers themselves leaned over backwards not to take advantage of their monopoly position.

Thus, the American Friends Service Committee was at first worried that the centers organized from London put too much emphasis in their nonsectarian service on Quaker advancement, but under the chairmanship of Rufus Jones, an American Quaker historian and professor of philosophy whose broad vision of Quakerism made him embrace Carl Heath's concepts, the committee came to support the centers with finance and personnel. As we will see, some of the tension between the two approaches lingered on and came up at times of evaluation and decisions on priorities.

The Work of the Centers
As the relief work tapered off in the early 1920s, offices purely for relief were closed and the remaining centers took on a more general peacemaking role under Carl Heath's guidance. A pattern of intentional diversity grew out of the traditional Quaker idea that persons with a concern should be freed to do what they thought best with a minimum of direction from the home office. Centers were expected to be as different as the countries and situations in which they were located and as the interests and abilities of the secretaries sent

to carry on the work. For example, the Paris center in the twenties was much involved with prison work, the Vienna center with refugees, the Nurenberg center with student groups, and the Warsaw center with an embroidery enterprise.[32]

In Carl Heath's rhetoric, the centers were links in a chain, reinforcing each other in spreading good-will, but actually they were only occasionally involved in joint endeavors. A single theme with variations did, however, run through the work of all the centers: —"the ministry of reconciliation." Of paramount concern in several locations were the minority problems produced by the peace treaties ending the First World War. Quakers, along with many others, worried that the new boundaries might bring about future wars. Thus, for example, after the first rush of refugee work had tapered off, the Berlin and Warsaw centers collaborated in cross-border programs to bring better understanding between Poles and Germans. Joint conferences were held in 1925, 1926, and 1927 bringing together a variety of educators and young people from the two countries to discuss the problems of the Polish Corridor, Upper Silesia, and other places where there were large German minorities. As a result, the technique of running seminars to promote understanding and to reduce tension was established as one of the center's programs.

Many of the minority groups were subject to cruel oppression as they sought to retain their national identity under an alien rule, and the Quakers in the centers became involved in various efforts of intercession to relieve the suffering of groups like the Germans in the Ruhr during the French occupation of 1923, the Austrians of the South Tyrol under an Italianization program, and the German political prisoners in

32. For a full treatment of the centers, see Willis H. Hall, *Quaker International Work in Europe Since 1914,* dissertation submitted to the University of Geneva (Savoie: Imprimeries Reunies de Chambery, 1938).

Memel under Lithuanian rule. Wherever persecuted minorities were, whatever their politics, the Quakers attempted to plead their case with the ruling authorities.[33] The Quaker workers were accepted by the authorities because of their general reputation for integrity and impartiality, earned to a large extent through relief work, and in many cases they were able to help, particularly, as in the Ruhr occupation, when the actions of lower officials were not in accord with higher policy.

After the Nazis came to power in Germany in 1933, the Friends were increasingly drawn into succoring Jews and other victims of Nazi persecution. Friends in Germany and Britain helped in many ways. The Friends International Center in Berlin aided many people to emigrate. After the Day of Broken Glass, when Jewish homes, stores, and synagogues were attacked with the connivance of the authorities, American Friends sent a mission composed of Rufus Jones, Robert Yarnall, and George Walton to gain approval of authorities in Germany for relief to Jews and for help in their emigration. They succeeded in reaching high officers in the Gestapo. Their plan was approved, and some emigration was expedited, but it was already late.[34] Quaker efforts were successful in helping many individuals, but the Nazi hurricane continued to sweep the world toward war and the Jewish people toward the holocaust.

The Geneva Center and the League of Nations

The Geneva Friends Center at the headquarters of the League of Nations had a different origin and purpose. Opened in Sep-

---

33. For more particulars, see Bertram Pickard, *Pacifist Diplomacy in Conflict Situations Illustrated by the Quaker International Centers* (Philadelphia: Pacifist Research Bureau, 1943).

34. The full story is given in Elizabeth Gray Vining, *Friend of Life, The Biography of Rufus M. Jones* (Philadelphia: J. B. Lippincott Co., 1958), chap. 26.

tember 1922 in neutral Switzerland, it was relieved of the large load of refugee and relief work carried by the other offices so that it could concentrate on a Quaker effort to support the League of Nations as an instrument of peace.

In the early 1920s a number of private international organizations seeking to influence world policies set up offices in Geneva. They were soon at loggerheads with each other as they vied for privileges of attendance at League sessions and submission of papers to League committees. Dr. Inazo Nitobe, the undersecretary-general of the League of Nations since its founding, was himself a Japanese Quaker married to Mary Elkinton, a Philadelphia Quaker. Active in the Geneva Meeting, Dr. Nitobe saw the Quaker center as a place for reconciling the differences among the international organizations. He helped to start a luncheon series in 1926 for the private international representatives to meet and talk together. Dr. Nitobe went to London to impress upon Carl Heath the importance of getting the right couple to staff the center and to carry on the luncheons. Largely at Dr. Nitobe's urging, Bertram and Irene Pickard were sent to Geneva in June 1926. Their combined graciousness, tact, and political acumen made the center a headquarters for Quaker knowledge and influence in international relations. The continuous lobbying activities of the Quakers who came to the center, such as working for the improved treatment of refugees, minorities, and stateless persons, constituted a sound footing for the later work with the United Nations both in Geneva and New York. Pickard sought to spread information about the League and the problems of international peace through syndicated columns in peace periodicals and in regular newspapers such as the Starmer group in England and the *Washington Post* in the United States.

Under the Pickards the luncheon meetings of international organizations developed into an important clearing house for lobbying activity, leading to the formation in 1929 of the

Federation of Private and Semi-Official International Organizations. Bertram Pickard served as secretary and treasurer. By working together, the private organizations were able to build good relations with the Secretariat and the delegations. They presented papers, listened in on sessions, and at times even participated in the formal discussions. When the United Nations Charter was being finalized in San Francisco toward the end of the Second World War, the informal practices developed under the League were formalized in article 71, which provided for nongovernmental organizations to have consultative status with the Economic and Social Council.[35]

In addition to influencing a wider public, the centers gave the Quakers a broader knowledge of world problems and prepared the ground for future international work. Traveling Quakers interested in postwar problems used the centers as headquarters during their visits and reported home in the Quaker periodicals. The cross-fertilization among the divided groups of American Quakers was facilitated because they all found attractive elements in the varied center programs. The centers were an important influence in the gradual process whereby various parts of the Society of Friends established in 1937 the Friends World Committee for Consultation, with headquarters in England. Carl Heath, appropriately enough, was the first general secretary. Quaker allergies to central control were respected in the smallness of the staff and budget and the looseness of the confederation.

Quaker International Affairs Work after World War II
One might think that the catastrophe of the Second World War would have discouraged Quakers from pursuing international work. The basis of the work, an appeal to the divinely ordered goodness of human beings, would seem to have been

35. See Bertram Pickard, *The Greater United Nations* (New York: Carnegie Endowment for Peace, 1956).

shattered. The effectiveness of producing a climate of good-will seemed by any objective index to be nil. Pacifist persuasion in the face of a phenomenon such as Nazism appeared hopeless. But just as the extreme hatred and cruelty of the First World War had brought a new dream of a world of good-will, so too the nightmare of the Second World War and the coming of the atomic age stirred the Quakers to see the greater urgency of international work, not only for relief, where the enormous problems were self-evident, but even more for plans to prevent future wars.

Two factors in Quaker thinking led to this reaction. First was the nineteenth-century optimism, which still had a strong hold in spite of the drastic events. Second, and more important, was the basis of Quaker faith, which was deeper than worldly optimism and had upheld the Quakers in dark trials from the beginning. When outward events denied the influences of the seed of God in man, the Quakers turned to the deeper levels of faith in the inward reality of God's love, which could not be denied even if men were blind to it. Thus, scientifically precise obliteration of human beings, as in Hiroshima, and planned genocide on a scale never before possible, as in Germany, became proof of the evils of modern society and arguments for renewed and increased efforts. There were more Quaker conscientious objectors in World War II than in World War I, and even before the end of the war committees were talking of new forms of peace work.[36] As soon as possible, Quaker workers were in Germany and Japan with relief for war sufferers and a little later with programs to promote the conditions of peace.

---

36. See Mulford Q. Sibley and Philip E. Jacob, *Conscription of Conscience: The American State and the Conscientious Objector, 1940–47* (Ithaca, N.Y.: Cornell University Press, 1952), where comparative estimates are given for all kinds of conscientious objectors in Britain (p. 5) and in the United States (pp. 83–84).

While several of the centers survived the war and continued with support from committees in London and Philadelphia, there was a growing feeling that with the diffusion of activity, the involvement with advancing Quakerism locally, and the lack of correlation, the centers made little impact on the international situation. The new postwar idea was to look for points of maximum leverage for influencing the nations for peace. The basic Quaker faith that God's love as witnessed by Christ could operate both in individual lives and in societal patterns was still the motivating force, but a search began to find influential groups the Quakers might reach, to single out the issues of greatest potential conflict, and to use the new resources in social science for conflict analysis and resolution.

The emphasis in the twenties and thirties had been on spreading good will from Quaker centers. The emphasis in the fifties and sixties was on bringing groups of potential leaders together across barriers of culture and national interest and exposing them to the new insights of psychology and sociology on conflict resolution, under the positive structuring of Quaker staff, so that they would be motivated to promote the conditions of peace. The first emphasis had developed largely under the leadership of British and Irish Friends at a time when the American Friends Service Committee was preoccupied with domestic problems of poverty, industrial violence, and peace education. The second emphasis after World War II came out of Philadelphia, although British Friends accepted and encouraged the trend.

The American Friends Service Committee was in a good position after World War II to reach out for broad financing of ambitious programs. The executive secretary, Clarence Pickett, was widely known for his work on problems of the Depression and immigration. After 1950, as secretary emeritus, he continued to be involved in international programs. The organization was known for honest reporting, economy in overhead costs, and absence of sectarian bias. Along with the (British) Friends Service Council it had been awarded the Nobel Prize for its work in reconciliation. While holding wide support among Friends, it reached far beyond the resources of the various participating yearly meetings. Ambitious plans require large resources, and it is no accident that the new program planning of the American Friends coincided with the opening of large new sources of income from non-Quaker donors and from foundations looking for ways to bring peace. Bold plans with a definite focus and a strong rationale appealed to the new leadership of foundations.

In the years from 1946 to 1953 three new programs particularly pertinent to our study were launched with foundation support: the International Student Seminars, the Washington Seminars in International Affairs, and the Conference for Diplomats. At the same time fresh thinking on the centers program brought increased emphasis on building the institutions of peace through the Quaker office at the United Nations and a more direct attack on particular conflict areas through the use of roving Quaker representatives.

Other ambitious programs in the international field were promoted in Philadelphia at this time: the School Affiliation Service, a program of pairing schools in the United States and abroad for exchange of teaching materials, students, and teachers, and the International Work Camps, bringing together young people of many countries for projects of village improvement. These, however, were less important in setting the stage for later conciliation efforts. Relief and rehabilitation endeavors continued to maintain the role of Quakers as healers of man-made suffering. For example, at the request of United Nations officials, after the Arab-Israeli war in 1948, the Quakers operated relief camps for 235,000 Arab refugees in the Gaza Strip for two years.

International Student Seminars
The first of the new programs was originated by an AFSC

peace worker who found donors to support international seminars on building peace. Large numbers of foreign students were coming to the United States for advanced training, and these students, it was reasoned, might be a strong influence for peace. Selected American students would also participate, but only as one national group among many. Immediate precedents for the program were two international student seminars organized in the United States by the peace program of the AFSC in 1943 and 1944. More remote precedents were the German-Polish seminars of 1925-27, organized from the centers of Berlin and Warsaw.

The first statement of purpose of the seminars,[37] given at a committee meeting of December 5, 1946, derived its inspiration from the quotation from the UNESCO charter: "Since wars begin in the minds of men, it is in the minds of men that the defenses of peace must be constructed." This quotation appeared frequently in the brochures of the Friends Service Committee in subsequent years. Appealing to religious and agnostic alike, the motto was noticeably more secular in tone than Carl Heath's call "to rebuild Europe as a City of God,"[38] but to the sponsors the same spiritual affirmation was implied.

In the summer of 1947 the seminars were started in the United States, with 249 participants in eight different groups. In the following three years ten seminars were conducted in various parts of the country, most of them lasting for seven weeks. The peak of participation was in 1949, with 320 students from fifty-nine different countries. The seminars involved intensive study, with a major consultant coming each week to lecture and lead discussion on some aspect of the general topic, "Laying the Foundations for World Peace." In

37. First called International Service Seminars, then International Student Seminars.
38. Heath, *Quaker Embassies*, p. 6.

the seven weeks the organizers sought to cover some of the psychological, political, cultural, economic, and religious bases for peace. Usually one week was devoted to the study of mediation in international relations and the functioning of the United Nations. Although the formal program attracted students seriously interested in war and peace problems, it was only part of the total experience, which, as the alumni testified, was rich in new insights growing out of the informal association with other students. The learning from inter-personal interaction was facilitated by work projects, group excursions, and small group discussions. The number of students from any one country, especially the United States, was kept small to prevent the formation of national cliques. In the friendly climate created in each seminar, students from traditionally hostile countries were brought together with quite positive results.

After the first four years participation fell off, largely because there were many other opportunities for foreign students to go to summer school or to earn money. The length and number of seminars was reduced, but the program in the United States continued until 1958.

In 1948 the program was extended to Europe, in 1949 to East Asia and South Asia, in 1963 in modified form to West Africa, and in 1967 to Southeast Asia. In places where a Friends International Center already existed, such as Paris, Geneva, Delhi and Tokyo, the seminar organizers maintained some contact with the center staff, but since their program involved wide travel to interview participants and resource persons and to seek out meeting places in various countries, their participation in local center activities was necessarily limited. Adjusting to regional needs, the program was modified to include, in addition to student seminars, groups of journalists, educators, social workers, rural development planners, and government officials brought together to discuss specific problems in which they were involved. The seminars were still international, but problems of development in less-developed countries came to be featured more than international disputes. The International Dialogue Program in West Africa was designed for the regional needs of the newly independent countries of sub-Saharan Africa. British Quakers played important leadership roles as individuals, but it was not until 1961 that the Friends Service Council of London became joint sponsor of the program. The Canadian Friends Service Committee and the Quaker Service Council of Australia joined in sponsorship later.

Through the Quaker International Seminars persons from all parts of the world came to know Quakers and were exposed to a broader understanding of world problems. As of 1961 there had been about 5,300 participants from 110 countries. The extent of the influence in changed attitudes and behavior is impossible to judge. Dr. J. Milton Yinger, sociologist of Oberlin College, reviewed the program in 1952 and recommended a "continuing study of the consequences of seminars on behavior over a period of years," but the AFSC was never in a position to implement this advice.[39] The priority for scarce funds was always to continue programs. Special funds for research were difficult to find, as was extra staff time to find them. An unplanned by-product, however, has been the positive reaction of alumni distributed throughout the world when asked to help in Quaker conciliatory work.

Washington International Affairs Seminars
In 1950 and 1951 a group of social scientists of various disciplines who had been working on problems of conflict in different universities were brought together at Princeton, New Jersey by the New Hope Foundation of Pennsylvania to

39. John Milton Yinger, "A Study of International Service Seminars of the American Friends Service Committee" (AFSC Archives, 1952).

explore the implications of current research in personal and intergroup relations for problems of international relations and especially United States foreign policy. The group produced a joint statement of principles on war and peace under the general heading "As the Social Scientist Sees It":

> Our view holds that war settles only the question of who will dominate whom. War never decides which values are best. It is an outmoded and increasingly futile device for seeking a resolution of human conflicts. The fact that most men deplore war and hope to discover means for abolishing it, is one of the scanty blessings of our times. We believe that if basic principles of social science are applied to national and international relations war can be eliminated. . . .
>
> The United States is in a position to make obsolete the traditional conception of diplomacy as a procedure whereby one nation seeks to outwit and outbargain an opponent for the purpose of selfish gain. Power is historically the concern of all politics. The time has come to revise this conception—within the nation and between nations—so that the values of understanding, accommodation, and charity become the leading objectives of politics.[40]

Directly out of this conference of social scientists grew the idea for influencing the foreign policy of the United States by a continuing seminar in which consulting social scientists would meet with government officials in Washington. Through the relation of Clarence Pickett, secretary emeritus of the AFSC, as a consultant to the New Hope Foundation, the Service Committee was asked to sponsor the project. Harold Snyder, who had been carrying on international projects for

---

40. "As the Social Scientist Sees It" (AFSC Archives, 1951), pp. 1 and 12.

the American Council on Education, worked part time to develop the program.

Key officials from the Civil Service Commission, the Bureau of the Budget, the State Department, the National Security Council, the Economic Cooperation Administration, and the Senate Foreign Relations Committee were present at the first meeting held in November 1951. The experts were limited to a brief presentation of the essence of their findings, which were then scrutinized for their usefulness to practicing officials and politicians. In the first meeting Professor Hadley Cantril summarized his research as director of UNESCO'S International Tensions Project on national stereotypes. Dr. George Gallup presented the results of his opinion research in Europe. The chairman of the meeting was Gilbert White, Quaker geographer, who set the tone of informality, flexibility of discussion, and disciplined pursuit of the topic which characterized the meetings from then on.

There was unanimous enthusiasm for the significance of the material presented and the format of the evening. The informal setting at the Friends Center of Davis House was considered ideal for entertaining a group of twenty-five for discussion at supper and after. After the first year of holding meetings about once a month, the question was raised as to whether the program should be carried on under other auspices. A special committee, asked to consult with participants, reported that the Quaker openness to highly controversial issues, their lack of vested interest in either research or government policy, and their general dedication to human values and peace made them uniquely qualified to sponsor the meetings. Their pacifist position was well known, said those consulted, but it did not limit thier ability to present issues objectively and to draw constructive views from many sources.

In 1952, Harold Snyder was engaged as full-time director and served until his retirement in 1972. To the monthly evening sessions for government officials and congressmen were added luncheons for Washington journalists and for government personnel officers. In 1959 weekend seminars for foreign diplomats and U.S. officials were started and continued through 1973. Over the years a large number of consultants from the United States and other countries were involved on the general theme "The Relationship of U.S. Policies and Programs to Other Peoples of the World." The initial emphasis on social science was early broadened to include presentations by persons with special experience and insights in the international field, such as Sir Zafrulla Khan of the International Court of Justice, Ralph Bunche, under-secretary of the United Nations, and Brock Chisolm, director of the World Health Organization.

The International Affairs Seminars of Washington were subject to constant informal evaluation by an advisory committee composed of participants and Quaker sponsors, but as in the case of the student seminars, no formal evaluation by an outside source was commissioned. It is fair to say that these seminars, carefully planned to insure significant contributions from consultants and maximum participation of the participants, held the interest of important people in Washington over the years and, as a by-product, brought respect for Quaker efforts for peace.

Conferences for Diplomats
The third program launched in these years grew out of the student seminars but was also strongly influenced by the Washington seminars. In 1950 the International Student Seminar Committee of Quaker and non-Quaker academicians drawn together largely by the staff, Burns Chalmers and Nora Booth, began discussing the extension of the seminar model to those already in positions of leadership in international affairs. A proposal to run a pilot project was approved by the Ford Foundation as part of a grant to the American Friends

Service Committee. Newly reorganized in Pasadena, California, under the leadership of Paul Hoffman, the Ford Foundation had a strong emphasis on work for peace. On the advice of Harold Snyder a proposal for a "leadership seminar" was drawn up. A consultative group was assembled in Paris at the end of March 1952. After considering various groupings of postwar leadership—educators, journalists, politicians, trade unionists—the group decided upon the small but significant world of diplomats, especially young foreign service officers.

The problem then was to convince the foreign offices of the various European countries that they should allow some junior officers to participate in an unofficial, unpublicized conference where there would be a frank airing of views on the topic "National Interest and International Responsibility." Martha Biehle, a member of the administration of Stephens College in Missouri, was responsible for securing participants, while Harold Snyder secured consultants and helped to run the conference. Though Martha Biehle was not herself a Quaker, she was helped by Quaker contacts to reach responsible persons in the capitals of Europe. The novelty of the enterprise was demonstrated by the refusal to participate of the British Foreign Office, scrupulously following the rulebook, which prohibited "any member of the Foreign Office from expressing his private views to anyone on any matter affecting the policy of his government in any area."[41] The other governments contacted agreed to the proposal, and the British joined after the first year.

The first conference, held that same summer, brought together twenty-five young diplomats from fifteen different countries under the joint charimanship of Gilbert S. White, American geographer and president of Haverford College, Pennsylvania; Dr. John R. Rees, British psychiatrist and director of the World Federation of Mental Health; and Alva

---

41. Report of Martha Biehle, no. 19, 14 July 1952 (AFSC Archives).

Myrdal, Swedish social scientist and director of social sciences for UNESCO. The participants were unanimously enthusiastic about the conference held in St. George's School at Clarens, near Montreux, Switzerland. The school accommodations were in the Quaker style of comfortable simplicity, and the location on the northern side of Lake Leman provided a view of the spectacular Dents Du Midi to the southeast and the Savoy Alps with Mont Blanc to the southwest. The ambiance was an important ingredient of Clarens conferences, and many alumni later said that the environment contributed to the discussions in creating a new vision of their work in international relations.

The value of the program has been attested by many participants. Writing in the *Foreign Service Journal* in the United States, one early participant expressed appreciation for the Quaker thought and care and identified three important parts of the learning experience. First, the consultants and chairmen, such as Ralph Bunche, Paul-Henri Spaak, and Gunnar Myrdal, emphasized "the importance of idealism in international affairs and the responsibilities of the individual official to be loyal to his ideals and to work for their achievement," yet not a "naive idealism" unaware of the manifold practical problems. Second, the participant learned from the discussions that "in defending one's national policies in foreign affairs, you find there is much more room for accommodating the views of others, without harm to one's own legitimate national interest." A third and final factor in the learning experience was the warm friendships created, which would be a great help in the future official relationships: "a bond, an easy entree, and broad basis of understanding to facilitate the official transaction of business."[42] Another expression of the value of the conference for younger diplomats was given by

42. Charles E. Hulick, "Friends at Work," *Foreign Service Journal,* July 1954.

the deputy permanent secretary in the Ministry of External Affairs of Nigeria in an interview with AFSC staff in April 1964: "The conference made it possible for us to take policy positions and postures of the Department, put them into a melting pot and check against realities presented by firsthand, frank, informal and extended contact with people from a non-Nigerian environment."[43]

During the late fifties and sixties the European conferences emphasized East-West relations and included participants from the Soviet Union and all the socialist countries except Albania and China.[44] The pattern of Clarens conferences was extended to South Asia in 1955 and to Japan in 1965. The program is much the same today, although topics have become more specific, and participants now include a proportion of nondiplomats. The 1974 directory of program alumni lists 1,770 diplomats in active service from ninety-three countries. Many of them have reached positions of distinction in the diplomatic field.

The Quaker United Nations Office

After the horrors of the Second World War, the world looked with anticipation toward the United Nations for a new start in organizing peace. American Quakers, moved by hope and a sense of responsibility for world issues, established an office in New York to serve as a center for Quaker influence on the world organization. As we noted, a provision was included in the UN Charter for the consultation of nongovernmental organizations. The assorted and scattered Quakers, constituting over fifty yearly meetings around the world, used the channel of the Friends World Committee for Consultation,

43. Trip report of Robert O. Byrd, director of International Dialogues in West Africa (AFSC Archives, April 1964).
44. The part played by Diplomats Conferences in the conciliation between the two Germanies is described in chapter 2.

formed in 1937, to apply for NGO status to the Economic
and Social Council of the UN. The application was approved
in March 1948, and in October of the same year, Elmore and
Beth Jackson of the AFSC staff in Philadelphia became the
first full-time staff, with their home in a large apartment near
the UN serving as both office and Quaker center.

The practice of submitting carefully prepared memoranda
to organs of the United Nations was begun with a paper addressed to the Human Rights Commission seeking the international community's recognition of the conscientious objector's right not to participate in armed combat. Staff and
short-term associates over the years continued research and
presentation of issues relating to peace such as disarmament,
slavery, the status of women, and development in the Third
World.

The study of issues occasionally led to the publication of
analyses and position papers. One early effort was the multinational group of specialists in labor disputes and in international conflict assembled to find techniques and procedures
that might be translated from industrial relations conflict to
conflict between nations. This led to the publication of the
book by Elmore Jackson, *Meeting of Minds*.[45]

Although British Friends were closely consulted and participated integrally from the beginning, the major initiative for
Quaker work at the United Nations was in the hands of the
American Friends Service Committee. There was some resentment of Anglo-Saxon dominance of the UN office in other
parts of the Quaker world, but there was no practical alternative for administration or financing. The Friends World Committee for Consultation, intentionally weak in finance and
decision-making power to conform with Quaker distaste for
strong central control, was content to leave the day-to-day
operation of an effective lobbying program to the AFSC.

45. New York: McGraw-Hill, 1952.

Mindful of their position as representative of all Quakers, the AFSC organizers tried from the beginning to make the staff and short-term volunteers as international as possible. In 1950 the first Quaker team gathered to attend the General Assembly meeting. It included Agatha Harrison, who had been involved in conciliation work between India and Great Britain; Elsa Cedergren, well known in Swedish government circles for her contributions to social welfare; Gerald Bailey, founder of the Britain–USSR Association; Heberto Sein, Mexican Friend with a strong but tactful voice for Latin American views; Clarence Pickett, just retired as executive secretary of AFSC; and Elmore Jackson, program director. During the three months that the Assembly was in session the team followed committee discussions with intense concentration, talked with delegates about issues such as expanding the scope of the United Nations High Commissioner for Refugees beyond just legal assistance to European refugees, and sought out the spokesmen of opposing sides in conflict situations such as the Arab–Israeli dispute, where the Quakers had some background for serious and meaningful discussion of the problem.

The most distinctive feature of the Quaker activity at the United Nations was the Quaker living center. Through the generosity of wealthy non-Quakers donors, first a large apartment and then a brownstone row house were obtained close to the United Nations. To preserve the tranquillity of a home and a Quaker center, the bustle of office work was transferred to the Carnegie Building, opened in 1953 across from the UN to house NGOs. Elmore and Beth Jackson acted as director and hostess for most of the years from 1948 to 1961, with the assistance of Sydney and Brenda Bailey, who came from London several times during this and later periods. Carl Heath's inspiration for the "Quaker Embassy: From the City of God to the City of Man" was embodied here more fully than in many former Quaker centers. Protected from the usual heterogeneous nature of Quaker activities, the primary function of Quaker House was to serve as a place where members of the UN delegations and the Secretariat could find refreshment, inspiration, and frank discussion in the informal atmosphere of a home. In the house on Forty-eighth Street small gatherings would discuss topics of special interest to delegates in a quiet, conciliatory atmosphere. At times outside experts would be called in to share their knowledge with the community. Many representatives of the international community over the years spoke about what might be called the pastoral function of the Quaker representative and the value of Quaker House as a place to retreat from the intense atmosphere of the world forum and to revive flagging courage in the cause of peace.

The program continues today in much the same pattern. As the United Nations has focused more on Third World views, the interest of the Quakers has also turned toward support of the claims of the have-nots and the search for justice as a basis for peace.

Quaker International Affairs Representatives
The Friends International Centers were revived after the war, continuing their varied work with special emphasis on the problems of refugees. The focus of Quaker House at the United Nations—to reach persons who could influence trends towards war or peace—became the model for other centers. The center in Geneva, which had operated under the direction of the Pickards during the time of the League of Nations, was reactivated in 1949 under the leadership of Colin and Elaine Bell, veterans of the Friends Ambulance Unit in China in the early forties, and became the second Quaker contact with and influence upon the fledgling United Nations Organization. The Quakers found themselves dealing with Bertram Pickard, now employed by the United Nations as the European liaison officer with consultative NGOs. Duncan and

Katharine Wood followed the Bells in 1953, and their abilities and twenty-five years of service made them an important
part of the Quaker network for the issues and problems
having special reference to Geneva. Duncan Wood, following
in the footsteps of Bertram Pickard, became chairman of the
Conference of Consultative NGOs.

The implementation of the centers' new concentration on
key issues and areas of conflict was accelerated after an evaluation of the centers sponsored by the AFSC in 1945–46.
Some centers were selected for special support from Philadelphia as a result of their international significance; others
continued to gain support from London for their local Quaker outreach. Cooperation between the centers was promoted,
and Colin Bell from Geneva spoke of realizing Carl Heath's
dream of "a chain of international centers" through "linked
centers" which would take concerted action on a limited
number of the world's problems.

The trend was clearly evident in an appeal for funds to the
Ford Foundation in 1951. Although some of the vagueness
and diffuseness of the center programs of the twenties and
thirties was still evident in the appeal, "a senior representative" was suggested for each center who would

> undertake to exchange views and information on a limited
> number of the world's problems and to bring the Quaker
> position to the attention of persons in government or in
> the United Nations. This phase of the work is relatively
> new and modest in scope. Experience to date suggests
> that it may well be one of the most important aspects of
> the work of the American Friends Service Committee.[46]

As the memorandum predicted, the "senior representatives," called Quaker international affairs representatives in
1953, soon came into prominence, although the old-style

46. Memorandum, "International Centers" (AFSC Archives, 1951).

centers continued to be the site of various Quaker-related activities until phased out or devolved on local groups. The acronym QIAR led to various puns referring to their harmonizing activities and to the quires of paper created as their reports to the Quaker constituency and a limited public were mimeographed in Philadelphia and London under the title "Quaker International Affairs Reports."

David C. McClelland, a social scientist called in as a consultant by the Ford Foundation, wrote almost entirely of the Quaker international affairs representatives in his report on centers. He described their objectives and methods of work in terms of conflict resolution: "The basic assumption is that, especially when tensions are high, people tend to believe about their opponents what fear leads them to believe, especially when their fear and anger prevents them from finding out the *facts* about what their opponents are thinking." Thus, he said, the Quaker intermediary worked to bring more reality perception to each side. McClelland described in detail the work of Eric Johnson, a QIAR loosely attached to the Paris center in 1952 and 1953, who was trying to bring better understanding between French colonial officers and Moroccan nationalists by interviewing many leaders in Morocco and Paris and interpreting the views of one side to the other. The Quaker United Nations office was also involved in this effort at conciliation, for Johnson sent his reports on key issues to Quaker representatives who could sound out Arab delegates on possible solutions. While his efforts were not crowned with immediate success, McClelland reports, "There is no doubt that he had done a lot of interpretation back and forth between the disputing parties, which may later form the basis for a useful settlement."[47]

---

47. David C. McClelland, "Report on the Activities of the Quaker International Centers Supported by the Ford Foundation," 17 September, 1953 (AFSC Archives).

By the 1960s the pattern of QIAR work was well established in both Philadelphia and London. A committee memorandum of 1963 spoke of continuing "the role of a Quaker Ambassador without confining him to the traditional Quaker embassy of the past."[48] Thus, the 1939 prediction of Carl Heath was fulfilled:

> It is not, however, to be imagined that the Quaker Service can be confined to "Centres" in the sense of institutions. Spiritually the Quaker embassy is a centre of personalities given to the ministry of reconciliation. But not a few such personalities are called at times to lonely and individual service.[49]

In this way the pattern was set for the work of the Quaker representative in Berlin (chapter 2) and the work of the roving intermediary sent to India and Pakistan on the recommendation of the Friends Mission in 1966 (chapter 3). The conciliatory work in Nigeria (chapter 4) was not confined to one QIAR but was at different times performed by three persons functioning in this capacity.

East-West Relations
Much of the impetus for the development of the post-World War II programs came from Philadelphia, yet one must not overlook the leadership given by the British committees to the problems of conciliation between Socialist and Western countries at a time when the dangers of a nuclear war dominated the headlines and American Quakers were inhibited by the atmosphere of McCarthyism. Following the early contacts made by Quaker representatives at the United Nations with

48. "Report to the Board of Directors; International Centers and Quaker International Affairs Representative Program," March 1963 (AFSC Archives).
49. Carl Heath, *The Quaker Centre* (London: Friends Service Council, 1939).

diplomats from the Soviet Union, the East-West Relations Committee established in London in 1950 held a conference with representatives of the World Peace Council, an organization sponsored by the Soviet Union, to discuss frankly the misunderstanding and rival ideological claims that divide Europe. The leader of the Soviet delegation invited Friends to send a group to visit the Soviet Union, and in July of 1951, seven Friends were chosen. They visited factories, mines, farms, hospitals, and schools; they talked with the deputy foreign minister and the minister of education. Their report received prominent headlines throughout Britain. It was one of the first openings between East and West after the barriers were erected during Stalin's drastic efforts to organize and collectivize the country and the first significant opening for Friends since the Friends center in Moscow was closed in 1930 after several years of tenuous existence.[50]

Other European initiatives can be only briefly mentioned. Swedish Friends arranged a meeting with Russian Baptists in 1953, and Friends from the East-West Committee and other European Friends kept up an important liaison through the fifties and sixties with the Eastern-oriented Christian Peace Conference of the World Peace Council. All these contacts were helpful later in obtaining the inclusion of persons from the Eastern bloc in conferences for diplomats, international seminars, and work camps.

Thus, the Quaker religious concern to work for peace, the historical precedents of going to top leadership in seeking peace, and the organizational framework briefly summarized here formed the basis for intensive Quaker conciliation efforts during the 1960s. There was no concerted plan to perform third-party functions in international conflicts. In the experiential manner typical of Friends, concerns arose for specific situations and the way opened for fruitful work.

50. Scott, *Quakers in Russia,* chap. 19.

Chapter Two

Quaker Work between the Two Germanies

Background

The Berlin Wall in Perspective

On Thursday, December 21, 1972, the *Grundvertrag,* or basic treaty, acknowledging the existence of two separate German states was formally signed in East Berlin. Egon Bahr, special assistant to Chancellor Willy Brandt, signed for the Federal Republic of Germany, and Michael Kohl, state secretary of the Council of Ministers, signed for the German Democratic Republic. Thus a major step was taken toward ending twenty-five years of resolute nonrecognition of the other Germany by the Federal Republic and persistent insulation of itself by the German Democratic Republic.

An observer in the quiet streets by the Opera House on that December day would have found it difficult to recall the crises of previous years in which Berlin had been the center of potential world conflict: the Berlin blockade of 1948, the Khrushchev ultimatum of 1958, the Berlin Wall of 1961. Nor was it easy to understand the potency of the illusions to which Western policy was rigidly attached all those years. While the treaty implied some concessions by the Eastern government, it marked a complete about-face in West German policy. The Berlin Wall marked the beginning of a transition in policy from Adenauer's nonrecognition and isolation of East Germany to Brandt's accommodation to the Democratic Republic. From the perspective of December 1972, the Wall, denounced throughout the Western world as a symbol of oppression, could be seen as a tragic but necessary event for the building of peace in Europe. To understand this and the Quaker effort in third-party conciliation, which was intimately connected with the changes of policy signalized by the Wall, we turn briefly to the origins and later stages of the cold war in Germany.

While the Allied generals on the eastern and western fronts were in the throes of the hot war against the Third Reich, their political leaders were making plans to prevent the resurgence of another German menace. Unconditional surrender and military occupation of the country were the policy guidelines for victory. The German armies collapsed in March and April of 1945, and Berlin fell to the Soviet attack on May 2 after a desperate house-to-house resistance incited by Hitler, who committed suicide on April 30.

In the tough bargaining over deployment of occupation forces and division of territory between the Western Allies and the Soviet Union, the cold war, already in the making, became manifest. Behind the boundaries finally agreed upon, the Allies, with the United States dominating, set about refashioning a new Germany in their own image. The Soviets did the same in their sector. Dr. Adenauer, first chancellor of the new Federal Republic, asked for a unified Germany strongly tied to the Western defense system. The popular slogan was "Self-determination of the German people with free elections." The Soviet Union called for a neutral and demilitarized confederation of Germany. The Allies thought that an unarmed, neutral Germany such as the Weimar Republic of 1919–33 would create a vacuum that would soon be filled by the Soviet Union, which seemed to them to have aggressive designs on all of Europe. To the Soviet Union, "Free elections in all Germany" might mean the loss of a useful ally and the possibility of a reconstituted Reich, which they mortally feared. Thus, while lip service was paid on both sides to German unity, actual policies tended toward the separation of Germany into two regions and eventually two states, each with a quite different political-economic system.

The former allies and unconditional victors, falling out over the spoils, created separate governments in the zones in which they had military control. On the Western side the *Bundesrepublic Deutschland,* or Federal Republic of Germany, was established in 1949 with a two-house legislature, a chancellor serving as head of the party in power, and a president elected by the two houses of parliament in joint session. In the Soviet sector the *Deutsche Demokratische Republik* was established in the same year with a *Volkskammer,* or People's Assembly, strongly dominated by the *Socialist Einheits Partei,* which in turn was dominated by the Communist party.

Although in theory the country as a whole continued to be governed by the Military Control Commission, which held final sovereignty, in fact the commission did not meet or act, and each side gave its client state more and more power, just short of full sovereignty. The Federal Republic was recognized in 1955 by the Soviet Union, but the Western Allies and West Germans continued to deny recognition to the Democratic Republic and dealt officially only with the occupying power, the Soviet Union.

Berlin, the historical *Hauptstadt,* was a significant symbol both of the defeat of nazism and the victory of the allies; all four powers wanted a piece of it. At an allied ministers' conference in London in September 1944 plans were made for carving up Berlin into three sectors. Later a fourth piece was cut out for France. The division was for occupation purposes, and the whole city was to be governed by an Inter-Allied Governing Authority. As it happened, when the Germans finally surrendered, the Soviets had all of Berlin, while American and British forces were occupying large parts of the agreed-upon Soviet sector of Germany. It took some time to sort out an exchange of territory in the Soviet sector in return for pieces of Berlin, and not until July 1, 1945, seven weeks after the German surrender, did Western military representatives arrive in Berlin to establish with the Soviets the governing authority, which became known as the Kommandatura.

The administration of Berlin required close cooperation between the former allies and was the first point to show the stress of the cold war. As each side tried to extend its power, ideology, and social system, a series of actions and reactions brought the division of the city into two parts. The German Communist leaders and parties who were put into political control of the whole city by the Soviet military in May 1945 soon found themselves in control of only the Eastern sector. A landmark in this process was the election of city and borough councils in October 1946 in which the communist-dominated Socialist Unity Party (SED) received less than 20 percent of the citywide vote. This statistic of the "last free election" was an index of the unpopularity of the SED leaders at the time and was cited for many years as unassailable proof that the Eastern side lacked popular support.

The former capital of Germany remained for many years a prime source of contention between the two successor states. Although a hundred miles within the East German borders, West Berlin was considered by the West Germans a part of the Federal Republic. Moreover, Berlin was considered the symbolic capital of Germany, so Bonn was made a temporary capital. The Federal president maintained an official residence in Berlin, and the historic Reichstag building was rebuilt just over the border from the Soviet sector for possible future use in a unified country. The Soviets and East Germans, on the other hand, minimized any connection of West Berlin with the Federal Republic. They insisted that according to the Potsdam agreement, West Berlin was an "independent political entity with a special relation to West Germany." East Berlin, contiguous in territory with the Democratic Republic, eventually became its capital.

An early confrontation over the status of Berlin came in 1948–49. In June 1948 the currency reform, which the Provisional German Government in Frankfurt proposed to introduce to West Berlin, was seen as the last straw in East Berlin. This action emphasized the linkage of West Berlin to West Germany, which was strongly opposed in the East, and it underlined the strength of the economy of the West, which represented a threat to the Eastern sector. The Soviet forces and German Communist leadership countered by closing the land access to West Berlin. The intent evidently was to force West Berlin to capitulate and become part of the capital city of East Germany. The United States responded by a massive airlift still remembered by West Berliners, who read on a large monument the figures of the record day that brought 12,849 tons of produce to the airport by 1,383 planes landing at sixty three-second intervals. The airlift indicated the strong resolve of the Western Allies to keep West Berlin a symbol of Western freedom, affluence, and anticommunism. Eleven months after the interference on the *Autobahn* began, the East gave up and allowed normal traffic to resume.

The drastic action of the airlift led twelve years later to the drastic reaction of the Berlin Wall. The airlift saved a Western enclave as an irritant in the heart of the German Democratic Republic, an infectious point, in the Eastern view, which finally had to be sealed off by the Wall. The miscalculation by the Eastern side in 1948, thinking that West Berlin could be forced into East Geramny, was matched by the Western policy during the next decade, which sought to wrench East Germany from the Soviet sphere of influence.

Using West Berlin as a major center for subversion, the Federal Republic, with the support of NATO allies, sought to hamper the development of the Eastern side in any way possible with the hope that eventually the "Ulbricht regime," which they thought had little popular support, would collapse or come to terms. Thus, the reunification of the Germanies so fondly wished by all would be accomplished, and the people of the "Eastern Zone" would be "liberated" from communism.

The policy of not recognizing the legitimacy of the second German state was carried to great lengths in the Federal Republic. Official transactions were carried on with the Soviet Union as occupying force long after the Soviet High Commission was withdrawn from the East in 1954. The passports of the citizens of the GDR[1] were not recognized either by the FRG or the NATO countries or other countries in the NATO orbit. For travel to such countries citizens of the GDR had to get special travel documents from the Allied Travel Office, which was operated by the three Western occupying powers but under the close scrutiny of West Germany. Applying a policy known as the Hallstein doctrine, the FRG sought to limit the international role of the East. Other nations, except the Soviet Union, who wanted to have any relations with the Federal Republic—a much stronger trading partner than the Democratic Republic—were told that it would be "an unfriendly act" to recognize the GDR. The government of the East was called "the regime"; the official name of the state was nowhere acknowledged by Federal Republic officials or the press. It was called "the Soviet Zone," "the Eastern sector," or "Middle Germany." Even in private conversations it was customary to use the official name German

---

1. Hereafter it will be convenient to use the initials GDR for the German Democratic Republic and FRG for the Federal Republic of Germany. The German equivalents appear in some quotations: DDR for Deutsche Demokratische Republik and BRD for Bundesrepublik Deutschland.

Democratic Republic only with the adjective *sogenannte,* or "so-called."

In the absence of any general peace treaty, the Adenauer government did not recognize that one-quarter, or 40,000 square miles of the former Reich, was awarded by the Potsdam agreement to Poland and a bit of East Prussia to the Soviet Union. The presence in the Federal Republic of 2.5 million expellees from these provinces led to strong voices of revanchism, the movement to regain areas of original territory lost through war. Though these voices became more and more muted during the fifties and sixties as the refugees were absorbed into an economically and politically flourishing state, they still made themselves heard by virtue of the free press of the West and brought counterblasts from the other side of the boundary. Official and unofficial maps of "Germany" posted in the West showed the solid boundaries of 1937, with dashed lines setting off the Eastern side as "the Soviet Zone" and with the pieces of prewar Germany east of the Oder-Neisse line designated as "territories under foreign administration." All of these devices emphasizing that the division of Germany was unnatural catered to the century-old urge of German nationalism and were looked upon from the Eastern perspective as ominous signs of renascent Hitlerism.

The Western policy of reunification on Western terms was directly contrary to the policy of the Soviet Union, reinforced by many divisions of troops stationed in the GDR, to develop a Socialist[2] state in the eastern part of Germany and to prevent a unified, and therefore strong, Germany from ever threatening the borders of Russia. The government of the

2. We use here the practice of the countries themselves, which base their society on Marxist-Leninist doctrines. They call their present systems "Socialist" and use the term "Communist" to apply to a future, more advanced state of social development. "Communist" however, is applied to the party members and leaders of the movement.

GDR denounced West Germany for imperialistic, revanchist, and neo-Nazi designs, insulated itself as much as possible from Western subversion, and worked to solve the many problems of wartime devastation, reparations to the USSR, shortages of resources, and widespread antipathy to Russian occupation and socialization. The more rapid economic development and greater degree of individual freedom on the Western side were a constant and ever present threat to the creation of the Socialist state. Those who opposed official policies for reasons of conscience or of convenience had only to slip across the border to be greeted with open arms by the citizens and officials of the Federal Republic, which claimed to be the only legitimate government for all of Germany. When concrete and barbed-wire barriers along the borders of East Germany were reinforced by the government of the GDR in 1952, there still remained the "escape hatch" in Berlin.

As ever, the rivalry between the two Germanies was most acute in Berlin. During the decade after the airlift the disparities between the two Berlins had grown. The Western world threw its resources into making West Berlin a showcase of the wonderful opportunities held out in the "free enterprise world," while the rebuilding of East Berlin as the capital city of a new Socialist Germany lagged behind. In the summer of 1958 each side reiterated its position. The Western powers called for reunification of Germany through free elections. They insisted that the "regime" in the Eastern sector was not a legitimate government; it had been set up by a foreign power against the will of the people and maintained in power by foreign troops. The flight of three million people since 1945 was cited as evidence of the real wishes of the people in the East. The Soviet Union and the GDR on their side claimed that the Western powers were rearming West Germany and creating a revived nazism contrary to the Potsdam agreement. They stated readiness at any time to negotiate a peace treaty with the Federal Republic of Germany, provided the two German states could get together through a joint commission and decide the future of their relations. In the midst of this belligerent standoff, in November 1958, Premier Khrushchev proposed a "free city" of West Berlin, which would be demilitarized with security guarantees from the four powers and possibly the United Nations. If by the end of six months no agreement was reached on the proposal, then the Soviet Union would turn over its occupation powers to the GDR, and full sovereignty over the approaches to West Berlin would be in the hands of the GDR.

West Berliners and West Germans considered the "free city" plan just another Soviet plot to take over West Berlin, and they braced themselves for another blockade. Khrushchev's deadline was soon removed, but the stalemate continued and the flight of dissident East Germans accelerated. Each month from 1958 to 1961 thousands drove, walked, or rode the underground from East to West Berlin, where they were provided with free transportation and resettlement in West Germany. The figures were highlighted each month in the West German press as "fugitives from the prison" and "new recruits for the free world." In the summer of 1961 the air of crisis accelerated. Quaker visitors in East Berlin were told by high authority that something was going to have to be done to stop the flight across the border in Berlin.[3]

On the night of August 13, 1961, a huge roll of barbed wire, soon to be replaced by concrete blocks, was uncoiled along the zigzag border through the heart of Berlin. Berliners woke up in the morning to find only a few checkpoints open. Soon a system of passes was established, which kept tightening up, until in a few weeks crossings for Berliners in either direction were forbidden. Families were separated, roads

3. Eric Tucker, "Confidential Report on a Visit to Berlin, April 20–27, 1961," Peace Committee of London Yearly Meeting, Friends House Archives, London.

severed, trolley lines stopped, the underground cut in pieces. The traumatic experience of that night still remains fresh in the imagination of most Berliners. The Wall itself stands out as a crude and inhuman construction severing the arteries of a great city. As one person interviewed by Quakers in 1963 said, "It was like a surgical operation without anaesthesia."

And yet the Wall marked a turning point toward recognition in the two Germanies of the postwar realities that had been ignored since 1945. On the one hand, the Socialist Germany could have the security to develop an economically egalitarian system of controlled socialism among a people most of whom had been brought up in the system of capitalist enterprise. On the other hand, the belief of Westerners that the GDR would wither and fade away was forcefully crushed. It was clear that the Soviet Union was not going to allow a unified Germany under Western auspices.

Background to the Quaker Response
In the Quaker world the Berlin Wall emphasized the need for outsiders to help local Quakers in conciliatory work between the two Germanies. The opportunities that opened up for Quakers in the 1960s must be viewed in light of the prior forty years work of relief and reconciliation. The story begins with the Quaker child-feeding during the postwar famine of 1920 and 1922 and the inflationary collapse of 1924. At the height of this program over a million children were being fed in 1,640 communities, with 8,364 feeding stations all administered by a small staff of foreign Quakers and 40,000 German helpers.[4] More intensive Quaker contact came through a number of centers established in those years by British Quakers catering to the needs of students and others, but it was the child-feeding, *Quakerspeisung,* which made the

---

4. Mary Hoxie Jones, *Swords Into Ploughshares* (New York: Mac-Millan, 1937), pp. 75–84.

widest impression. During the days of Nazi power after January 1933, American and British Quaker organizations worked quietly though steadily to assist Jewish and political refugees.

After World War II the Quakers returned again to the task of rehabilitation, helping the German people in the Western sectors, who were afflicted with destruction and demoralization. An additional burden were the numerous displaced persons, non-Germans stranded in Germany, and the millions of expellees, Germans moved forcibly into West Germany from the borderlands of the new Poland, the Sudetenland of Czechoslovakia, and other parts of Eastern Europe. From the first team of British Quakers called in to the catastrophe of Belsen camp right after liberation in April 1945 to the last neighborhood center devolved on local management in the early 1960s, the extent and variety of personal assistance was impressive. The impact of the teams was less in mass distribution than in activating German organizations to work together in the interests of the whole community. The teams frequently included foreign workers who had themselves suffered at the hands of the Germans, and the witness of reconciliation went with the aid. An example of the inclusiveness of Quaker ministry to friend and foe alike was the action of William Hughes in bringing help to the 50,000 suspected Nazi leaders in the new internment camps. Hughes, an English Quaker, had been evicted by the Nazis because of his efforts on behalf of threatened Jews.[5]

These various activities over the years meant that Quakers were better known in Germany than in any other country of the world. In these circumstances continuing work of reconciliation seemed expected and hardly questioned. As the

5. For a description of the work in the British Zone, see Roger C. Wilson, *Quaker Relief* (London: George Allen and Unwin, 1952); and Magda Kelber, *Quakerhilfswerk, Britische Zone 1945-48* (Bad Pyrmont: Leonhard Friedrich, 1949).

report of the mission who visited Germany in 1963 says:

> A number of the people interviewed by the mission both
> in East and West Germany expressed gratitude for "Quak-
> er food" that they had eaten as children following World
> War I. Others expressed interest in and approval of various
> current and past international Quaker activities. The mis-
> sion members were keenly aware of the fund of good will
> that the Quakers enjoy in Germany and of their responsi-
> bility to preserve it.[6]

As the work of rehabilitation was phased out or devolved in
the fifties, the work of mediation between the hostile spheres
of East and West became increasingly significant. The call for
this work came directly from German Quaker leaders.

The chairman of the Peace Committee of German Yearly
Meeting from August 1954 to November 1962 was Margarethe Lachmund. While many other German Quakers were
active in peace work and related concerns, Margarethe Lachmund was outstanding in her inspired and intelligent concern
for Quaker work in East-West relations. In her own life she
had spanned the gulf between East and West. She lived with
her husband, Hans Lachmund, a judge, in the Eastern part of
Germany when the Soviet troops took over at the end of
World War II. She organized the civilian relief in the university town of Greifswald, boldly approaching the occupation
authorities to get food for starving children and for the great
many refugees coming across the Oder-Neisse boundary as
they were replaced by Polish people. Under the Nazis she and
her husband had been constantly suspected and occasionally
threatened for their help to Jews and opposition to the
regime. In spite of this, Hans Lachmund was also suspected
by the Soviets because he had been a judge under the Nazis

---

6. American Friends Service Committee, *Journey Through a Wall*,
(Philadelphia, 1964), p. 5.

and because of his contacts with Western Freemasons, so he was taken away to prison. Margarethe worked for over eight years for his release. She never wavered from her faith that all human beings should be approached in the spirit of love and truth and that many times they would respond. She could find the human core in the hardest commissar or military officer. She combined childlike trust with sharp political acumen.

Willy Wohlrabe and Margarethe Lachmund, as clerks of German Yearly Meeting, which embraced all of Germany until a separate yearly meeting for the GDR was set up in 1969, called upon the American Friends as early as 1949 to send a person of stature to concentrate on the problems of United States policy in occupied West Germany and rising East-West tension. The response finally came thirteen years later. During the interval, Margarethe Lachmund herself acted to a degree as international Quaker representative in Berlin. She had the help of several German Quaker associates. The Office of German Yearly Meeting, which was reopened after the Second World War in an obscure corner of a shabby building in Planckstrasse, East Berlin, provided an opportune meeting place for Friends from East and West. Occasional visits of traveling Friends helped the German Quakers to understand and to meet the manifold problems of a divided existence.

Even during the years when relief was a primary emphasis, East-West politics intruded abrasively. All relief supplies were used as political levers by each side to win adherents. Margarethe Lachmund was determined that Quaker distribution should be for human welfare and peace, rather than political gain. A shipment of clothing came from the American Friends Service Committee in 1949. The Friends had no organization for direct distribution, and the two major local relief agencies were strongly political. The *Arbeiterwohlfahrt* was aligned with the Social Democratic party of the West, and the *Volks-*

solidarität was an arm of the Marxist Social Unity party. Since each agency operated throughout Berlin at that time, each wanted to distribute all the goods on both sides to promote its own political aims. Lachmund succeeded in placing responsibility for distribution in the Western sectors with the Social Democrats and in the Eastern sector with the Communists, thus minimizing the propaganda sideeffects. The pattern of Quaker reconciliation in Berlin grew out of a long heritage of Quaker work, but it carried the immediate imprint of Margarethe Lachmund's beliefs. Truth and love were the guidelines: courage to tell the truth and the spiritual resources to do it with love.

When the Wall came in August 1961, Frau Lachmund, living in West Berlin, could no longer go to the *Quäkerburo*. The sporadic efforts made during the fifties to raise money and to recruit staff for a Quaker representative in Germany took on a new urgency as Berlin emerged as the most critical flashpoint in the world. Several Quaker visitors from the United States and Britain returned to say that the Wall, however inhuman and tragic, was the East German government's answer to a situation it found intolerable. These visitors reported that an outside Quaker representative was needed to promote more realistic discussion of the divided Germany on the Western side and work toward constructive contacts between the two sides.

Responding to these voices in December 1961, the board of the AFSC urged vigorous efforts to find a well-qualified person and sufficient funds to send him or her to Germany. Writing to Friends in Britain and the United States on December 30, 1961, Margarethe Lachmund said, "I think that all these greater complications of the situation will show that only an experienced, highly-respected, weighty Quaker personality of great inner security may become accepted from the Eastern side."[7]

7. Letter in AFSC archives.

The Quaker concern found a response from Roland Warren, who left a post with the New York State Charities Aid Association and took two years out of his career in sociology and community organization to become Quaker representative in Berlin. That he had to make his own role and develop his own methods without close direction from headquarters made the post all the more appealing.

Willy Brandt and the Turn toward Accommodation
When Roland and Margaret Warren and family took up residence in Berlin in the summer of 1962, the debate in the West over policy toward Berlin's Wall was at its height. For the general public of Western Germany, West Berlin, and indeed the Western world, the Wall was the latest monstrosity of "Stalinist communism."

The high point of rhetoric was reached by President John F. Kennedy in his famous speech to a million cheering people before the city hall of West Berlin on June 26, 1963. At the climax of his speech he said:

> Freedom is indivisible, and when one man is enslaved, all are not free. When all are free, then we can look forward to that day when this city will be joined as one and this country and this great continent of Europe in a peaceful and hopeful globe. When that day finally comes, as it will, the people of West Berlin can take sober satisfaction in the fact that they were in the front lines for almost two decades.
>
> All free men, wherever they may live, are citizens of Berlin, and, therefore, as a free man, I take pride in the words *"Ich bin ein Berliner."*[8]

The response of Willy Brandt, governing mayor of Berlin, was

8. *Public Papers of the Presidents of the United States, John F. Kennedy, 1963* (Washington: U.S. Government Printing Office, 1964), p. 525.

an echo of the high emotional tone: "This is a great day in the history of our city."

Mayor Brandt voiced with sincerity the dominant feeling of the people at the time, and his political prestige grew as a spokesman for Berlin's freedom. At the same time he was too much of a pragmatist to fly in the face of the facts. Already in the 1959 Social Democratic party congress of Bad Godesburg, he had been one of the leaders in a renovation movement to make the party a serious contender in German politics. In 1962 and 1963, along with his deputy mayor, Heinrich Albertz, and his information officer, Egon Bahr, he started the move toward accommodation to the Wall.

Roland Warren was in close touch with these three men from the time of his arrival in 1962. His paper for the Quaker International Affairs Reports series on the "Background of the Berlin Wall" supplied a new way of looking at the division of Berlin. Up to that time each side had justified its position and had caricatured the other's. Warren outlined the official Eastern conception of the "Protective Wall" in ways that would be most persuasive to the West. He then outlined the official Western view of the "Wall of Shame" with equal persuasiveness for the East. His own conclusion was that the Wall was there to stay. Its necessity was interwoven with general East-West tensions, and there could be no overall improvement without détente at higher levels. He suggested that in the meantime things could be done locally to prevent dangerous incidents and to ameliorate family separations. Roland Warren talked this paper over with Heinrich Albertz, deputy mayor, who privately endorsed it.

Warren's June 1963 paper on "Possibilities for a Berlin Settlement" analyzed Mayor Brandt's six points on Berlin and Ulbricht's seven points on relations between the two Germanies, sorting out the vital nonnegotiable interests and the secondary interests on each side. This analysis revealed a basis for negotiating a temporary, partial solution for Berlin, but one major obstacle was the Western policy of nonrecognition.

> In combination with the "Hallstein doctrine" of breaking diplomatic relations with countries which recognize the GDR, it has hampered West Germany in exercising the influence in Eastern Europe which it might otherwise bring to bear both economically and politically. It has led to repeated stalemates on the question of negotiating an easement of the conditions at the Berlin Wall. It has placed the Federal Republic in increasingly embarrassing postures in international sports events and in cultural exchanges. Most discouraging of all, it has not brought Germany any closer to unification, but now operates to widen the breach.[9]

At this same time Egon Bahr, Willy Brandt's close associate, presented a paper called "Wandel durch Annäherung," or "Change Through Rapprochment"[10] at the Tutzing meeting of the Social Democratic Party (SDP).[11] His thesis was that the desired transformation in East Germany would come through steps of accommodation to relax tensions rather than through nonrecognition. In effect, he was saying that since

9. Roland Warren, "Possibilities for a Berlin Settlement," Quaker International Affairs Reports, vol. 10, no. 3, American Friends Service Committee, unpublished in archives.

10. See Philip Windsor, *Germany and the Management of Detente* (London: Chatto & Windus, 1971), p. 141. He translates *Wandel* as "transformation."

11. It will be convenient to use the following initials for the German parties:

SED: Socialist Unity Party (Eastern Communist)
SDP: Social Democratic party (Western)
CDU: Christian Democratic Union (Western)
CSU: Christian Social Union (a sister party of CDU operating in Bavaria)
FDP: Free Democratic party (Western).

the cold wind had not worked, why not try the warm sun? Egon Bahr struck boldly and forcefully at the illusions of the West:

> The conditions for reunification can only be arranged with the Soviet Union. They cannot be obtained in East Berlin, nor in opposition to the Soviet Union, nor without the Soviet Union. Whoever develops ideas . . . that reunification can be effected via East Berlin is indulging in illusions and ought to imagine himself faced with twenty to twenty-two well-equipped Soviet army divisions. If the zone cannot be taken out of the Soviet Union's sphere of influence, then it follows that any policy leading directly toward a collapse of the regime there is without hope of success. This conclusion is horribly inconvenient and goes against our sentiments, but it is logical.[12]

The only alternative, Bahr said, was to hope that the "improvement in the internal situation would bring with it a general relaxation in the Zone." To promote this improvement, Bahr advocated a succession of small steps such as trade agreements and travel exchange. In making his statement Egon Bahr was still careful to use the phrases and the dicta of the reigning policy of nonrecognition and reunification. He assured his audience that he was not advocating recognition of the German Democratic Republic, not giving up on reunification. He was only showing how small steps of negotiation short of recognition would bring a better atmosphere for eventual reunification. "The obvious reluctance to recognize the Zone as a *bona fide* state—which no one questions—must not be allowed to paralyze us," he wrote, "Reunification is not a matter of a single transaction which can be activated by

12. Typed copy of speech in archives of American Friends Service Committee, translation by M. C. Morris.

one historical decision on one historic day at one historic conference, but a process of many steps and many stages."[13] He was also careful to invoke President Kennedy's policy of détente.

The West German politician could not allow the emotive symbol of the unity of German culture and nation to be captured by the opposition or by extremists. No politician who wanted to be reelected could raise a question regarding reunification, much less speak against it. Symbols move people more forcefully than logic, and indeed conflicts are often about symbols.[14] The danger of a Neo-Nazi insurgence playing on the symbols of nationalism was always in the minds of party leaders, with the inconsequential but stridently rightist National Democratic party on hand to remind them. Thus, Brandt and Bahr professed to be working toward the unity of Germany East and West, but in the long-range future by gradual accommodation to the GDR, rather than by refusing to have anything to do with it. The emotions of German nationalism had a strong appeal on both sides of the Wall. The leaders of the pluralistic society in the West tolerated but channeled them; the leaders of the more centrally organized East tried to suppress them by denouncing nationalism as nazism.

At the time of Bahr's trial balloon of July 1963, the German people were not ready to defer symbols to logic. The speech aroused a storm of protest. The right-wing Springer press attacked in force. Brandt, Bahr, and Albertz suspended speech making for the time being and worked on practical accommodation to conditions in Berlin. They tried, for example, to negotiate pass agreements so that West Berliners could visit relatives in East Berlin at Christmas or Easter.

13. Ibid.
14. Kenneth E. Boulding, *Conflict and Defense, General Theory* (New York: Harper and Row, 1963), chap. 5.

Quaker Mission to the Two Germanies

Planning and Purpose

At the time when passions were most strongly aroused in the Western world against East Germany, the American Friends Service Committee was invited to send a team to visit in the East. The first letter of invitation on June 20, 1961 came from Emil Fuchs, a prominent German Quaker who had accepted an offer to become professor of philosophy at Leipzig University in 1949 and moved from West to East. The indispensable official sponsorship came shortly after in a letter from the German Peace Council, of which Dr. Fuchs was a member.

The Peace Council (*Friedensrat der Deutschen Demokratischen Republik*) was a citizens' organization affiliated with the World Peace Council and with close relations to the Peace Committee of the Soviet Union. This invitation was undoubtedly made possible by a whole series of earlier Quaker contacts, starting with meetings of British Quakers with the World Peace Council in 1950 which led to the invitation from the Soviet Peace Committee for the British Quakers to visit in the Soviet Union in 1951, followed by the American Quaker visit in 1954, the East-West seminars in Vienna in 1955 and 1956, and the series of Quaker visits to Moscow to negotiate exchanges which started in 1960. The peace committees of the Socialist countries, while nongovernmental and not formally affiliated with the Communist parties in control, are nevertheless strongly associated with the foreign policies of their respective countries and, through the World Peace Council, with the foreign policy of the USSR.

Under the circumstances the American Friends Service Committee took a considerable time to mull over this invitation. The delay and caution indicated the delicacy of the venture. It showed how thoroughly the Adenauer view that all communication with the GDR was tantamount to support of an "illegitimate government" had permeated American thought. An overriding suspicion was that any such visit, however well intentioned, would be used by the "Communists" for purposes incompatible with Quaker aims.

Some preliminary talks were held in the fall of 1961 with the Peace Council, but not until after the appointment of Roland Warren in February 1962 as a field representative who could carry through with negotiations and arrangements did the home committee go ahead. In the fall of 1962, Barrett Hollister, director of international affairs for AFSC, and Roland Warren again went over the particulars of the invitation with the Peace Council officers in East Berlin. The Quaker objective of moving around freely and seeing the persons in the Democratic Republic that they wanted to see was soon accepted. To their desire to limit publicity and minimize the danger of being misquoted, the Peace Council responded that there would be no minutes of meetings and no communiques, just a simple press statement telling who was in the group and what officials they were visiting, with nothing said about the content of the discussions. When Hollister suggested that even a simple factual statement should have mutual agreement, the Peace Council officers demurred, indicating the Quakers could depend on their good faith. The issue loomed large in the minds of board members on the special committee in Philadelphia. The final aide-mémoire that expressed the agreement of all parties stated, "The wording of any such notice [simple factual press account] should be agreed upon by the Quaker mission prior to its scheduled departure from the GDR."[15]

The negotiators on the Eastern side never made stipulations about the report that the Quaker team planned from the beginning. When published this included a whole chapter on

15. Roland Warren, Letter to Philadelphia, 24 October 1962, AFSC Archives.

the substantive items discussed with the Peace Council. This was not cleared with the Peace Council, nor was there any expectation on either side that it would be. The committee in Philadelphia paid deference to the asymmetry in this situation:

> While the publishing of a report might seem to be inconsistent with an agreement regarding no publicity, it was felt that since the invitation was extended in order that we might learn, it would be necessary to publish a report and that this would be understood by the Peace Council.[16]

In order to make the team's report more acceptable in the United States as a treatment of the views of both sides, visits in West Berlin and West Germany were proposed and accepted by officials in East and West. West German officials, with their basic values favoring free communication, did not oppose the visit to the East or refuse to talk to the Quakers themselves, but they warned that the Quakers would only be allowed to see the favorable aspects of East Germany and their trip would be used by the East German press to show that Americans approved "the regime." Direct third-party conciliation between contending opponents was only a part of the proposed activity. A major emphasis was on learning and reporting back to the citizens of the United States in order to influence U.S. policy toward a more conciliatory stance in Central Europe.

Selection and Functioning of the Team

The members of the team were carefully selected to have a good knowledge of Germany and to represent different specialties and interests. This brought the total to a some-

---

16. Minutes, Ad Hoc Committee on Germany, AFSC, 30 January 1963, AFSC Archives.

what unwieldy eight. All members of the mission had worked for Friends in Germany or Austria; together their experience there covered a period of over thirty years before and after the Second World War. Irwin Abrams of Antioch College was a specialist in European history. Morris Keeton was dean of the faculty at Antioch College, and Francis Dart was a professor of physics at the University of Oregon. Hertha Kraus, recently retired professor at the Bryn Mawr School of Social Work and the one emigré in the group, was well prepared to appraise social welfare programs, while Clifford Maser, dean of the School of Business and Technology of Oregon State, was well versed in economic matters. William Barton, head of the Friends Service Council, London, and Finn Friis, retired Danish Foreign Service officer, added European to American views. Roland Warren was an ever present help in interpreting the social-psychological aspects of the German split. At least four had firsthand experience of the serious problems of dialogue with representatives of Socialist countries, where the value assumptions and methods of discussion were very different. No one, least of all the members themselves, felt uneasy about calling the team "a group of Quakers," although two were not members of the Society of Friends: Morris Keeton, who was made chairman, and Finn Friis, who had been Quaker representative in Vienna and had gone on the Quaker mission to Poland in 1957.

The team spent one week in West Berlin, one week in East Berlin and East Germany, and then one week in West Germany, mostly in Bonn. They visited with the highest officials in East Germany and West Berlin. In Bonn, President Heinrich Lubke was called away at the time of their appointment, and they talked with two assistants to the president. Of the 76 people seen, 27 were German officials (11 in the GDR, 16 in the FRG and West Berlin), 11 were foreign diplomats posted in Germany, and 38 were private persons on the two sides. Church leaders were particularly sought out in order to report on the state of religious activity in East and West. Five were seen in the East and eight in the West. Not included in the above figures are six people who constituted the core of Quaker advisors in East and West Germany and a number of other Quakers seen at meetings in Leipzig, Karl Marx Stadt, Frankfurt, and East and West Berlin.

Since each of the eight highly competent members had strong opinions on a great variety of topics, it was a considerable feat for the group to function as a unified whole. The AFSC board clearly intended that they operate as a team, producing a single report rather than several. Quaker processes for harnessing individual insights into consensus were utilized effectively. There were many long discussions and frequent periods of quiet worship. Roland Warren and Morris Keeton were hard taskmasters. The team had little spare time in any part of the three weeks. After a strenuous two weeks in West Berlin and East Germany, when they might have expected a breathing space, they secluded themselves in an island hotel in Grunewald, a suburb of West Berlin. There they shared impressions of East Germany, reported on those trips and interviews that a few had done for the whole group, and discussed the contents of their final report. This process continued during the next week in Bonn. Drafts of interview reports were passed around for revisions, and a detailed, confidential journal of 145 pages was produced. On the final weekend in Frankfurt the leaders held as much of the group together as possible so that the final report would be truly a team product.

Worship occupied a prominent part in the life of the group. It was the time for renewal of inspiration and heightening of sensitivity in the delicate aspects of the mission. It was a time for the submission of individual and group will to a higher Will. A typical quotation used in the worship is one from Isaac Pennington, early Quaker writer:

> Give over thine own willing, give over thine own running,
> give over thine own desiring to know or be anything and
> sink down to the seed which God sows in thy heart, and
> let that be in thee and grow in thee and breathe in thee
> and act in thee. . . .[17]

One interview with a high official in Bonn produced considerable tension. The official was impatient and condescending in his defense of policies of reunification and all-German elections. In their questions, the team members conveyed some of their irritation with his manner and rigid line. In the worship period later they asked themselves if they had conducted the interview in the true Quaker spirit.

The report itself was a good example of the way individual expertise and opinions were harmonized into a group production. As the team engaged in the last week of interviews in Bonn, the question of the scope and character of the report was discussed intensely. Some called for long and expert reporting. Two members of the group had collected considerable data on economic and social welfare matters in East Germany. Others wanted to produce a short, readable report directed to a wider public interested in foreign policy. Some wanted to emphasize the practical experience of the mission, while others wanted to deal with the underlying philosophical problems of confrontation and communication between two worlds. The chairman, Morris Keeton, skillfully steered the group to a consensus on a short report which would "present our seasoned judgment as a group as to the preconditions basic to finding of solutions to the problems" . . . "refute important misconceptions, in so far as we are able" . . . "emphasize the raising of questions," and be limited to "that which would have the full benefit of the interaction of our minds

17. "Journal: Quaker Mission to Germany, September 8–30, 1963," AFSC Archives, p. 85.

while we were together.''[18] Within these guidelines the individual knowledge and insights of the team members were utilized by assigning sections of the report to different members, subject to the final editing of Morris Keeton, Irwin Abrams, and Roland Warren. The prior experience of several in Marxist-capitalist dialogue insured a valuable treatment of the underlying problems of communication.

Conciliatory Activity

From the mission's journal we can separate the types of conciliatory activity that were carried on into four inexact though convenient categories: listening and asking questions; message carrying; understanding and assessment; and making proposals. Any particular conversation might include a mixture of these, and the listing is only helpful in discerning different aspects of conciliation and trying to assess degrees of intervention. Listening and asking questions is the least threatening of third-party procedures. Message carrying arises from the direct request by a spokesman on one side to make some point to persons on the other side and includes no element of clandestine spy activity. If handled with discretion, message carrying can be of great importance, though it is less threatening to the parties and less dangerous to the intervenor than the more independent roles involved in the last two types of activity: assessing the different perceptions of the situation, and making proposals for settlement.

A central part of all these efforts, but particularly related to the last two, was the process of bringing the one-sided, mutually exclusive perceptions of the two sides closer to each other and to reality. In the German trip the conciliation was directed to two sets of antagonists, the Democratic Republic versus the Federal Republic, and the Democratic Republic versus the United States, with its Western allies.

18. Ibid., p. 89.

A great deal of time was spent listening, particularly in the East. A notable instance was the first meeting with the Peace Council. Instead of the give-and-take discussion that the group expected, they were treated to a succession of ten-minute speeches about the misdeeds of the West. Western authorities, Peace Council members said, claimed to favor free travel and cultural relations but had refused permission for a scientist to attend a conference in the U.S. and had cancelled an East German play production in Frankfurt. The "freedom" the West Germans vaunted only allowed, they said, the same old militarists to get back in power, supported by war propaganda that would be illegal in the GDR, with its Law for the Protection of Peace. The Wall, they said, was necessary because of the propaganda, espionage, and black-market operations carried on from the Western side of Berlin. All this had to be spilled out to the captive Western audience before any further communication could take place. The group was disappointed with this first meeting and were not sufficiently aware that they were performing their first function of conciliation: to listen. Fortunately, a second meeting brought substantive and meaningful interchange for which the team was looking.

On the Western side they also had to listen over and over again to explanations of the West German view: the "Ulbricht regime" were Soviet puppets with no consent from the people; for the sake of future peace, Germany must be reunited; and any dealings with "the regime" that implied recognition of its legitimacy was a betrayal of the German people.

Listening led to understanding and assessment of the situation. As the process went on, the listeners asked more pointed questions, based on what they had learned or what they had heard from the other side. On each side, for example, they asked whether a policy that led to separation of families was really necessary for the state.

One particularly important area of assessment was the question of the "legitimacy" of the Ulbricht government. Did it rule only by the force of Soviet arms? Or did it rule with a degree of consent of the East German people? The mission members did a great deal of thinking on this question during the island weekend. The previous week of interviewing and visiting in schools, factories, farms, and social service institutions gave all information on which to test their preconceptions. They had not come away with uniform impressions. They agreed that the leaders were sincere in their efforts to build a new state based on socialism and emphasizing a more equitable distribution of goods and services rather than individual freedom. They found, however, evidence of popular dissent from official policies along with a fear of criticism and a sense of restriction. One of the group thought the government was more unpopular than the government of Nazi Germany had been, though he sensed that many individuals were not as fearful or anxious as they had been in 1935. Others pointed out that it was difficult to tell how much of the discontent was based on the lack of comfort rather than a conscientious opposition to government policies. It was hard to accept the austerity of economic life and the limitations on personal liberty in the East when living so close to the luxury and personal freedom of the West. Thus, the common assertion in the West that 85 percent of the people opposed the regime was found inadequate to cover the intricacies of the situation.

These impressions were faithfully reported in the published pamphlet in a chapter on "East Germany Today," which raised questions about the accuracy and wisdom of the popular Western view on the government of the GDR, but which avoided any precise answers. On the closely related question of whether Western countries should recognize the Democratic Republic, the team was cautious and came to no conclusion. Some were more ready than others to advocate specific steps toward recognition, but as a whole they felt there was sufficient evidence of popular dissent in the Democratic Republic to make it unwise to advocate recognition. The team only raised the question of whether the policy of nonrecognition might lead to further separation and alienation rather than to the dream of unity.[19]

Issues such as recognition fell under a self-imposed limitation on dealing with "political issues." The group inherited this guideline from the tradition of Quaker good-will visits. These visits were thought to have a broadly humanitarian rather than a political purpose. As stated by Morris Keeton on several occasions, "Our competency, if any, lies rather in identifying conditions within which political solutions may be effectively sought and the preconditions for the political solutions not the solutions themselves."[20]

Avoiding broad political judgments, the team looked for small steps of communication and contact which would lead to a better climate and eventual solutions. A number of specific proposals from the team itself or from the people they talked with found no response. Small steps of accommodation suggested by the mayor's office in West Berlin ran into hardening opposition in the East. The position of the GDR government, made clear by Mr. Ulbricht himself in the interview with the Quakers, was that individual hardship cases could be settled quietly, but changes in regulations could be made only if the Federal Republic and its allies stopped threatening the absorption of the Democratic Republic and recognized it as a separate state.

A considerable quantity of factual information was conveyed across the abyss of ignorance, misinformation, and stereotypes. A major Bonn official who asked about the persecution of Christians in the East was given some informa-

19. AFSC, *Journey Through a Wall*, p. 63.
20. "Journal," p. 87.

tion to correct his overdrawn impression. Eastern officials were told of the genuine desire of Berlin officials for practical compromises. The major conciliatory activity of message carrying involved the issues of travel restrictions on East Germans going into NATO countries and restrictions in the East on travel between East and West Berlin.

Travel Restrictions in the West and the East
The issue the team pursued most assiduously in the West was that of the restrictions on travel óf East Germans. Even fifteen years after the war, East German residents who wanted to travel in NATO countries had to seek temporary travel documents (TTDs) from the Allied Travel Office, since their own GDR passports were not recognized. After the Wall was built, the NATO powers, looking for some means to retaliate, issued orders drastically restricting the issuance of TTDs; only certain clergymen, trade representatives, and those who applied for "compassionate reasons" could receive them. The result was to reduce visitors from East Germany to an even smaller trickle. In theory, the Allied Travel Office was operated only by the occupying powers—U.S., Britain, and France; in practice, however, there was close consultation with Bonn.

After listening to long explanations of this policy, the members of the team raised serious questions with U.S. representatives in Berlin, Bonn, and Washington; the FRD Foreign Office in Bonn; and the British representatives in Bonn and London. Finn Friis made a similar effort in Denmark. The team argued that the GDR government for its own reasons severely restricted foreign travel of its citizens, and therefore the restrictions imposed by the Allied Travel Office merely put an additional restrictive device in the hands of the Eastern authorities, who could tell GDR citizens not to apply for the humiliating permits. Thus, an act of retaliation against the East German government boomeranged, aiding the isolation policy of that government and negating the Western ideas of open communication.

In several interviews the Quaker representatives pushed very hard on this issue. The most aggressive line of questioning was taken with the head of the Office of East German Questions of the Foreign Office in Bonn, who was well known to Roland Warren. When the spokesman said that the restrictions were necessary to keep the GDR propagandists out, he was asked if this did not mean attributing motives to a person before the fact and forbidding entry before any illegal act. Other questions were pressed: "If not now, when can the restrictions be relaxed?" The group mentioned people they had talked to—the university rector, the scientist, and the doctor—who were kept from international contacts by the policy. The Foreign Office spokesman argued that the measure was a necessary retaliation for the Wall and was expected to bring concessions from the other side. After three hours of polite sparring, the interview ended with the spokesman thanking the group and saying that he was trying to apply the policy with some flexibility.

The deliberations of the group on this travel issue led to a carefully drawn document by Roland Warren giving the official reasons for the policy along with a careful rebuttal of each point. This paper was sent to the German Affairs Office of the State Department in Washington and then discussed in person with three officials. Although these men gave careful attention to the points made, and particularly to the proposals made to Mr. Ulbricht at the same time, the final answer was that the government must back its ally, the Federal Republic. The answers would have to be sought in Bonn. In Germany Roland Warren sent a copy of the memorandum to the West German Foreign Office and arranged an interview with the same man the group had argued with before. This spokesman said the memo had been taken "very seriously" and alluded vaguely to processes of change which he was unable to discuss. Again he was cordial and friendly. In March 1964 an announcement was made that the restrictions would be lifted for nonpolitical groups such as musicians, actors, and sportsmen. In a letter to Irwin Abrams, then back at Antioch, Roland Warren gave this judgment:

> We can be confident that our Mission was a significant factor in the changes. I might add that, without explicitly saying so, the Americans here and the West Germans seem to indicate the same. Likewise several G.D.R. officials have mentioned the change in close relation to our visit. Although the official line is still very definitely that they believe the Allied Travel Office should be done away with entirely and G.D.R. passports should be recognized directly (as I do, personally), they nevertheless express gratification regarding the part we played in the development.[21]

The team made a parallel proposal to the East for the relaxation of travel restrictions for certain specific categories of people. These proposals were put forth first in the one-and-a-half-hour interview with the chairman of the Council of the State, Walter Ulbricht, which was the climax of the visit to East Germany. In preparing for this interview the group decided on a series of questions to be sent in advance and an introductory statement to be presented orally. The statement was the subject of earnest discussion in a last-minute special session. Some members urged a stronger tone favoring the relief of family separations and opposing restrictions on personal freedom. In the Quaker tradition of "speaking truth to power," this mood prevailed. In the interview Mr. Ulbricht did not respond directly to the concerns, but in the course of wide-ranging remarks about the deficiencies

---

21. Roland Warren, Letter to Irwin Abrams, 28 April 1964, AFSC Archives.

and misdeeds of the Western political and social system, he implied that the West was more guilty of cutting off contact and restricting freedoms. A deputy added that human relations could thrive only in peace, which would come through political arrangements.

There was no opportunity to pursue these questions in detail at the time, so the group decided to write Mr. Ulbricht a letter setting forth specific suggestions for state action in the relief of human suffering. The letter, dated November 12, 1963, urged the government of the GDR to start the small steps that would move the nations away from the impasse created by policies of noncommunication. Four specific measures were proposed. The first involved visits by GDR citizens to the West for compassionate reasons, such as illness or death in the family: "Where there is reasonable assurance of the visitor's return."[22] The second asked for visits in similar cases by West Berliners to East Berlin and the GDR. Two others involved permission to emigrate for wives, husbands, or fiancées of persons separated at the time of the Wall. A fifth point was deleted in the final edition when it was learned that permission had already been granted for children in East Germany to rejoin their parents in the West. The effects of this letter were not in any way measurable. There was no official acknowledgement, and no policy change was announced, though the humanitarian actions called for were attended to over the course of time on a case-by-case basis through the Red Cross.

Aspects of the Two-Sided Approach
The two letters with their proposals and persuasive arguments, one to the United States State Department and the other to the chairman of the State Council of the GDR, were the major effort in direct third-party conciliation by the

22. AFSC, *Journey Through a Wall*, pp. 70–71.

team. A significant feature of the overture was that each letter outlined the parallel effort on the other side. The State Department showed great interest in what the team had learned on the other side. The spokesman went so far as to say that if Ulbricht accepted the Quaker proposals, then he felt the Allies should remove the restrictions of the Allied Travel Office. This was a considerable step, since the official position was that travel restrictions would end only with removal of the Wall. On the Eastern side there was marked interest from the beginning in the Quaker message to the West and evident appreciation for the Quaker position on the ATO when the first relaxation of restrictions seemed to follow.

The different approaches of the two letters reveal an accommodation by the Quakers to the different values of the two parties and an effort to mix arguments of principle with arguments of expediency. The letter to Mr. Ulbricht proposed unilateral actions justified as humanitarian actions not threatening to state power, though also advocated as a means of relaxing political tensions. The letter to the State Department argued from Western values of freedom for a unilateral relaxing of ATO restrictions, denying that the restrictions could be used to extract concessions since they only played into the hands of the East's own policy of restricting travel. In the last draft of the letter, however, a small note on reciprocal bargaining crept in: "We feel that the possibility of extracting certain modest but important 'concessions' from the East for a change in Allied Travel Office policy should be most thoroughly explored."[23] This non sequitur was picked out by the State Department spokesman during the discussion that was arranged. He said that he agreed that it was advisable to seek a quid pro quo. The Quaker representatives tried to clarify their position, in effect contradicting this one

23. Ibid., p. 68.

sentence, by saying that the policy of the ATO was bad both in principle and practice and should be changed unilaterally whether Mr. Ulbricht made any concessions or not.

Each of the two letters was written in deference to the policy presuppositions of the addressee. The letter to Ulbricht argued for emigration by individuals not on the basis of an inherent right of freedom, but as a relief of suffering, which could be allowed in the few instances covered without danger to the interests of the state. The arguments said nothing about "restrictions on personal freedom," which had been mentioned in the interview. The letter to the U.S. State Department argued against restrictions because they were contrary to the Western idea of freedom and were also ineffective or unnecessary. This writing in different idioms raises the question of integrity. Was the team exposing one face to one side and another to the other? The issue is dealt with by the team itself:

> If we appeal to our own basic values in trying to persuade our adversary of the worth of the proposal, he may be unconvinced, because those values are not his. But if we appeal to his values, we may appear to him or to ourselves to be deceptive, insincere, or opportunistic. The difficulty can be overcome by full and frank recognition of the situation and by building upon shared goals and upon diverging but compatible vital interests.[24]

In the appeal to Mr. Ulbricht, then, the team was depending on the background of understanding built in previous talks with people on the Eastern side, in which the full Quaker position was set forth, to provide "frank recognition of the situation." The same difficulty does not occur in assessing the Quaker arguments on the Western side, since there could be a common assumption of values in human freedom and

24. Ibid., p. 61.

open intercourse. But the Quakers had a different kind of problem in persuading Western officials to align their policy with Western assumptions of freedom rather than with considerations of power politics. In one instance already pointed out, the Quaker argument was flawed by a too cunning appeal to the supposed realism of the power struggle.

Consequences of the Report

The publication of the report, *Journey Through a Wall,* in February 1964 was designed to influence American public opinion and thereby American policy. An AFSC press release featured the Quaker proposals, and as a result, the opposition to travel restrictions of the ATO received wide press coverage in the United States and in both Germanies. The seventy-one page pamphlet was by no means a best-seller, however, and was only one of many small breezes contributing to the growing wind of détente that blew, albeit fitfully, from 1963 to 1972.

In this study we are particularly interested in the effect of the published report on the subsequent conciliatory work of the Quaker representative between the two Germanies. From the beginning it was realized that the publication of analysis and recommendations in print might impede the ongoing work. In such a polarized situation it would be hard to please both sides, and the crystallizing of views might stop communication with either side or both. Part of the motivation for continuing to talk to a third party is often the desire to convince him of the rightness of "our side." When views are committed to print, one or both of the parties in the conflict may lose interest. Evaluation of public opinion in the GDR and of the accomplishments of its government in economic change and social welfare were particularly sensitive areas. Fortunately the man in the field was given the last word, and Roland Warren scrutinized every paragraph, while Margarethe Lachmund gave wise and cautious assistance. The only part that Warren did not screen was the cover art work and the map inserted at the last moment, so of course these two oversights were what almost wrecked the whole effort.

The cover had been designed by the publicity office in Philadelphia with a view to catching the public eye. The design suggested barbed wire and rock walls to set off the title, *Journey Through a Wall*. To the officials of the East this gave the appearance of just another cold war propaganda pamphlet like the pamphlet of RIAS (Radio in American Sector) published in 1962, with barbed wire on the cover, boasting of its support for the free world and its broadcasting to "the captive peoples of the Soviet Zone." Roland Warren explained that the designers in Philadelphia had no intention of giving this impression; after all, the first chapter brought out clearly the psychological wall erected by the West, and the journey was through both walls. This explanation might have been more acceptable to the Eastern point of view had there not been further problems.

The map was even more troublesome. It was not sufficiently recognized by the production staff in Philadelphia that any map was bound to be highly controversial because of its political connotations. In the last-minute rush to the printer, a map of "Germany" was inserted without any clearance by the team. They were alarmed to find that the shadow of prewar Germany appeared in an area of the new Poland east of the Oder-Neisse boundary marked off with dotted lines as "Polish Administration," and a small section on the Baltic Sea of the former Prussia now in the USSR was marked as "Soviet Administration." The map did not differ greatly from the official West German map, which was technically correct, since a peace treaty settling boundaries had not been negotiated, but was considered by people in the GDR, Poland, and the Soviet Union as a symbol of West German ambitions to restore the Greater Germany.

The head of the American Section of the Foreign Ministry

of the German Democratic Republic said this map could only indicate that the Quakers supported the expansionist tendencies of the Federal Republic. In addition, he said, the fact that Berlin itself was not divided by a line indicated support of the united Berlin promoted by West Germany. All the Quaker representative in the field could do was to apologize profusely, saying that the map was a sad mistake and that readers of the report would see that there was no support for the claim to Eastern territories or for the takeover of Berlin.

The map caused some damage to Quaker relations in Polish circles. In April a letter from an influential person in Warsaw acknowledged the Quaker excuses but said, "The very fact that in 1964 such a map could be included in a publication of this kind proves once more that it is not merely our 'obsession' with the revisionist trends in Western Germany which point to their political implications."[25] The first answer of the Quakers to East Berlin and Warsaw was that the map would be left out of any future editions. But in June, after a direct remonstrance from the head of the Polish delegation to the United Nations, the Quakers replied by removing the map from all copies that could be found.

After registering complaints about these unfortunate errors, spokesmen for the GDR Foreign Office and the Peace Council pursued other instances of what they considered bias in the report. In dealing with internal conditions in the GDR, they said, the report gave credit for social welfare improvements but failed to acknowledge all that had been done to suppress militarism and war propaganda. The economic analysis, they thought, was made in terms of capitalist standards of productivity and material consumption, but did not acknowledge the great task of socialization that was in process or the checks on economic exploitation. The treatment of the inter-

25. Letter to Alun Davies, 24 April 1964, Friends House Archives, London.

view with the chairman of the Council of State, Mr. Ulbricht, was thought inadequate, probably because it repeated the Quaker statement to the chairman but gave no report of his message to the Quakers. Several Peace Council members indicated that the report did not give an accurate and fair account of what they had said. There was textual criticism of words used and, finally, a general criticism that the Quakers had not made their position clear on the important issues of recognition, future status of Berlin, peace treaties, militarism in West Germany, and others—hot political issues the team had intentionally skirted.

After such a storm of criticism, Warren was assured that the Foreign Office and the Peace Council remained open to continued relations and cooperation with the Quakers. They were disappointed by the report, but not to the point of cutting off contact. Roland Warren estimated the net result of the report:

> I am greatly relieved to report that—with the exception of the Meeting for Intellectuals, a bitter blow—I do not believe our relations have been impaired, even with the Peace Council. In addition, my round of friendly farewell visits this past week . . . indicated nothing but cordiality and a very definite interest in building on the foundations already laid in participating in such other programs as the work camps and seminars.[26]

The major casualty of the Meeting of German Intellectuals East and West will be considered later.

On the Western side the report was received more favorably. Copies were distributed to West German officials and received acknowledgements varying from polite to cordial. The deputy mayor of Berlin remarked that the mission had surely made a

26. "Confidential Memorandum of Conversation with Officials of Peace Council," 9 April 1964, p. 3, AFSC Archives.

contribution to new developments. The spokesman from the FRG Foreign Office with whom the team had argued so vigorously on travel restrictions was quite positive and asked Roland Warren to come for another talk.

Some voices in the West attacked the document for being naïvely uncritical of conditions in East Germany. An editorial in the *American-German Review*, published in Philadelphia, took the report to task for being critical of Allied Travel Office operations and far too uncritical of various aspects of East German policy.[27]

As several commentators stated, perhaps the greatest contribution of the mission in mitigating the climate of suspicion and accusation was the fact of the visit itself. Time and again Western officials were surprised to learn of the degree of freedom the team had in moving about and the way in which the stipulations regarding publicity were respected. Even the team itself was pleasantly surprised; the meeting with Chairman Ulbricht, over which the Peace Council had said they had no control, produced no fanfare of publicity. All that the public in East Germany knew of the whole visit was a brief account in *Neues Deutschland* on the evening of departure cleared in the agreed manner. This experience was the best refutation the team could give to the frequent charges in the West that the "Communists" would exploit any opportunity to gain recognition and would not hold to agreements.

Work of the Quaker International Affairs Representatives

The Quaker mission to the two Germanies was only one short episode early in the long effort to understand and conciliate.

---

27. "The Wall that Wasn't Pierced," *The American-German Review* 30, no. 4 (April–May 1964):3–5.

The work of the Quaker representatives in Berlin spanned the eleven years from the spring of 1962 to the summer of 1973. Roland Warren was succeeded by Robert Reuman, thus covering between them the four critical years of the gradual thaw before the "grand coalition" of November 1966. A lapse of two years ensued before the fortunate coincidence of available staff and a gift of money brought William Beittel to Berlin in the fall of 1968. Lore Horn, a German Quaker who had worked with Roland Warren as secretary and also helped Robert Reuman, provided a valuable connecting link and kept up correspondence as a volunteer during the hiatus.

The three representatives were quite different in skills and background. Roland Warren, formerly professor of sociology at Alfred University, New York, came directly from the position of research director of the New York State Charities Aid Association. Robert Reuman was on leave as professor of philosophy at Colby College in Maine. William Beittel, after extended youth work in Europe during the early fifties, was the director of American Friends Service Committee work camps in Paris from 1960 to 1963. When called to the post in 1968 he was working on a doctoral thesis for the University of Pittsburgh.

Each specialty seemed particularly well adapted to the needs of the time. Coming right after the Wall, when the break in communication was almost complete, Warren used his insights on conflict interaction as well as his Quakerly understandings to develop a procedure of interviews on each side. His academic and intellectual stature as a sociologist helped initiate a mission of conciliation with top-level people, who needed to be persuaded of the Quaker role.

The German academic world was particularly receptive to Robert Reuman's emphasis on moral and social philosophy. He was interested in the underlying forces of the spirit that moved people, "the great confrontation of values" between East and West, mentioned by one of the Quaker visitors in

1961.[28] Reuman's interest in people in all walks of life enabled him to relate to a cross-section of persons, from policy-makers to church leaders to academics, who could promote the broad change of thinking on the future of the two Germanies that was needed.

William Beittel, younger and with less academic prestige, commanded respect for his analytical ability and knowledge of Germany and Europe. With his interest in political sociology, he came at a time when the mutual shunning of the two Germanies had turned into an awkward courtship in which an overture from one side brought cool rebuffs from the other. He was an indefatigable matchmaker intent on seeing that the union came off by counteracting the stereotypes of each side. He recorded the details of encounter and his own interpretation with great care.

All three men had important experiences in Germany. Roland Warren had taken a doctorate at Heidelberg University and had gone back to Stuttgart from 1956 to 1957 on a Guggenheim fellowship to study citizen participation in community activities. Robert Reuman had directed the Quaker Student House in Freiburg from 1951 to 1953. William Beittel, from his post in Paris, had traveled frequently in the two German states and Eastern European countries. He had been in Berlin at the time the Wall bisected the city. Each was fluent in German, and each had a wife who contributed in important ways to the enterprise. Margaret Warren, with a doctorate from the University of Heidelberg in history, literature and art, provided another dimension to their joint observations of German life. Dorothy Reuman was a discerning observer, helping on the occasional trips when she could accompany her husband. Hanne Beittel had experienced the vicissitudes of postwar German life in her own growing-up period. She digested news and made reports, especially during

28. Grigor McClelland, "Report, April 1961," Friends House Archives.

the period when Beittel was on partial leave to work on his thesis. All three were good partners in the daily exercise of confronting frustrations, assessing situations, and planning next steps in an exacting and lonely enterprise.

The representatives reported fully and frequently to the Philadelphia home office, with carbon copies going to Friends Service Council, London. Their queries and requests usually received prompt replies. Suggestions were made to the field staff by the Centers and Quaker International Affairs Representatives Committee and staff in Philadelphia, but the initiative was in the field, where the worker operated with a great deal of latitude on questions of who to see next, what responses to make, what projects to pursue.

The relation of the Quaker representative to local German Friends was complicated. He was not directly responsible to any local body, and yet he could not ignore their views. He needed to be both detached and yet in touch. As in many such situations, he had to be free to act as an outsider, German Friends were inevitably conditioned by their environment. There were Friends in the West who shared the prevailing view that the government of East Germany was a foreign imposition which should not be recognized. Some Friends in the East were strong supporters of the new socialism, arguing that it was working for a new society which was basically more Christian than Western capitalism; others in the East were strongly critical in private. Thus, the Quaker representative had to be discreet without appearing aloof, to listen without agreeing. He could not divulge the details of who he was talking to or what they were saying, and this led to an aura of mystery. While many German Quakers generally appreciated the Americans, some were uneasy that an outsider was making "Quaker policy" without clearing with locally responsible bodies.

To counteract these negative feelings, each of the Quaker representatives made overtures to Friends on both sides. They attended the local meetings in West Berlin and East Berlin. Roland Warren and Robert Reuman made major presentations to yearly meetings at Bad Pyrmont. William Beittel produced a program description especially for German Friends in December 1969. A few local Friends in both East and West were close consultants and strongly supported the Quaker workers whenever the issue arose among local Friends.

The major amount of the work was in personal visitation to individuals and small groups on both sides of the political barrier. Roland Warren tallied a total of 245 conversations during his two years. He saw 151 different persons, 94 being repeats. One hundred and fifty-three conversations were with officials, and 92 were with nonofficials; 95 were in West Berlin, 71 in the FRG, and 79 in East Berlin and the GDR. Reuman and Beittel did not keep an exact count, but Reuman estimated 300 to 400 talks divided evenly between East and West and Beittel estimated 700 to 800 over his five years, during one of which he was on leave.

A prospective visit required careful preparation. As Robert Reuman said, "Vital to the depth and value of QIAR conversations is extensive, accurate and up-to-date information." In preparing for an interview, Beittel made a practice of picking out at least three issues he wished to raise. These issues were gleaned from records of previous interviews with the person, knowledge of his or her background and position, and general reading in newspapers and periodicals. In this process Beittel was helped by his wife and secretary, but all three representatives reported that the time and assistance they had was often not sufficient, and this resulted in lost opportunities and some uneasy moments. Roland Warren, usually well prepared, was caught off guard in a difficult interview because he had only a vague knowledge of Ulbricht's recently announced "seven points."

The three men carried on their daily contacts in quite

similar ways with a wide range of people, but there were differences depending on the individual style of the Quaker worker and the changing relations between the two Germanies.

Roland Warren and Social-Psychological Analysis

Warren's use of social-psychology is well revealed in two speeches he gave before groups in the East and West in which he applied the analogy of individual neurosis to society. A whole society, rather like a neurotic person, he said, could have a concept of historical trends and present events that was at variance with reality and sure to bring conflict with the quite different perceptions of the same realities held by the opposing group. Societies, rather like individuals, are unable to face the realities of a problem and resort to mechanisms such as projection (blaming their failings on the enemy) and phantasy (finding satisfaction in a dream world) to enable them to adapt to a situation. But their adaptation is unrealistic and only succeeds in making their adjustment to reality worse. As a result, reality appears so different from each side that negotiation and compromise are not possible until the area of common perception is expanded.

In this first speech in the East, Warren tactfully avoided offense by not pointing to specific examples from the internal or foreign policy of the GDR.[29] Nevertheless, he was heartened to find that the audience of fifty or sixty, including doctors, medical students and others, responded positively. They understood his thesis, and instead of dwelling on the failings of the other side, they discussed ways to improve reality perception in the East.

29. Roland L. Warren, *"Krankheit, Konflikt und Gesellschaft; zum Gespraech zwischen Soziologie und Medizin,"* Stimme 15, September 1963.

A year and a half later, in March 1964, he presented a similar thesis in the West and analyzed the schizoid thinking that advocated German reunion while refusing to have anything to do with the other Germany.[30] This application of social-psychological concepts to political analysis was realitvely new to popular German thinking and came at a time when people were receptive.

In an article published in the *Journal of Conflict Resolution,* Warren described in social-psychological terms his activity of talking to leading spokesmen on both sides of the wall.[31] The pattern of beliefs and consequent actions on each side of the wall he called "belief-action" systems, which were opposite and yet mirror images of each other. Each system, he said, contained a complete explanation for the deterioration since 1945 of the hopes for a unified Berlin as the capital of a unified Germany. "Thus though the content varies, the systems purport to describe the same events."[32] He formulated a series of nine propositions that applied for either side, a condensation of which follows:

> The other side is completely to blame for the failure of reunification and continues deliberately to thwart this purpose. We have a true picture; theirs is distorted to confuse the issue. We are willing to negotiate; they have either ignored overtures or set impossible terms. They have provoked incidents which risked war and war might have occurred were it not for the patience of our side. They have revived elements of Nazism and wish to destroy our social order and set up their own instead.

30. Roland L. Warren, *"Der Ost-West-Konflikt und die Problematik der psychischen Stoerung,"* translation by Annette Carlsohn, AFSC Archives.

31. Roland L. Warren, "The Conflict Intersystem and the Change-Agent," *The Journal of Conflict Resolution* 8, no. 3 (September 1964): 231–41.

32. Ibid., p. 233.

He showed how the "belief-action" system of each side is a unified, interrelated whole, based on an ideology—Marxism—Leninism or Western capitalism—each with its own interpretation of history and social structure, supported in the East by the Soviet Union and in the West by the Western Allies.

Warren discussed the mechanisms for control and reinforcement of the system; the "pull" of the official "line" was reinforced by the social need to present a united front against a dangerous enemy. Devices of selective perception and impugning the motives of the other side, he explained, protected the distorted images. While the method of control in the pluralistic "free" society and the monistic controlled society were different, the results were surprisingly similar; both produced a pervasive image distortion.

He also discussed the surprising fact that the "two systems, though logically mutually exclusive, are from the standpoint of social process reciprocally supporting. Each is sustained in part by the existence of the other system and by the pattern of hostile interaction with the other system.... In Adenauer's time there was a cynical saying among disenchanted Germans on both sides of the divide that Adenauer needs Ulbricht, and Ulbricht needs Adenauer." This mutual reinforcement of hostile systems, Roland Warren wrote, "is almost puncture proof the opponent is damned if he does and damned if he doesn't. If he does something which our side believes he should do, then that proves that our side's hard policies are having a beneficial effect. If he does something which our side believes he shouldn't do, then this proves his moral culpability and serves as a reason for redoubling our efforts against such inhumanity."[33] What limited communication existed between the two systems, Warren explained, consisted of official pronouncements and reports through controlled media that reinforced the stereotypes.

33. Ibid., pp. 234, 235.

Thus, it was the purpose of the Quaker "change agent" to suggest a new look at the common realities each side needed to face. Roland Warren, using the natural curiosity of the official who for the first time had someone before him in direct touch with the other side, selected the arguments that seemed to have most validity and presented them not as his own opinions, but as those strongly and sincerely held by the other side. At times the Quaker representative would inject his own views of possible alternatives. At times he would use historical analogies: on ideological warfare, Roland Warren often used the example of the Protestants and Catholics, who had once fought fiercely and now coexisted peacefully. Although some persons interviewed were impervious to this method, with others it led to a serious dialogue and an exploration of alternatives.

In November 1962 Roland Warren talked with a high official of the People's Assembly of the GDR, who stated that the GDR had freed itself from militarism, fascism, and revanchism and until the same was done in West Germany (Warren's mental note: "until West Germany likewise became socialist"), there was little hope or sense in trying to ease tension or make slight adjustments. A step such as exchange of newspapers would only be possible if war propaganda was eliminated, as the official claimed it had been in the East. While the conversation was pleasant enough, Warren felt he could accomplish little more than to indicate clearly that this continual oversimplification of issues left Warren unsatisfied. After talking with a person of similarly dogmatic views at a later period, William Beittel said: "I left Mr. S wondering to myself how one can cut through the shield of words and images reflecting only one part of the truth that surround and permeate such individuals (in East and West) and hoping that communication at another level occurred even when I thought my discussion partner did not or would not listen to another view."[34]

34. Confidential Report, 3 June 1970, AFSC Archives.

As an example of the more open-minded officials he met, Warren reports on an interview in January 1964 with an important GDR political leader with whom he felt free to propose a list of possible contributions toward relaxation which the GDR could make without affecting its vital interests. The steps proposed ranged all the way from liberalizing cultural exchanges to tempering certain foreign policy demands such as the GDR's insistence that occupation forces be withdrawn from West Berlin and that West Berlin's ties with the Federal Republic be severed. Both demands, Warren indicated, cut so close to vital interests of the West that their presentation shut off all possibility of negotiation.[35] During the three-hour conversation the East German official took extensive notes, saying that he would accept and consider these suggestions from Warren even though he would not have accepted them from a Western official. This demonstrated a well-known psychological fact that the adversary relationship cuts off constructive communication, but a trusted third party can present the same ideas and have them considered rather than immediately rejected.

Integrity of the Conciliator and the Religious Dimension
In talking to both sides the third-party conciliator is put under considerable strain to retain his personal integrity. The pulls of each side tend to stretch the listener into two different persons. Warren defined integrity operationally as "trying insofar as possible never to say anything or agree with any point on one side of the Berlin Wall which was inconsistent with anything said or agreed to on the other,"[36] or in biblical terms, "Our Yeas must be Yeas and our Nays must be Nays."[37] Warren found that assuming a person from the other side was

35. Letter of 10 January 1974, AFSC Archives.
36. Warren, "The Conflict Intersystem," p. 232.
37. Roland L. Warren, "Quaker Peace Work in a Tense International Situation," *International Affairs Reports from Quaker Workers* 10, no. 1 (January 1963): 6.

looking over his shoulder was a constant antidote to the one-sided thinking that can easily slip by when one is not alert to the basically different assumptions from which conclusions are drawn. For example, in the interview cited above, Warren might have agreed with the hard-line *Volkskammer* leader that the belligerent and inflammatory statements of extremists in the West which he called "war propaganda" should be curbed, but before answering, Warren asked himself how he would then argue for this position on the Western side. Could he really advocate a system of censorship which would violate all the Western standards of free speech? In the circumstances he remained silent. With a more open-minded discussion partner he might have elaborated the reasons why such curbs were not possible in the West.

Any such self-discipline as Warren proposed had to be applied with tact and flexibility. Warren himself said, "Rigid adherence to it [the discipline] in all cases would perhaps be undesirable."[38] In other words, a certain amount of inconsistency in the role of the third-party may be inevitable for social interaction with such varied and opposing conversation partners.

While listening with real sympathy to both sides and spending much of his time relaying other people's views on issues, the conciliator could not be completely neutral toward values or morals. Integrity required him to show at times what he believed. At these points the Quaker representative might support his position by alluding to elements of Quaker philosophy—pacifism, the ultimate value of all persons, the constructive power of love in human relations. But integrity is not conveyed by words; it comes from the impact of the whole person, and too many words about one's own beliefs may detract. In describing his interview experience, Roland Warren found religious terms were needed to bring in a new

38. Warren, "The Conflict Intersystem," p. 232.

dimension beyond the social scientific process. In some indefinable and not wholly communicable way, Warren said, the Quaker worker feels that two persons talking together stand under a higher authority and that the goal is to speak with honesty in one's own position and a loving understanding of the other person's position. He elaborated this point in a speech to the annual meeting of the AFSC in January 1963.

> This word "love" will hardly seem strange to this audience. I use it simply to mean an attitude which seeks that of God in the other person and addresses that of God in the other person and listens for that of God in the other person. The attitude with which one approaches a Communist is crucial, just as is the case with approaching anyone else. As one high Communist official expressed it to me, "You don't need to be a communist or even to agree with the fundamental social order of socialism in order to be welcome here. We can tell who comes to us with friendly intent, and who comes to us as an enemy." How can he tell? I do not know. What I do know is my own side of the relationship. I know how I ought to feel and behave toward that Communist—with the realization that we are both children of one heavenly father who loves us both and wants us to love each other.[39]

The Quaker representative did not require any deference to this religious dimension in his discussion partner, but he sought it for himself. Under the best of circumstances it made him more courageous, more perceptive of his own internal conflicts and those of the other person, more aware of his own limitations and failings.

The two disciplines of social science and religion were complementary in this enterprise. While the one stresses thorough logical, historical, and analytical preparation, the

39. Warren, "Quaker Peace Work," p. 6.

other stresses thorough internal, emotional, and spiritual preparation. Looking back on his interview experience, Roland Warren identified guidelines to the approach which were based both on psychological insight and on religious discernment:

1. "To acknowledge the truth—and there was at least a kernel truth—in the point which the conversation partner mentioned."[40] (For example there was a danger of neo-Nazism in West Germany though it was exaggerated out of all proportion in the East.)

2. To avoid explosive issues where "his relationship to his conversation-partner was not sufficiently strong to bear the weight."[41]

3. To avoid self-righteousness by respect for the other person: —"I find it helps to remind myself that among these highly placed officials many are more intelligent and capable than I, and have demonstrated much more than I have a basic devotion to principle which withstood the test of concentration camp and possible death. Certainly, a self-righteous attitude toward such persons is not only unjustified but extremely harmful to the relationship."[42]

4. To understand the role of an official: "I made it quite clear to him that we feel our contribution lies in speaking our minds frankly, as Friends, but with a full realization that we do not bear the decision-making responsibility and also we do not have to weigh in all the factors which officials do and that we are undoubtedly unaware of some of these. We appreciate their listening to our point of view."[43]

5. To avoid fear through the sense of "nothing to hide" in

40. Warren, "The Conflict Intersystem," p. 239.
41. Ibid.
42. Warren, "Quaker Peace Work," p. 6.
43. Letter of 25 November 1963, AFSC Archives.

one's activities between the two Germanies and no ulterior motives of personal gain or organizational gain. "Fear is perhaps the greatest hindrance to Christian love."[44]

The approach of truth and love in human relations can be described and broken up into various segments, but these attributes cannot be learned from a guidebook or put on as a cloak. Acting as a medium for exchange between opposite poles in conflict is an art. Analytical description can help marginally, but it cannot provide a prescription for the kind of temperament and character that enabled the Quaker representatives to fulfill the role.

What is the difference between a Quaker approach in third-party conciliation and some other approach? Perhaps a hint comes in noting that the Quaker conciliator does not try to detach himself from the conflict as something that he observes at arms length, surveying it with all his mental powers but not becoming involved. Such detachment is necessary for some types of mediation, and Quakers themselves may assume such a role at times, but in these case studies it is evident that the individuals involved, after doing their intellectual analysis as thoroughly as possible, felt it important to immerse themselves in the conflict, viewing the people not as pawns in a chess game, but as real persons. This makes for severe strain, and the words of Robert Reuman would be echoed by the others

> It has not been a relaxing experience. Sometimes one feels as if he were trying to resolve German tensions by taking them into himself and carrying them there. This is, of course, fruitless, but it is to a degree unavoidable when you try to listen with compassionate concern and clear understanding to the people on both sides of the many walls of distrust and fear, when you struggle continuously

44. Warren, "Quaker Peace Work," p. 7.

for the requisite knowledge of facts and attitudes, and when you try to speak to and of the people on both sides with sympathy and respect which spontaneously demand the honesty of founded criticism.[45]

Robert Reuman and the Problems of Recognition in West and East

While Warren stressed the symmetry and mutual reinforcement of misperceptions, Reuman laid more stress on the rigidities of the Western position, which sought the collapse of the Eastern government in spite of the fact that it was supported by Soviet troops and increasingly secure in its own right. Adenauer, the embodiment of this policy, had stepped down as chancellor in 1963, but although his successor in the party and in national leadership, Ludwig Erhard, made some modest changes, official policy toward the East still aimed at reunification through isolating and weakening the GDR. While eager for private openings to influence citizens of the other Germany, the West was spurning all official contact. The East, on the other hand, bent on securing international recognition, was eager for official contact and averse to private communication.

By 1964, when Reuman came, it was abundantly evident to observers and to many West Germans that a change in the stalemate would come only with major concessions in the foreign policy of the West—moves toward recognition. On the Eastern side it was less a change in foreign policy that was needed than a change of the relations of the government to its own citizens. "Internal recognition" was the term applied, meaning that the government needed to increase its popular support and not depend on Soviet arms. The two factors were closely interlinked, since the West German

45. Robert Reuman, "Reconciliation in Germany," *Middlebury College Newsletter,* Summer 1966.

policy of nonrecognition was based partly on the argument that any gesture toward the "so-called" German Democratic Republic would betray the large majority in the East who, it was assumed, were opposed to their own government and opposed to any support for it from abroad.

In terms of the conciliator's role, Reuman was engaged more in analysis and proposal than in mediating between the reality perception of the two sides.

Reuman found his proposals were taken more seriously when he wrote them out. As he said in his final report:

> Undoubtedly the best conversations were those centered around such papers as the reunification proposals, where the person had had time to read them first, and could see the balance of the critique and sympathy. In this way it was possible to establish the proper balance of agreement, which by itself can be quite puerile, with criticism and disagreement, which by itself can too easily appear to be hostile and unacceptable.[46]

In his first report in June 1965, Reuman attacked a major buttress of the Western nonrecognition policy. He attempted an evaluation of the attitudes of East Germans toward their own government and toward the foreign policy of the Federal Republic. While the earlier mission "through a Wall" had raised questions on these points, Reuman made some conclusions. His observations were based on a three-week visit in East Germany, where he moved about freely and talked in confidence with approximately two hundred people, and were supplemented by his many visits to East Berlin and general reading. Although he still found a high degree of impatience and criticism of the government, most people, Reuman wrote, "have come to accept the relative per-

46. Robert Reuman, *"Rechenschaft und Ausblick,"* Memorandum, August 1966, AFSC Archives.

manence of the present state of affairs and are making their accommodations to it."

The most important "news" in this report was his observation, contrary to Western assumptions, that the Western non-recognition policy was condemned by a large majority of the citizens in the East. As Reuman summarized:

> There is a high degree of rejection [by East Germans] of official West German policies toward the DDR [GDR] government, and very little support to be found within the DDR groups for the Western claims that recognition of the DDR government would be betrayal of the non-communist citizens there. On the contrary most saw non-recognition of the DDR government as helping to maintain illiberal pressure and recognition as a pre-condition of any kind of reunification.[47]

Reuman sent this paper as a QIAR report to a wide circle of contacts on both sides and in the United States. Many interview reports confirmed the careful attention given it, and several times Reuman was called by Western journalists planning trips to the GDR who needed background information.

Reuman's March paper, "Proposals on German Reunification," also received high-level attention. Egon Bahr, assistant to Mayor Willy Brandt, called the Quaker office to ask if he could discuss it with Reuman, but he had already departed. Reuman's subtle reasoning was appreciated in the West, since he did not propose to give up the goal of reunification but showed how a united Germany could only come about in the far distant future after a period of rapprochement. The writing was criticized by Eastern officials, who wanted outright

47. Robert Reuman, "Attitudes in the DDR (East Germany)," International Affairs Reports from Quaker Workers, vol. 12, no. 6 (30 June 1965), AFSC Archives.

recognition, not the small steps Reuman advocated, and who found it hard to distinguish in the speeches of their opponents between the necessary political lip service to the image of a united Germany and an aggressive policy of absorption.

William Beittel and the Process of Détente
In his first interview in 1968, Beittel played a go-between role similar to Warren's. In the uncertain movement of détente, extremist spokesmen on one side provoked similar statements on the opposite side, while gestures of accommodation by the politicians in power were often misinterpreted. The Quaker role was to interpret the reasons for these reactions.

In early 1964, after his efforts to negotiate with East Germany for some humane relaxation of barriers in Berlin had been thwarted in Bonn, Willy Brandt, the mayor of Berlin, increased his efforts to gain power in the national arena. He was elected head of the Social Democratic party in February 1964, and although the elections of October 1965 did not bring his party to power, its position improved and he became leader of the Social Democrats in the Bundestag. The big opportunity came in November 1966 when the Erhard coalition of Christian Democrats (CDU plus CSU) and Free Democrats fell apart in a debate over the budget. In the ensuing party crisis Erhard resigned as head of the CDU and Dr. Kurt Georg Kiesinger was elected his successor. Kiesinger, finding the Free Democrats still unbending, formed a coalition with the traditional opponents, Willy Brandt and the Social Democrats. Much to everyone's surprise, the "grand coalition" was inaugurated. The left wing of the SDP felt that such a marriage would lead to the party's downfall and the betrayal of socialism. The philosopher Karl Jaspers warned of a new dictatorship, since there was no effective opposition party.[48] The grand coalition provided Brandt, as vice-chancellor and foreign affairs minister, and his close associate Bahr the opportunity to start the steps toward *Annaeherung* that Bahr had proposed in his Tutzing speech of 1963. Brandt announced a new *Ostpolitik* (policy toward Eastern Europe), which sought to make overtures to Eastern European countries, though leaving the other Germany far down on the agenda. The Hallstein doctrine, providing that the Federal Republic would not deal with countries that recognized the Democratic Republic, was put on the shelf.

Although Willy Brandt was given considerable latitude in foreign affairs by Dr. Kiesinger, his policy could be misinterpreted in the East as a more clever expression of the old CDU policies. Thus, when Beittel arrived in 1968 he found the GDR showing a particularly hard face toward the blandishments of the Kiesinger-Brandt coalition. Their fear was that small steps of rapprochement would benefit the politicians of the West without exacting any changes in the basic policy of nonrecognition. In East Berlin Bonn's overtures toward the other Eastern European countries seemed a continuation of the CDU objectives of isolating and undermining the Democratic Republic. Furthermore, the Soviet Union's suppression of the Czechoslovak "spring" in autumn 1968 had brought repercussions in the GDR, where the leaders felt a hard line was needed to maintain internal controls.

Thus, again and again William Beittel found himself listening to diatribes in the East, which lumped together all political leaders in the West from Willy Brandt to Franz Josef Strauss, the right-wing leader of the conservative CSU, and condemned them as "imperialist," "revanchist," "capitalist," "neo-Nazi" oppressors just as intent on destroying the GDR as Adenauer had ever been. Beittel would listen patiently and

48. Karl Jaspers, *The Future of Germany* (Chicago: University of Chicago Press, 1967).

then quietly disagree, pointing to important differences
among the West German party leaders and attesting to the
realistic acceptance by many of the GDR. He explained that
even the terminology of the cold war was going out of vogue
and the name of the German Democratic Republic was coming into greater use. Many times he felt that his rejoinders fell
on deaf ears, but in later visits someone occasionally would
pick up on a point made by Beittel on a previous visit and
indicate a change of view.

In the spring of 1969, William Beittel's message seemed to
be contradicted by the provocative action of Bonn in calling
a meeting of the Federal Assembly in West Berlin to elect a
new president and thus dramatize their view that West Berlin
was a part of the Federal Republic. Although previous elections had been held in Berlin, the East saw fit this time to
capitalize on the event as a major challenge to their official
stand that West Berlin was an "Independent Political Entity"
and not part of the *Bundesrepublik*. Traffic on the Autobahn
routes was interrupted intermittently, raising the specter of
the Berlin blockade twenty years before. Threats and counter-
threats were exchanged. Official protests from the East that
the holding of a Federal Assembly in Berlin was against the
Potsdam treaty and international law brought the reply that
any interference on agreed traffic routes by East Germany
was contrary to the Potsdam treaty. Beittel discovered that
no one on the Western side was very enthusiastic about holding the election in Berlin—not the city leaders, or the Bonn
government, or, least of all, the U.S. Mission in Berlin.
Nevertheless, any change of plans, it was thought, would be
viewed in West Germany as a sign of weakness in face of
Eastern harassment.

Bill Beittel participated in the search for a face-saving
formula to ease the tension. Several possibilities were considered, and Beittel visited both sides to interpret these proposals. A suggestion was made by the Soviet ambassador that

Easter passes be offered to West Berliners for a visit to East
Berlin in exchange for cancellation of the Federal Assembly.
All efforts were too late to stop the election, but they did
help to relieve the tension and show that neither side wanted
the crisis to lead to an ultimate showdown. Dr. Gustav Heine-
mann, an elder statesman very much in sympathy with the
policy of *Annaeherung,* was elected as the first Social
Democratic president since the Weimar Republic, which
ended in 1933.

On the Western side William Beittel tried to interpret the
oversensitivity and suspiciousness of the East in terms of
history and current internal politics. He suggested that the
Ulbricht government still had strong remnants of a siege mentality, seeing foes without and foes within. Patience was
necessary, and provocative acts such as the holding of elections for the Federal president to the Bundestag in Berlin
could not help.

The general elections of October 1969 brought a new
coalition of Social Democrats and Free Democrats. With a
majority of only twelve votes, Willy Brandt, now chancellor,
sought to pursue his *Ostpolitik* more directly and openly. In
his initial speech before the Bundestag on October 28, 1969,
Brandt offered to discuss outstanding issues with East Germany and to negotiate nonaggression pacts with East European states, including the GDR. In deference to West German dreams of reunification he proposed "a two in one"
formula. He acknowledged the existence of the other German
state, but insisted that both entities were part of a single
German nation; thus, the two states would not be "foreign"
to each other and would have a special status under international law.[49] This was followed by an active policy of

49. Lawrence L. Whetten, *Germany's Ostpolitik: Relations Between
the Federal Republic and the Warsaw Pact Countries* (London and New
York: Oxford University Press for the Royal Institute of International
Affairs, 1971), p. 116.

negotiation with the USSR and Poland leading to treaties that renounced German claims to Eastern territories.

Brandt's policies were still subject to the old suspicions in East Berlin. The effort of the Brandt government to change policy toward "the other German state" while still claiming one "German nation" was thought in the East to be the same old expansionist nationalism aimed at a united Germany. The overtures to the Soviet Union and Poland were interpreted as efforts to undermine the GDR's position in the Warsaw Pact. Beittel kept probing the position in the West and then reassuring his contacts in the East.

Organizations in the forefront of the old reunification policy now were trying to revise their image. For example, the Ministry for All-German Questions, dealing with the problems of German refugees, was established from the beginning under the Adenauer theory that the Federal government represented all Germans in the world at large. In May and September 1969 an official told Beittel that the hardest job the ministry had was living down its old reputation. He said they no longer held to the sole representation formula (*Alleinvertretung*) and were not trying to woo citizens in the GDR away from their own government. Rather, they wanted to make them more loyal to the GDR in the hope that the Eastern government would become more flexible. This leader asked the Quaker representative to make clear in the GDR that his ministry was not "revanchist" or "neo-Nazi."

Bill Beittel assured the minister by saying that he encouraged all the people he spoke to on both sides to differentiate between past and present and to abandon the stereotypes that had controlled their past thinking. But Beittel went on to point out that his task was made more difficult by the events at the annual rally of refugee organizations called *Tag der Heimat* (Day of the Homeland), partially financed by the Ministry for All-German Questions. At this rally many boos and epithets of "traitor" and "quisling" were hurled at Klaus

Schuetz, mayor of West Berlin, when he said that the Federal
Republic must recognize the Oder-Neisse boundary.

Leaders of the *Kuratorium Unteilbares Deutschland* (literal-
ly, Caretaker for Indivisible Germany), a private agency set
up with strong government support in the early postwar years
to work for reunification, also sought Quaker help. New
leaders saw their task as one of preparing the German people
to accept a separate Socialist state. As the chairman, Wilhelm
Wolfgang Schutz, put it in a memorandum in 1968, the GDR
should be recognized as a second state within one German
nation. When Beittel came, he found that KUD leaders
deplored the provocative act of holding the Federal Assembly
in Berlin. Beittel carried the message that the KUD wanted to
make contact with organizations in the East. Although there
was no positive response then, that such a message was sent
stirred considerable interest in the East.

A climax in the activity of encouraging détente came in
Bill Beittel's efforts in 1972 to support the *Ost Vertraege*
(Eastern treaties). The Brandt-Bahr policy had moved ahead
to the point where treaties with Poland and the Soviet Union
had been signed and were up for ratification by the Bundestag. Chancellor Brandt was never quite sure of how much support he had. In the legislature he was dependent on a fragile
coalition with the Free Democrats. His twelve-vote majority
was gradually being whittled down. In the spring of 1972 the
CDU-CSU opposition hoped to defeat the governing coalition
by appealing to the still-lingering postwar fears of the West
German public. They did not have a constructive alternative
to propose, as Beittel learned in talks with them, but they
were doing their best to cast the SDP-FDP coalition government in an unpopular light as the betrayers of the German
nation to communism.

At this point the Quaker representative moved from cautious phrasing of possible alternatives to outright advocacy
of particular positions. Beittel talked with U.S. representa-

tives in Bonn and Washington to find out how United States official support could be secured for ratification of the treaties. He talked with persons in West Berlin on support for ratification that might come from a big rally to be addressed by the popular former mayor, Willy Brandt. He helped leaders of the *Kuratorium Unteilbares Deutschland* to make contact with an official in East Berlin, which he had not succeeded in doing two years earlier. Bill Beittel emphasized in his contacts that the issues were much broader than just the German question. They related to the security of Central Europe and the avoidance of another world war. It is hard to say how much influence Beittel's urging in key spots may have had; for the most part the trends were well established by major political and economic developments, so that the election in the fall of 1972 turned out a stronger vote for Brandt's policies than anyone expected. The treaties were well on the way to full acceptance.

Projects of Direct Communication

As he tried to provide a relay point between opposite poles of thought, the Quaker representative frequently wished that the persons he was talking to on each side of the boundary might meet face to face. Such a meeting, arranged with careful preparation and favorable auspices, might lead to an educative breakthrough as each side encountered the misperceptions of the other. A number of projects of this kind were proposed, and some were worked out by the Quaker representatives in Berlin.

Conference of Intellectuals
Roland Warren early on began to nurture contacts with the intellectual leaders on both sides. He had friends from previous days of study and research in Heidelberg and Stuttgart,

and his standing in the field of sociology opened up many contacts. His affiliation with Quakers led him to seek out influential churchmen. These contacts were more numerous on the Western side, though not lacking in the East. The idea for a conference in which intellectuals of East and West would exchange views arose on both sides. There was no difficulty in developing lists of well-qualified persons who wanted to participate. Questions of official clearance and possible venue were more difficult.

Clearance for Western intellectuals to attend a meeting was not necessary, since individuals were free to travel wherever invited, but the Federal government might try to obstruct the project by preventing East Germans from attending if the conference were held in West Germany or in a country, like Switzerland, open to influence from Bonn. Roland Warren, following his policy of candor, told Foreign Office officials at Bonn and U.S. embassy members what he was proposing, not for their approval or disapproval, but to inform them. There were mixed reactions, but no suggestions of interference.

Intellectuals from the Eastern side would need permission from their own government to travel, and so Roland Warren, with some persuasion, secured the official auspices of the Peace Council and the preliminary approval of the Foreign Office. Planning had progressed to the point of reserving the St. George's School at Clarens, Switzerland, for the meeting, when in March 1964, Warren found officials in East Berlin raising objections and making counterproposals. Before these new elements could be sorted out, *Journey Through a Wall* reached the Peace Council and Foreign Office. On the next contact in April 1964, Warren was told that the Peace Council was no longer interested in the East-West meeting.

One can only speculate on the real cause for the veto. The proposal had been considered in high party circles, where foreign policy at the time was governed by the aim of securing any small sign of recognition. For this reason, the authorities may have initially favored the idea, just as some officials on the Western side opposed it for fear it would give too much recognition. A completely unpublicized conference of private individuals held under Quaker auspices was hardly a step toward recognition, and it is probable that on second thought, officials in the GDR considered the risks of discussions outside party control between intellectuals in East and West outweighed the advantages. There had been tension in the recent past between the Ulbricht government and intellectual circles over the suspension of a professor at the Humboldt University. The publication of *Journey Through a Wall* was probably the last straw and a convenient reason for withdrawing approval for the meeting.

Robert Reuman, coming to the field in July 1964, tried without success to revive the plan. At the same time the Foreign Office sought Reuman's help in securing Western participation for an international writer's conference planned in the GDR. Reuman was more successful in this effort. The differences between support for these two events showed clearly that the Foreign Office thought nonofficial, middle-level contacts as proposed by the Quakers were either of no value or too sensitive, while a publicized large gathering under party control would lend some international prestige to the Democratic Republic.

Other Projects

In addition to promoting face-to-face communication, another reason for pursuing "projects" was to give the Quaker representative something to talk about in his interviews. Robert Reuman especially felt the need for a "handle" for his discussions in the period of 1964 and 1966, when any movement in relations between the two Germanies was glacially slow and new messages few.

The Berlin representative could discuss a number of possible projects in connection with the varied international programs of the American Friends Service Committee. The School Affiliation program, for example, had arranged pairings of American and West German schools for several years, resulting in exchanges of teaching materials, student products, students, and teachers. There was the possibility of extending this project to East Germany. Another AFSC program sent a few volunteers to West Germany and other parts of the world for two years of service in neighborhood centers, schools, and agricultural development projects. Reuman's efforts to extend these programs to East Germany did not get past the initial talking stage with officials. The time was not propitious for exchanges that would bring Westerners to live and work for extended periods in the GDR.

The Quaker representative had more success in planning short-term youth involvement in seminars and work camps. Through a long series of negotiations with the *Freie Deutsche Jugend,* the official agency in the GDR for international youth contacts, participation in international seminars outside Germany was secured for East Germans starting in 1963. In 1964 the *Freie Deutsche Jugend* put on a tour for six American and English young people in East Germany. The association of the six Westerners with the two tour conductors and the bus driver provided some opportunity for dialogue, but the major impact of the project was to give the visiting young people a better understanding of Socialist development in East Germany. In 1965 a jointly sponsored work and study project was carried on in Guestrow, Mechlenberg, attended by twelve British and American young people and nine East German students. A similar program planned for 1966 was cancelled by the GDR because of an outbreak of hoof-and-mouth disease among the cattle in the area. Because of policies of the GDR these projects could not include West Germans, so the only occasions the Quaker could arrange for East-West dialogue among German young people were the International Student Seminars outside Germany. After the hiatus in Quaker representation in Berlin from 1966 to 1968, William Beittel was unable to find much interest in Quaker projects in the youth agency, while the Foreign Office was taking greater interest in the diplomats conference.

GDR Representation in the Conference for Diplomats

The European Quaker Conferences for Diplomats carried on from the Geneva office had West German participation from the beginning in 1952, and by the end of 1965 a total of forty-five officers of the Federal Republic's Foreign Service had participated. No one from the GDR had attended. A major focus of the conference after 1956 was East-West dialogue. In 1960 the conference organizers were asked to arrange a conference in Poland, and in 1964 the practice of holding one conference a year in an Eastern European country was begun. While one of the objectives of the meetings was to bring together representatives of officially noncommunicating countries for informal conversations, in practical terms the organizers knew that the inclusion of certain countries would prevent the participation of others.

While Robert Reuman was in Berlin and Paul Johnson and Franklin Wallin were working on conferences from Geneva, a beginning was made. The first step was a special conference arranged by Wallin of members of scholarly institutes of international affairs close to the foreign offices of various countries. Two participants from West and one from East Germany could attend this 1966 conference at Gars-am-Kamp, Austria, because they were not considered official representatives. A second step was made possible by the long term practice of having three or four consultants who were not usually officials of their home countries at each conference for diplomats. Negotiations were in progress with the Rumanian Foreign Ministry for a diplomat's conference to be held in that country in 1966. The Rumanians, willing to accept diplomats from all countries, including Spain and Portugal, brought up the question of inclusion of the GDR. Johnson and Reuman found a solution to the dilemma by inviting consultants from both Germanies and diplomats from neither. A third step was taken near the time of the conference when Paul Johnson, thinking that a lone GDR consultant might be all the more defensive and rigid, asked the East German ambassador in Bucharest to send an officer of his embassy—not as a participant but as a personal guest of the director. The official selected was a fortunate choice, since he was not a career diplomat but an educator in charge of the GDR student exchange programs in Rumania. He did not attend the small morning groups nor talk in the plenaries but, along with the consultant professor, participated fully in the intensive informal discussions which went on to the small hours of the morning. Participants from the Western countries appreciated this opportunity to talk to able spokesmen from the GDR, and the experience was considered a great success. At Clarens later in the summer, however, the usual pattern of two diplomats from the Federal Republic and none from the Democratic Republic was repeated.

In 1967, when there was no Quaker representative in Berlin, East Germany was not included in the diplomat's conferences. The device of "guest of the director" was used again in 1968. This time it was agreed in both Bonn and East Berlin that the nominee would participate fully but not be listed as a regular member of the conference. The representative from the GDR Foreign Office was an active participant—all the more since he had been at the Gars-am-Kamp seminar as a scholar from the Institute for International Relations.

The devices for including the GDR on a less official basis than the other members of the conference were wearing thin. In 1968, William Beittel in Berlin and the new conference director in Geneva, Stephen Thiermann, conferred with

Philadelphia headquarters and decided that the logical next step was to invite an official GDR diplomat to be a regular participant in one of the two Clarens conferences. Although the hope was that Bonn would agree, there were no assurances that they would. With this decision in mind Thiermann and Beittel went to the head of the American Affairs section of the GDR Foreign Ministry. The Foreign Office spokesman took the occasion of this first contact with the two new Quaker workers to deliver a long lecture on the limits within which Quakers would be allowed to work in the GDR. The implied threat was that if the Quakers did not accept certain facts, such as the equality of the GDR, there would be no further cooperation. When he had a chance to speak, Stephen Thiermann presented the plans for the summer conference in 1969, which included for the first time the full participation of a GDR representative. Beittel said that the policy would have to be discussed in Bonn before they issued a formal invitation, but the Quaker organizers planned to go ahead, hoping that there would be no West German or NATO objections. The Foreign Office spokesman seemed surprised and pleased at this development.

The plan was not received as warmly in Bonn, where the "grand coalition" of Kiesinger and Brandt was facing critical elections in the fall of 1969 and did not want to give any fuel to anti-Communist elements in its own ranks or in the opposition. Talks in Bonn by Thiermann in early March and Beittel in May produced the answer that diplomats of the FGR could not appear in a meeting, however private and unofficial, with diplomats of the GDR where matters of recognition and the status of Germany as a nation might be discussed—whether on the agenda or not. Several highly placed officers who were alumni of Clarens voiced their own unhappiness with the policy, but explained that it was made more rigid by the pending elections.

The conference staff in Geneva soon heard rumors of a

NATO boycott. Efforts to stave it off with visits to U.S. missions in Berlin, Bonn, and Washington and to British officials in Berlin and London had no result. The matter had evidently been considered at a high-level, four-power meeting. Canada joined the boycott at the last minute when a participant and an ambassador who was to act as a consultant sent regrets. Italy and France also joined the boycott; Norway and the Netherlands did not.

Another innovation had been planned for this conference as a result of the suggestion from alumni that nondiplomatic participants with particular experience on the topic discussed should make up one-third of the conference. To discuss the topic "Violence and Nonviolence as Methods of Change,"—very timely in the ferment of 1969—Stephen Thiermann had brought together an assortment of individuals ranging from young revolutionaries and freedom fighters to staid diplomats of the Soviet Union. Included were three persons from the GDR, one of them official, and four private citizens from the FRG and West Berlin. The usual politesse of the diplomat's conference was marred by a number of sharp encounters. So many new factors were included in the plan that the result was quite different from any previous conference. As the director said in his report, "Clarens was something like the stew prepared by a newlywed housewife who tries too many interesting ingredients so that the final product has good morsels, but overall there is too much for anyone to digest."[50] The NATO boycott resulted in a lack of symmetry between East and West, a preponderance of nondiplomats in the whole group, and the loss of an important consultant from Canada. The foreign service officer from the GDR was disappointed in the lack of counterparts from the West, but said he found the conference valuable as a whole.

50. Report, "Conference for Diplomats and Other Specialists in International Affairs XXXV," AFSC Archives.

The presence of an East German married couple, both able theologians and church workers, was an important plus; they were open to discussion of all issues, while convinced of the merits of the Socialist system and the role Christians had in the construction of such a system in the GDR. Both appreciated the opportunity and were pleased that husband and wife had both been allowed to attend the same conference. Their presence was the result of the direct intervention of a highly placed officer in the Ministry of Church Questions of the GDR and was certainly contingent on the new Quaker policy of inviting diplomats as regular participants.

In the debate in the Quaker Service bodies before and after the summer program, some argued that the staff had moved ahead too rapidly in an awkward year when the pending elections in the Federal Republic had assured a rigid position. On the other hand, others insisted that it was time the Quakers paid deference to the principle of equality in representation of the two Germanies. The setback to East-West dialogue caused by the Western boycott proved temporary, and the argument among the Quakers was resolved by the election of October 1969 in West Germany when the new Brandt-Scheel coalition of Social Democrats and Free Democrats won a narrow majority of twelve votes. When William Beittel and Stephen Thiermann went to Bonn in January 1970, they found the atmosphere changed. An official high in Chancellor Brandt's office indicated they expected the Quakers to continue with their new policy and that the FRG would participate in meetings with persons from the GDR. In the conferences of 1970, 1971, and 1972 there was strong representation from both Germanies.

The GDR's eagerness to participate clearly grew out of the striving for any sign of recognition that could be gained. The Quakers, on the other hand, were promoting communication, not recognition. Their judgment was that GDR officials were so confined to ideological stereotypes that they were in danger of blocking moves toward peace. They knew that stereotyped thinking about the "East Zone" in the West was also dangerous. By 1972 the objectives of the GDR Foreign Office and the Quaker organizers had grown much closer. As recognition drew close, GDR officials were eager to give their young diplomats a chance to learn how to operate on the international stage. A discerning GDR participant commented that the government had spent all its energy on gaining recognition and little on the substantive issues of international affairs. Again and again in interviews with Eastern participants, Beittel was told how much the conference had meant to them in personal growth and in improvement of their ability to represent the Socialist state to the rest of the world.

Bridging the Gap between the United States and the German Democratic Republic

The United States was, as we have seen, a partner of the Federal Republic in keeping the German Democratic Republic isolated. Anticommunism in the United States and anticommunism in the Federal Republic reinforced each other.[51] A one-hundred-and-eighty-degree swing was needed for both countries to move from a policy of ignoring to a policy of accepting the GDR. The Quaker probers were never quite sure whether the State Department was encouraging Bonn in this swing or lagging behind it. In any case, the Quaker representative frequently found himself engaged in promoting a change of perceptions in the United States.

Many opportunities occurred in the Berlin setting where members of the American community were returning to the United States and itinerant leaders from the United States

---

51. An AFSC book, *The Anatomy of Anti-Communism* (New York: Hill and Wang, 1969), translated into German, was distributed to a number of people in West Germany by Beittel.

wanted to learn about East Germany. All three Quaker representatives had frequent contacts with journalists. In his book on East Germany, the NBC correspondent in Bonn, Wells Hangen, quoted Roland Warren's statement that Christian churches were basically healthier under the hostile regime of East Germany than under the protective regime of the West.[52]

In one of his early conversations with the Foreign Office of the GDR, Roland Warren was asked whether one or two U.S. senators might be interested in attending the Leipzig Fair. He had to report that in view of prevailing American attitudes he doubted that they would come. Two years later in Berlin (1965), Robert Reuman briefed Congressman Henry Reuss of Wisconsin on East Germany and arranged for him to visit with three or four intelligent and informed spokesmen for East Germany. This was probably the first visit in fifteen or twenty years of an American official of national status to the GDR.

Over the years the Quaker representatives frequently visited the United States Mission in Berlin and the Embassy in Bonn, where they found their firsthand knowledge of the East eagerly solicited by the frequently changing staff, a number of whom had been to Clarens conferences. By the time William Beittel came to Berlin in 1968, direct contact with the East by U.S. officials was in the realm of possibility. Carefully clearing the meeting with individuals and authorities to avoid embarrassment, he arranged in 1969 for some officials in West Berlin to talk with church leaders in the East. Then, in 1971 he opened the way for talks between U.S. officials and lower-level officials of the GDR in East Berlin. In 1972 the Washington International Affairs Seminar arranged a meeting in Washington, D.C. of U.S. officials with traveling scholars from an institute in East Berlin that was closely

---

52. Wells Hangen, *The Muted Revolution: East Germany's Challenge to Russia and the West* (London: Gollancz, 1967), pp. 181–82.

linked with the Foreign Office. Not all of these face-to-face encounters produced better understanding. One Western diplomat used his first meeting with an East German counterpart to denounce the Wall and the iniquity of shooting fleeing Germans. The contact flagged after that but was picked up later.

By far the most ambitious undertaking of communication between the United States and the German Democratic Republic was the mission of September 1963 described above. This led naturally enough to the proposal for a return visit of East Germans to the United States. It was in fact the first question asked by the Peace Council in the second session with the mission,[53] and it was brought up by Chairman Walter Ulbricht in the session that the American delegates had with him.[54] The Peace Council and Foreign Office continued to pursue the idea of an AFSC-sponsored visit in the United States until 1973. Even at that late date, when both sides were gearing up for recognition, interest was expressed in a Quaker-sponsored tour. The East German disappointment that the Quakers were unable in all those years to arrange this visit was often expressed, at times as an accusation that the Quakers had gone back on a promise. The only answer was that the Quakers were never in a position to promise, but had tried hard.

At the time of the first major effort, in 1965, even sounding out the idea might have led to a rebuff from one side or the other, so the Quakers had tried to explore the matter tentatively without making any formal requests or applications that could be officially turned down. On the Eastern side there were few obstacles. The Peace Council was so eager for the opportunity that they were willing to accept fully the

---

53. AFSC, *Journey Through a Wall*, p. 52.
54. "Journal," Interview, 20 September 1963.

Quaker stipulations for off-the-record discussions and no public platforms. Furthermore, they agreed that Peace Council representatives would apply through the hated Allied Travel Office and would "under no circumstances use this as an occasion for making publicity against the ATO."[55]

On the Western side the proposal ran into a major roadblock arising from West Germany's policy of nonrecognition of the GDR. Friendly persuasion was exerted in West Berlin, Bonn, and Washington. Participants in a major parley with officials of the Office of German Affairs in the State Department in Washington included Roland Warren, former Quaker representative, and the chairman of the Quaker Mission, Morris Keeton. From previous exploratory talks they had learned that visas for the delegation would depend on who was invited. Robert Reuman had therefore sent a list of eight names which the Peace Council staff hoped would be acceptable. Half were SED party members; half were not. Half were Peace Council members; half were not. They represented a variety of professions and religions. From the Quaker point of view it was a good list of able, informed and relatively flexible supporters of the GDR. The head of the delegation was to be a highly esteemed retired director of the East German bank system. Also included were a prominent evangelical clergyman, an influential Quaker woman, a writer, a scientist of international reputation, and three academics. The Peace Council had gone along with the scheme of submitting a trial list without informing the individuals they might be invited.

State Department officials approved of the idea in general terms, but on seeing the list they raised objections. Several delegates, especially the party members, would require waivers from the Justice Department assuring that their ad-

---

55. Memorandum: "A Brief Description of the Nature of a Proposed Visit," 1965, AFSC Archives.

mission to the United States was "in the national interest."
As names were tossed back and forth, it became clear that
any group GDR officials might pick for a dialogue on political
issues with Americans would not be approved by the State
Department, and that this decision was primarily one made
by officials in the Bonn government with the strong support
of the United States ambassador to Bonn.

The Quakers argued that their purpose was to promote
dialogue with an isolated government and people and that
under the circumstances only persons in good standing with
the GDR government would be allowed to come; indeed,
such persons would provide a much more realistic basis for
discussion than opponents of the Socialist government. They
pointed out that such a visit under the agreed limitations
would have a minimum of propaganda risk and a maximum
of possibilities for enlightenment on both sides. It might even
give the State Department a chance to try out a change in
their policy toward East German visitors with the least risk.
The spokesmen for U.S. policy praised Quaker efforts to
develop communication with the Soviets and other East
Europeans, but, they said, East Germany was different. It was
an illegitimate government and the only reason the "regime"
wanted to send representatives was to "make propaganda."
This seemed in reality to mean that if such a group went to
the United States, the GDR press would play it up with their
own people. As the ambassador in Bonn put it, "it will make
them [East German Government] look respectable." The intervention of Congressman Reuss was unsuccessful. In summarizing their disappointment about the final decision, the
American Friends Service Committee wrote:

> We realize that the decision of the Department is con-
> sistent with present U.S. policy. However, we seriously
> question whether a policy which requires such a restric-
> tion of communication is not in danger of becoming

sterile and uncreative of the new approaches and solutions which we need to find.[56]

Summary and Assessment

Acceptability of Quaker Good Offices

A paramount question for the study of conciliation is the basis on which a third-party gains acceptance as a go-between in any dispute. In dealing with nonofficial, self-appointed intervention, which might well be characterized as "meddling," the question is all the more important. The Quaker background was good for a first introduction, but continued acceptance had to be earned.

The nature of acceptance was quite different on the two sides, owing to the differences in the sociopolitical systems and the fact that the Quakers were more identified with the Western side. In the West many private persons and most officials expressed understanding for the Quaker third-party role. The Quakers were thought to be "one of us" and "on our side." Some appreciated the religious basis of the Quaker efforts and valued what they were doing. The decision makers in the West did not necessarily agree with particular Quaker points of view and would argue that the Quaker proposals were "too idealistic." The Quakers occasionally would meet hostile attitudes, such as the member of the Bundestag who said he would be eternally grateful to the Quakers for the material help they provided him when he was down and out, but they were a lot of pipe dreamers who did not understand what they were doing and didn't know the realities.[57] United States officials generally appreciated the

56. Letter to Director of Office of German Affairs, U.S. State Department, 2 August 1965.

57. William Beittel, "Bonn Trip Report, 2–10 May, 1972," AFSC Archives.

contacts with Quaker representatives, who could travel where they could not. They understood the Quaker approach well enough so that they never pressed the conciliators for any information that might have been considered classified in the East. Only occasionally did they ask questions concerning the views of individuals in the East that the Quaker representatives did not feel free to answer.

On the Eastern side different assumptions prevailed and affected the work of Quaker conciliators. The Quaker background was acceptable for an initial introduction, but its religious overtones probably aroused suspicion in official circles. The basic stance of the Quakers must have seemed alien and even subversive to the system of centralized control imposed in the East in a theoretically transitional period of proletarian dictatorship. Along with the Western world the Quakers believed in the values of open communication as a process by which ideas are sifted and the truth is sought. Their religious tradition declared the freedom of the individual conscience not only for themselves, but for all others. In the East the doctrine prevailed that at a certain stage of historical development when socialism was threatened by external and internal enemies, communication should be controlled by authorities who knew best the requirements for the new Socialist state. Discussion was possible as to the details, but the major lines of the blueprint must be set out with authority by those who knew. The pluralistic social ideology and structure of the West, with its emphasis on the individual, was a threat to the construction of a new value system in the East. The religious bodies in East Germany, including Quakers, were part of this threat and were the only organized groups somewhat beyond state control.

From the Eastern standpoint then, Quakers were suspect. They might be in touch with dissident elements in East Germany and might even be a screen for direct CIA activity. Denunciations of Western "bridge building" were voiced

sporadically in the official journals of the Warsaw Pact countries and particularly after the Czechoslovakian crisis of 1968.
In view of this situation the Quaker representatives in Berlin
were careful to accept certain Eastern expectations as the sine
qua non of their activity.

Because of the possible suspicion that the Quaker workers
might be enemy agents, their relations with United States
officials were a particularly sensitive matter in the GDR. The
Quaker representatives made very clear in the East that they
talked with United States officials about their impressions of
general conditions and attitudes in the GDR and the official
views of the government as an essential part of their conciliatory function. But they had no military or otherwise secret
messages to give, and their Western conversation partners
knew better than to ask for such.

Quaker workers got to know the East German border in-
spectors quite well, for each crossing brought a new test of
their credibility. A first rule was that they would never
violate the censorship, customs, or currency rules. Requests
to do little favors came frequently: "to sneak in" a book,
carry a letter, buy something on the Eastern black market
with West marks. Even strong Eastern government supporters
occasionally expected such favors, but the Quaker workers
had to disappoint them. Beittel made it a practice to inform
border guards of the general scope of his work. He would
open his briefcase and show them everything he had. Usually
the car search and glance in the portfolio would be perfunc-
tory, but occasionally the guard searched thoroughly. On one
occasion, soon after Beittel had started his work, he was
searched and questioned for over an hour in a most hostile
manner. In talking to a Foreign Office official after this
incident, Beittel used it as an example of actions that
produced hostility and reinforced stereotypes of the "prison
state." He said he had no objection to being searched and
knew this was the function of the guards, but he questioned

the hostile and suspicious manner. The official wrote this all down without comment.

Certain interviews with East German officials stand out as testing sessions. At first the officials probably thought they could convince the Friends workers of the rightness of the Eastern point of view. Warren reported that in an interview in 1963, officials in the Ministry of Church Questions seemed intent on convincing him of the correctness of their thinking and the error of Western ideas. Warren saw that his judicious answers, carefully weighing the plus and minus factors, did not satisfy them, and he had the impression that his work might be threatened.

It also appeared on that occasion that the official wanted to use the Quaker representative to gain information on the opinions of East German Friends. The Warrens had just been on a two-week trip in East Germany, a trip authorized only after considerable questioning and delay. The Secretariat asked what Warren's impressions of the GDR were. Since they knew that the chief contacts of Roland and Margaret Warren had been with Quakers, any specific negative reactions might lead to questions attempting to find out the source of these views. Thus, Warren's answers were general and guarded. Going a step further, these officials asked how the GDR Quakers felt about the peace policy of the government as outlined by Ulbricht in his seven points. Warren also answered this in the most general terms, trying to indicate without saying it that he would not be an informer.

Later interviews were more relaxed. Indeed, the same officials in the Church Secretariat in 1964 were cordial and went out of their way to say to Warren at the end of his stay that they had all been impressed by the various activities and particularly the frank and friendly discussion of differences.[58] The publication of *Journey Through a Wall*

58. Letter to Philadelphia, 16 April 1964, AFSC Archives.

caused, as we have seen, difficult discussions, but they were carried on in a spirit of frankness and mutual understanding. The officials expressed disappointment that the Quakers were violating their own premises of fair dealing and nonprovocation on certain points.

Following Roland Warren, Robert Reuman was never subjected to a special grilling, and his trip to East Germany was approved without difficulty. William Beittel came after a lapse of two years. His first interview with the major figure in the Foreign Office with whom the Quaker staff had visited over the years was the most threatening and constrained of any in the eleven-year period. It was a time of heightened cold war tension in February 1969 when the Federal Republic was planning to elect a president by holding the meeting of the combined Federal Assembly in West Berlin. Furthermore, it was shortly after the clampdown in Czechoslovakia when Western "bridging" activities were subject to new denunciations in the Eastern press. Stephen Thiermann of the Geneva office was also present, since this was the meeting to talk about conferences for diplomats referred to earlier. Both reported that the official appeared to have been charged with impressing certain points on the Quakers. He spoke sternly, as if from the record, and made the following points:

1. What the Quakers did was carefully watched by the authorities.
2. Attempts to seek out individuals for Quaker conferences who had different opinions or ideas than those selected by his office would be of no avail. (A previous seminar director in Geneva was cited as having traveled too freely in the GDR.)
3. The working relationship that had existed with Roland Warren and Robert Reuman could continue and grow provided Herr Beittel did nothing secretive or undercover.
4. In particular, any kind of research such as Herr Beittel had

carried on in Yugoslavia would be completely out of the question.

5. He could expect searches at the border, and the hostile attitudes of border guards were only natural when persons came from a state that refused to recognize the very existence of the GDR and that engaged in illegal activities such as holding the election of the next *Bundespraesident* in West Berlin.[59]

The two-hour session ranged widely over cold war issues, but the points listed indicated the particular sensitivities of the GDR to the Quaker operation. Evidently there were fears that the Friends might increase dissidence in the East, fears that they might be making harmful reports in the West, and perhaps even fears that they were recruiting espionage agents. A particular suspicion attached to Beittel because of his earlier research work on decision making in a Yugoslav commune. The Foreign Office was evidently afraid that he was coming to Berlin to carry on such activities under the guise of Quaker conciliation. Suspicion of foreign-sponsored research had caused trouble for a number of scholars in East Germany.[60] It was likely that these kinds of questions had reverberated around in party circles and the official was given the task of laying down the law to the new Quaker appointees. It is even possible that the search at the border which Beittel had cited as an example of reinforcing stereo-

59. Memorandum from Berlin QIAR, 10 February 1969, AFSC Archives.

60. For example, Frederick Pryor, a Yale professor, was accused of espionage activity and arrested in December 1961 shortly after the Wall was built. The minister of security of the GDR asserted that behind the screen of scientific work of a dissertation, this man had sought to provide information of foreign trade activities and other economic matters to the CIA of the United States. He was released after many appeals, including those of Emil Fuchs, Quaker professor in East Germany, and Clarence Pickett, honorary secretary of the AFSC.

types had been ordered to reassure certain persons that the Quakers did not operate in a clandestine way.

Beittel remained calm and unruffled, deferring but not conceding. When openings came he assured the inquisitor that he had nothing to hide, had no intentions to do research, and would certainly keep the ministry informed of his activities.

On this same day the Foreign Ministry junior officer appointed as liaison with the Quaker representatives offered to accompany Beittel with auto and chauffeur on the interviews he was arranging for the next day. Beittel said that he saw no need for this, but acquiesced when he saw it was very important to the junior officer. Beittel found it helpful to have the officer along on the interviews to reassure the Foreign Office that all was clear and aboveboard.

The testing process and the suspicions lasted into the fall. Beittel's application for a visa for himself and his wife, Hanne, to travel in East Germany to attend the first session of the separated East Germany Quaker Yearly Meeting was turned down, with no reason given. This was the one occasion in five years that Beittel got angry and registered his irritation in a letter to the ministry of Church Questions. Otherwise he worked on quietly expanding the areas of freedom of movement beyond those seemingly laid down in his first talk, careful to clear all that needed to be cleared, but keenly aware of the subtle differences between an official position for the record and the actualities of control.

The session that William Beittel had in March 1972 with the same official he had first interviewed showed his success. Beittel reports: "The first half hour was a *tour d'horizon* of developments in the U.S. in the past months . . . an interesting exchange devoid of the sharp attacks and polemics that have characterized previous visits. . . . This pleasant tone characterized the full two hours we met."[61] The official

61. Memo of 21 March 1972, AFSC Archives.

showed a wide-ranging knowledge of Quaker work, including the Quaker lobby in Washington, the Quaker UN program, and the Quaker work in the Middle East. This relaxed atmosphere must have been due largely to recent major policy and leadership changes in the GDR. The détente was proceeding well on both sides. But it also indicates that the Quaker worker had passed all tests and had become fully persona grata to the Foreign Office.

A startling incident in February 1970 gave warning of the possible misunderstanding of Quaker work that might arise in the East. The Quaker international representative in the Vienna Center, who had only been on the job a few months and was not sufficiently aware of the political pitfalls of East-West conciliation, undertook a visit to Czechoslovakia. On his way back to Vienna he was stopped at the border, seemingly in a routine way. When border guards looked at a number of the documents he was carrying, they detained him for questioning by higher authorities. He was put up at a hotel and questioned intently, though politely. The interrogators kept his card file of contacts in Czechoslovakia and some confidential documents written by Quaker workers giving judgments on the Czechoslovak "spring" and the intervention that followed in autumn 1968. In July 1970, an article appeared in the Czech party organ *Rude Pravo*[62] giving a detailed account of the seizures and the questioning of the Vienna-based Quaker representative and cleverly twisting statements to build a case for the notion that the Quakers, under the guise of genial, religious, peacemakers, were actually operating a far-reaching intelligence system, which must surely be of aid to the enemies of the Socialist states.

The incident caused much dismay among Quaker workers. They were worried about the repercussions befalling Czech

---

62. "Whose Friends? Strange Interests of the Sect of the Quakers in Czechoslovakia," *Rude Pravo*, 31 July 1970.

citizens. They were worried about effects on all other conciliation work. A German translation of the article was cir-
culated in West Germany by the Religious News Service, and
East German officials must have known about it. They never
mentioned it to Beittel, however, and he carried on in his
usual discreet, but open way. Czech diplomats continued to
come to Clarens conferences, and the storm blew over. Many
thought the publication of the article was timed to warn
citizens within Czechoslovakia as well as other Eastern countries of the danger of contacts with foreign organizations. It
was probably also intended to remind Quakers that in the
East their activities were suspect and potentially subversive.

It was precisely the delicacy of this relation with Eastern
authorities that made it difficult for Quaker workers to intercede for individuals thought by the West to be wrongfully
imprisoned. The general aspects of such intercession by third-
party conciliators will be considered in chapter 5. Here we
give two examples. Shortly after Roland Warren arrived he
was asked to find out about Heinz Brandt, an American who
had been tried and found guilty of espionage. Warren's quiet
inquiries at the Peace Council brought forth a long response
in writing from the general secretary asserting that Brandt
was rightfully sentenced and was no fighter for peace, but a
promoter of the cold war. Home committees in Philadelphia
pushed hard for the Quaker delegation to ask for a prison
visit to Heinz Brandt. Roland Warren was reluctant to pursue
this, and his view was sustained by the mission members, who
used some of their sharpest language in pointing out to the
Philadelphia office that such a request was inappropriate for
their particular task.

A similar question arose later in the matter of Mark Hussey,
a young American Socialist who was arrested, tried, and sentenced to seven years in prison for making statements in-
jurious to the GDR. Beittel looked into the matter and found
that Hussey probably had acted indiscreetly. Beittel found

that several persons were interceding quietly to reduce the harsh sentence, and Hussey would probably be released much sooner if there were not such a fuss made in the Western press. Beittel did not think that there was anything more that Quakers could do. Hussey was released not long after.

Conciliatory Activity

In this description of the work of the Quaker international affairs representatives in Berlin it is clear that the different types of conciliatory activity—listening, message carrying, assessment, and making proposals—were intertwined in any particular conversation. After initial stages of listening, a main activity was the assessment and reporting of antagonistic perceptions. It was not long, however, before the Quaker workers felt they had earned sufficient trust so that they could put forth tentative proposals. In formal mediation, which is officially agreed to by the parties in dispute, any proposals for solution by the mediator are likely to be highly threatening to one side or the other. Thus, they are not lightly given nor easily accepted.[63] For the unofficial third-party intervenor, such directed conversation is easier because he has no official position at stake and his discussion partner can feel free to explore alternatives without danger of public exposure.

The degree and range of solutions proposed was greater in the German case than in the other cases. This was no doubt due to the length and continuity of the effort, as well as to the fact that the disputing parties became more and more interested in practical suggestions. Many conversations with key persons had to do with tentative solution-making proposals offered to encourage cross-questioning. Indeed, proposing alternative paths of policy was part of the process of

63. Elmore Jackson, *Meeting of Minds* (New York: McGraw Hill, 1952), pp. 161–62.

checking reality perception. Were there conciliatory initiatives that the GDR could make in order to encourage the forces working toward accommodation in the West? Was there a difference in policy between Mr. Brandt and Mr. Strauss that the East should recognize? Different perceptions and different solutions went hand in hand. As already described, certain individuals on both sides were eager to try out unorthodox thoughts about new solutions on the Quaker listener, knowing that the confidence would be kept.

At the end of the enterprise, as we have seen, the last Quaker representative moved from making tentative proposals to active advocacy, a stage beyond conciliation that would have been either impossible or inappropriate in the beginning. Anticipating criticism by local Quakers, Beittel wrote a letter to a leading German Quaker saying:

> You will have seen from my letter, . . . that I have moved from the role of reporting to that of advocacy. This is not a new question, but it is one that I do not face this directly very often. I will not be surprised if there is some feeling that advocacy of this type is inappropriate and damaging to the "neutral" image of a QIAR, but I am concerned that a useful image not get in the way of a plea for reason. And in this case I consider the stance of the coalition government a plea for reason that warrants, no demands, broad support, to the extent possible by organized bodies of Quakers and their service bodies.[64]

Beittel's trepidations about the proper role of a Quaker representative have been duplicated in many a like situation. In this case his advocacy was amply justified by the circumstances, and he was fully supported by the Quaker home office. German Quakers were more divided in their views but did not object.

64. Letter, 23 March 1972, AFSC Archives.

Resources for the Operation

Quakers can well be criticized in these kinds of efforts for the meagerness of their budgets. Did the sponsoring organization provide the resources that Oran Young says are so essential for conciliation?[65] In the home office there is need for a continuing service of liaison, response to questions, coordination with other efforts, and general housekeeping aids to the field; in the field, logistic, secretarial, and analytic help is needed. Even though contributions from Friends and non-Friends have been generous, the organization tends to stretch every dollar or pound to the limit. Indeed, the generosity of donors is attracted by the Friends' reputation for care in spending: using volunteers, paying low salaries, economizing on expenses—all of which fits in with the Quaker testimony of simplicity.

The German case involved a long-term sustaining relationship between the home office and field workers. While the correspondence back and forth indicates excellent relations, with a humorous give and take and openness to all kinds of comment, occasionally the requests from the field office were met by frustrating delays. In addition to a more full-time servicing function, one might advocate a full-time analytical function with a staff member at headquarters to read relevant books and journals and applicable concepts from conflict research, all for the purpose of sending useful suggestions to the Quaker representative. Auxiliary aid of this kind can be helpful, but risks building up home office expertise and bureaucracy at the expense of the field. This is a phenomenon of the U.S. Foreign Service that worries observers. The Quakers, on the other hand, have a tradition of giving rein to the man in the field. He is expected to consult with the home office and keep them fully informed, but give leadership to

---

65. Oran R. Young, *The Intermediaries: Third Parties in International Crises* (Princeton: Princeton University Press, 1967), chap. 3.

the home committees and staff rather than await direction.
In the German experience the policy was amply justified.

A better case can be made for auxiliary aid in the field. The
Quaker representative had some excellent secretarial assistance, but there were many gaps between secretaries. An additional asset would have been the right kind of junior partner
with background in international politics who would read and
analyze current material so that two minds could be reacting
to the host of impressions rather than one. Such a person
would be in the field and not liable to the distance distortion
of Philadelphia or London. He or she could also do a lot of
the chores of arranging appointments and writing up interviews. A post of this kind tied in with university graduate
work was proposed at one time, but did not materialize for
lack of funds.

Appraisal of Results

The difficulty of assessing the results of this kind of work are
obvious. Yet a few comments can summarize the German
experience. The Quaker representatives and committees, with
the help of some perceptive German analysts, early saw the
Wall with all its grimness as a potential contribution to peace
rather than a hindrance.[66] The physical barrier was merely a
manifestation of a much greater psychological barrier that

66. Professor Dietrich Goldschmidt, professor of sociology at the
Institute of Pedagogy in Berlin, a close advisor to the Quakers, wrote in
October 1961:

> I have been expecting the erection of a "wall" or barrier for years.
> Federal German policy, at least since the Paris treaties of 1954,
> could not but lead to this result. . . . The Federal Republic has in
> fact helped to prepare the "wall" by refusing any kind of contact
> with the German Democratic Republic and by turning Communism
> into the Devil Incarnate.

("A Voice of Reason," *Alternative,* a West Berlin students periodical,
AFSC archives.

operated to prevent understanding and communication.

Since a great part of the psychological barrier on the Western side was the inability to accept the existence of a German Socialist state, the Wall brought the possibility of change toward recognition. Thus, the Quakers could set to work within their general hypothesis that improved communication is the essence of peace when the barriers are so high and the distortion on each side so great. In effect, they said, "Tear down the psychological wall and the concrete Wall will lose its significance." The process of détente would certainly have gone on without Quaker intervention, but the evidence shows that they may have facilitated the flow and, as far as one can judge, did nothing to hinder it.

In a series of interviews in December and January 1972–73, the writer and William Beittel asked for informal evaluations of the eleven-year effort from several key persons on both sides who had been seen many times over the years. A few highlights can be reported here.

Herr Heinrich Albertz, former deputy mayor of Berlin, who had played a role with Brandt and Bahr in changing the thinking of the Social Democratic party, said that the Quaker representatives were very helpful on two points. First and foremost was the support and encouragement they gave to leaders in the painful process of guiding public opinion to an acceptance of the reality of two Germanies.

> The years of 1961–64 were times of great tension and fear. Incidents at the Wall were happening all the time. Students and others in West Berlin were inflamed. To advocate contact and exchange with the builders of the Wall was equivalent to high treason, and we were exactly in the position of such advocacy. The Quaker representatives provided moral support of immense value, since we stood alone, without the backing of the three Western allies, of the West Berlin citizens and of the Bonn govern-

ment. Yet Willy Brandt, Egon Bahr and I knew it was necessary."[67]

The second function, less important in the view of Herr Albertz, but still helpful, was the function of a message carrier accepted and trusted by both sides. After the Wall, Albertz said, there were only two persons who could help through their access to both sides: Roland Warren and a Swedish pastor. Warren could report what the East thought of some of the provocative actions in West Berlin and interpret their conception of the Wall.

On the Eastern side similar questions of evaluation put to a Foreign Office spokesman brought a realistic and practical reply. He appreciated the Quaker willingness to take on difficult problems and seek solutions where others were not doing so. (This no doubt referred to programs he knew about in Vietnam and the Middle East as well as Germany.) Specifically, he valued the opportunities for GDR diplomats to gain experience with Western thinking and ways of working in the Conferences for Diplomats. To participate officially rather than as "guests" was considered of particular value. The continuing attempts of the Quakers to see the GDR realistically and to share these impressions with the West were also appreciated. On the negative side, the Foreign Office official mentioned his disappointment that the return visit of Peace Council delegates was not accomplished. He had thought the Quakers would have enough political sophistication to pull this off. He criticized the youth seminars and diplomats conferences for having too much the atmosphere of friendly get-togethers rather than meetings for "scientific" study of causes and solutions.

Thus, the Foreign Office official emphasized the aspects of Quaker work that helped his "business"—securing recogni-

67. Memo, 22 December 1972, AFSC Archives.

tion. Others interviewed in the East spoke of the value of interpreting Western attitudes and carrying messages. A noted scientist appreciated Friends' efforts to assist communication, but he also emphasized that efforts to build bridges between peoples or opposing philosophies may be harmful at times rather than helpful. What is important in East Germany, he said, is to build socialism. When the West tells Easterners to work for individual freedom, it is working against the philosophy of socialism. Personal aggrandizement at the expense of others cannot be tolerated in the Socialist Germany. Thus, the pros and cons from the Eastern standpoint were forcefully presented.

Another way to test the operation is to ask whether the Quaker efforts were ahead of the trend or behind. In general, the record gives a clear answer that the Quaker representatives in their analyses were pushing ahead rather than lagging behind. The report of the mission seems less clear than it might have been. In their eagerness to avoid "political" issues, the team's nonanswers were equivocal. One looks in vain for a forthright statement to the effect that the West needed to work on external recognition and the East needed to work on internal recognition. These were both highly sensitive points, and perhaps the Quakers were right at that time in not getting out too far ahead of the American public in a published report. The narrowing down on the Allied Travel Office as a major target was a brilliant tactical move. The ATO was the most vulnerable in the array of Western instruments of non-recognition and retaliation. All that the Quaker report said about it was corroborated in later years, and the office quietly folded up in early 1970.

An official of the United States Mission in Berlin who had known the Quaker work in various connections was asked whether it was not true that United States policy had lagged behind the realities and had failed on occasion to seek imaginatively for alternatives. A specific instance was the adamant refusal over the years to allow a return visit of the Peace Council. The spokesman said that in his opinion the answers given had been right in every instance for the times that they were given. He appreciated the value of groups like the Quakers who were continually acting as gadflies to the State Department, but by its nature the department could not have moved faster.

Both sides were unconvinced in this encounter and that is evidently in the nature of the case. The Quakers continue pushing here and pulling there trying to help conciliation where two parties of comparatively equal power are locked in conflict, hoping that their efforts are based on adequate knowledge and the right motion of the spirit.

Chapter Three

The India-Pakistan War of 1965

The Dispute over Kashmir

The dispute over control of Kashmir, a former princely state, was not resolved at the time of partition of the subcontinent in 1947, and India and Pakistan were soon locked in an undeclared war. Through the initiative of the United Nations, the Kashmir War of 1947–49 ended in a suspension of hostilities, with a UN-patrolled cease-fire line dividing the state into two parts, one under Pakistani and pro-Pakistan (Azad Kashmir) control, another under Indian and pro-Indian Kashmiri control. In the fall of 1965 the smouldering hostility that had prevailed between the two nations broke out into open warfare. At the root of the dispute were the contradictory nation-building concepts of the two nations. According to the Pakistani ideal of a Muslim state, the Muslim majority of Kashmir could not exist happily in a predominantly Hindu nation. India's theory of a secular pluralistic state insisted they should and could. These mutually exclusive assumptions were not just theoretical concepts, but rather a strong source of identity for ordinary citizens, a ready basis for mob action, and the guiding principle of popular journalism.

At first fighting in the 1965 conflict was confined to skirmishes between Indian army units and bands of so-called

144

infiltrators crossing into Indian-controlled territory from the Pakistani section of Kashmir. Then the Pakistani army made major incursions over the cease-fire line into the Indian sector, and the Indian army retaliated by crossing the internationally recognized boundary between India and Pakistan with a pincers movement at Lahore. Major battles with all the equipment of modern war ensued in the next few days, ending in an inconclusive stalemate. The secretary-general of the United Nations, under the authority of the Security Council, secured a cease-fire agreement on September 22. Bickering over the terms of the cease-fire continued, and a high state of tension prevailed until the Soviet-sponsored peace meeting in Tashkent from January 4 to 10 began a cooling-off period.

Background of Quaker Work

A century of Quaker humanitarian efforts before 1965 in the subcontinent present three strands of activity: the India Conciliation Group, the work of humanitarian relief and reconstruction, and the conferences and seminars program. There were other kinds of Quaker activity, such as the missionary work, with hospitals, farms and schools, and the individual efforts of Friends in various spheres, but they did not form as direct a background for the conciliation effort.

The India Conciliation Group

The work of the India Conciliation Group from 1931 to 1950 was the most important precursor of the Quaker India-Pakistan Mission of 1966. Although the principle of independence for India was recognized at the time of the Round Table Conferences of 1930–32, the rule of the British Raj continued as firm as ever through the thirties and forties. Nationalists clamored for self-government immediately, while British authorities in London and New Delhi insisted that the complex problems of the princely states, the rights of Muslim and other minorities, and the constitutional division of power between central and provincial governments should be worked out before independence was granted. As time wore on and the internal divisions intensified rather than abated, Indian leaders felt more and more that the men in Whitehall were only paying lip service to self-determination and would continue to dominate the subcontinent, thanks to the internal division among the people and their leaders. Thus, in the many misunderstandings that arose, the nationalists had little faith in British promises. On the other hand, the ministers in London and viceroys in New Delhi, many of whom were genuinely interested in promoting an independent India with close ties to Britain through the Commonwealth, felt continually betrayed and harassed as they carried on what they thought to be a responsible process of devolution.

In the crosscurrents of political policy and agitation, Mohandas K. Gandhi was the unquestioned but unofficial command center. In the flow of his life the world came to see a unique and extraordinary kind of power, power based not on any material possessions or position, whether appointed or elected, but only on "soul-force," *satyagraha*. Horace Alexander, a Quaker who visited with Gandhi many times over the years, said of him in 1929: "Gandhi's daily life is marked by an extraordinary care for detail, great courage in obeying the inner voice, and a marvellous humility of spirit. He seems always gentle, always self-possessed, always strong and determined."[1] In Mahatma (Great Soul), as he came to be called universally in India, was to the British rulers an enigma. Again and again they misjudged his political effectiveness and misread his aims. By interpreting Gandhi to the British leaders and public, members of the India Conciliation

1. *Friends and Young India* (London: Friends Service Council, 1929), p. 6.

Group played their most important role. Through their own
pacifist religious orientation they were able to value the
spiritual methods of the Mahatma. They brought a witness to
the Western mind of the sincerity and impact of Gandhi's
spirit and action.

Mahatma Gandhi came to London for the Second Round
Table Conference of 1931. The members of the conference
were chosen by the viceroy presumably to represent all the
various minorities and factions in Indian life. The Congress
party leaders were strongly opposed to the method of selection, since they felt they represented all of India, and many
of the leaders thought the party should boycott the conference. Only after much persuasion from Indian and British
friends Gandhi undertook the heavy load of representing the
whole of the Congress and hence, in their eyes, the whole of
India. Congress leaders agreed to be represented, if he was the
sole representative—for he alone would be trusted by all. This
put an impossible burden upon Mr. Gandhi, and he looked to
a small coterie of British friends for support. C. F. Andrews,
a saintly Christian clergyman who had long been a close associate of Gandhi in his campaigns for the oppressed, met
Gandhi in Marseilles and helped him to get established in a
modest suite in London. Carl Heath of the Friends Service
Council and Henry Polak, who had known Gandhi in his
South African days, worked closely with Andrews in arranging meetings and special opportunities for Gandhi.

The Round Table ended in failure, as the Congress leaders
had predicted. It was impossible to get any agreement among
the Indian leaders for dividing power among the various factions. Gandhi succeeded, nevertheless, in bringing his own
views before a wide segment of the British public. Knowing
that the struggle had only begun, he discussed with a group
of friends the need for continued interpretation of views of
the Indian National Congress party in Britain and of British
thinking to leaders in India. On the suggestion of Horace

Alexander, Gandhi asked Agatha Harrison, one of the small group that prayed and worked with Gandhi on the fringes of the Round Table Conference, to undertake a full-time job interpreting the independence movement. Her salary would be paid by an Indian manufacturer sympathetic to the Congress.

The Indian Affairs Committee of London Yearly Meeting had been doing this kind of work since its establishment in 1930. As a direct harbinger of the later conciliation efforts, the committee had sponsored a visit of Horace Alexander to India in the summer of 1930, when the major civil disobedience movement was launched. Alexander conferred both with Lord Irwin, the viceroy and the symbol of British authority, and in prison with Modandas K. Gandhi, the symbol of Indian independence. He interpreted one to the other and both to the British people in a remarkably understanding way.

The India Conciliation Group was drawn together by Carl Heath in December 1931. It was kept apart from the Indian Affairs Committee, both to be more inclusive of such key non-Quakers as C. F. Andrews and Muriel Lester and to take actions the Society of Friends as a whole might not approve. Friends were by no means of one mind on Gandhi's campaign for independence. In a letter to the Committee on Indian Affairs, Carl Heath summarized a situation not uncommon in Quaker committees operating in the controversial political arena: "I do not, I must confess, see any future of value for a Committee which, in spite of the extreme gravity of a situation such as now obtains in India, is yet debarred, as an official Committee, from any strong and straight action."[2]

The India Conciliation Group remained throughout its existence a self-constituted, informal organization of about thirty-five members, many of whom had roles in other

2. Letter, 16 August 1932, Friends House Archives, London.

organizations sympathetic to Indian independence. The chairman throughout the committee's life was Carl Heath, who operated first from his office as secretary of Friends Service Council, where he was promoting Quaker centers, and after 1937 from his office as chairman of Friends World Committee for Consultation. Agatha Harrison, having agreed to Gandhi's proposal, was asked by Heath to be the secretary of the group, and during the next twenty years, through independence and after, she worked tirelessly and selflessly for the peaceful liberation of India. Alexander Wilson, an English Quaker, was the indefatigable treasurer who sent out personal appeals whenever a new trip to India was planned or a pamphlet needed to be published. An inner core met and conferred frequently, and a wider group attended monthly meetings and was kept informed. The real work of the group was done largely by the writing, speaking or visiting of individuals. Although it was not officially a Quaker organisation, many key members were Quakers or, as in the case of Agatha Harrison, joined the Society of Friends.

In Great Britain the group undertook a job of public education: producing pamphlets, briefing politicians and journalists on the nationalist movement in India, and arranging for Indian speakers to speak to audiences in Britain. Through frequent visits to India, the more significant work of conciliation was carried on in a low-keyed unpublicized manner by Agatha Harrison and two or three others. Agatha Harrison carried messages back and forth between Gandhi and the viceroy, between other leaders, such as Jawaharlal Nehru, and government officials. Time and again when complicated incidents led to complete misunderstanding, the opposing parties would refuse all talk. When the Congress had an official policy of "no talk with the British Raj," Agatha Harrison would still find a way. When British officials could not be seen with "rebel leaders," she would nevertheless arrange it. Her description of the significance of Gandhi's fast in

March 1939 for the oppressed people of Rajkot is a good example of the way she and others sought to understand and explain the spirit of Gandhi's action:

> It was a strange sight seeing Gibson [British Resident in Rajkot State] drive up complete in evening kit—and being led out to the spot where, under the stars, lay the Mahatma. The talk was not completely satisfactory on either side—but the contact was good. After Gibson had left, he (Gandhiji) talked to me for some 40 minutes. At that point I think he felt as though his fast would go on to the end. He said some memorable things to me—things that made me aware of the deep significance—spiritually— this ordeal had for him. It was almost unbearable, for here was a man closely in touch with spiritual forces. He said he was glad I had been there, that I had been a help and that Gibson had also said this. And that if he was called upon by God to lay down his life—then my being there would make me a better interpreter in the future; that he would lay it down gladly—knowing it was His will.

Then, as the fast ended and Agatha Harrison's efforts to arrange for Gandhi to meet with the viceroy in Delhi succeeded, she says:

> And so this chapter ends—and I go on to Delhi to-night for the next one. I feel there is something I can do before the Mahatma comes. As in England—so here—most Britishers feel doubts about the ethics of Fasting. But being with Gandhiji through these days has taught me something; and I must pass it on. Unless they know something of the background of this ordeal for the man they are now going to deal with—they will not get far. I mean, if they approach him and in the back of their minds—they feel he achieved this by unfair means. When you see a man, as I did, believing he was called on to give the

supreme sacrifice of his life—in no martyr-like spirit—with
no feeling he was better than anyone else—but believing
absolutely he was called on by God to do this—then, one
must respect this even if one does not agree. To put any
other construction on this event would be criminal. It will
be a different Mr. Gandhi who meets them. A man who
has been close to death, and all the time in touch with
God in a way that was apparent if you were as closely in
touch with him as I was. I believe the Viceroy will understand. But it is no light thing for Gandhiji to go, after all
he has gone through, into the sophisticated, cynical atmosphere that surrounds many people in Delhi. It is a baf-
fling thing to be face to face with deep spiritual forces in
the midst of a political tangle. India understands better
than we do this method of the Mahatma. It certainly can
only be used by few people; anyone using this method
must be very spiritually prepared.[3]

The close bond that developed between members of the
group and India's future leaders can be shown in one further
incident. While Jawaharlal Nehru was in prison in 1935 his
wife went to Germany for medical treatment accompanied by
their daughter, Indira, who was seventeen. Word came at the
end of August from the German doctor that Mrs. Nehru had
had a relapse and was very ill. Unless her husband came immediately by air he might not see her alive again. As a result
of the work of Agatha Harrison and others in London and
Delhi, Mr. Nehru was quickly released to join his sick wife. In
the meantime, Agatha Harrison went to Badenweiler, Germany, to help out with Mrs. Nehru and her daughter until
Nehru could arrive. This kind of personal attention with no
aim of personal reward was not forgotten by the future prime
ministers of India.

3. Letter of 10 March 1939, Agatha Harrison to "Carl Heath and
members of the sub-committee," Friends House Archives, London.

Quaker Service

The more politically oriented work of the India Conciliation Group was complemented by the Quaker humanitarian work. Living with endemic poverty and disease, the millions of people on the subcontinent have suffered more than their share of natural disasters. Friends were involved in raising contributions for many of the catastrophes of the nineteenth and early twentieth centuries, but here it is sufficient to start with the flood and famine of 1942 to 1944. The first small group of Friends Ambulance Unit workers, some on alternative service as conscientious objectors, went to Calcutta from London to help the Indians prepare for Japanese bombing raids. Persons like Leslie Cross and Richard Symonds, who both had done air-raid warden work in the London blitz, got their first experience of India at this time. Horace Alexander was appointed leader of the unit, since he had been in India for extended periods from 1927. The air raids did not materialize as a major threat, but nature's own weapon, the cyclone, brought devastating floods in October 1942 to the lower reaches of the Hooghly River. Crop failure and the disruption of war added to the flood to bring the terrible Bengal famine of 1943-44. The American Friends Service Committee added its efforts to the London-based FAU in January 1944 and brought quantities of food and clothing.

This was a period of great political tension and civil disturbances in India, and Bengal was the most inflamed area. With the encouragement of Gandhi, large elements of the Indian National Congress were engaged in varying degrees of non-cooperation, insisting that the Britain that was fighting against tyranny in Germany should abdicate its tyrannous rule in India. It is significant that the Quaker team, though invited by the colonial government, touched base at the center of rebellion, Gandhi's headquarters, on their first arrival. With Gandhi's blessing they were able to work with organizations the government considered subversive. There were times when the Indian relief workers' only protection from police arrest was their association with the Quaker body. Part of the difficulty in organizing relief measures stemmed from the long-standing division between Muslim and Hindu communities. Here also the Quaker groups provided a mediating force by insisting on serving all equally. Thus, the work of conciliation across hard-drawn lines of conflict went hand in hand with relief. In August 1945 the war was over, but the needs were still so great that it was decided to continue the work. American and British units were merged into the Friends Service Unit. Thus, the staff were on hand to minister to the suffering that accompanied independence and partition.

The big issue before and during the Second World War was how and to what bodies the British would hand over control. The longer this process was postponed, the greater was the split between the Muslim League and the Indian National Congress. The Muslim League, under Mohammed Ali Jinnah, insisted on a separate Muslim state called "Pakistan," and the Congress party sought a single united India. The viceroy, Lord Wavell, and the cabinet mission sent out in 1946 from London had tried their utmost to work out an orderly transfer of power to a single Indian authority. But when continued rioting made this appear hopeless, Lord Mountbatten was sent out to succeed Lord Wavell and, should this seem the only practical solution, to prepare a plan for partition. The decision to divide and the process of working out boundaries led to mass migrations both ways, with people fleeing from rioting enemies. Gandhi spent most of his time in these last years of his life trying to quell the killing on both sides. As he said on the eve of Independence Day, August 14, 1947: "If the flames of communal strife envelop the country, how can our newborn freedom survive?"[4] Horace Alexander and Agatha

4. Horace G. Alexander, *Gandhi Through Western Eyes* (New York: Asia Publishing House), p. 156.

Harrison both worked with Gandhi on his trips of conciliation. The Friends Unit, which had worked from the beginning
with both Muslims and Hindus, was drawn into the succor
and rehabilitation of refugees.

An incident showing the close relation of relief and recon-
ciliation is described in Horace Alexander's book *Gandhi
Through Western Eyes.*[5] In September of 1947, the Friends
Service Unit was asked by Sardar Patel, home minister, to
come to Delhi to help the refugees streaming in from
Pakistan. Soon after coming, Horace Alexander and Richard
Symonds, who were helping in the work of the unit, decided
that they should investigate conditions in the transitional
camps on both sides of the border between Pakistan and
India. Sardar Patel saw no reason for them to help in Pakistan.
After all, they had not been invited there. When the Quaker
leaders insisted that they must work on both sides to relieve
suffering, Patel finally said that if Gandhi agreed, he would
also. Gandhi, of course, was in complete sympathy, and permits were secured from ministers in both Pakistan and India.

As the two successor states settled down to the task of
building their new nations, the Quaker service bodies in London and Philadelphia, with the help of the Canadian Friends
Service Committee, looked for a way to help the people of
the two countries. During the fifties and sixties multifaceted
village development programs were carried on in the central
state of Madhya Pradesh and in the eastern state of Orissa.
An urban program was started in the northern state of Gujerat
in 1964. Seeking to minister to both sides in the potentially
explosive situation, projects of urban community development were carried on at the same time in Pakistan. The
Quaker staff had just moved from Dacca in the East Wing
to Lahore in the west, when the war came to the outskirts of
the city.

5. Ibid., pp. 166–67.

Conferences and Seminars

The pattern of group gatherings across international boundaries discussed in chapter 1 was established in south and southeastern Asia beginning with student seminars in 1950. The
Asian Conferences for Diplomats organized after 1955 had a
major purpose of promoting Indo-Pakistan communication,
and to extend the contacts to other potentially influential
groups, the staff in Delhi initiated a series of "young leaders
conferences" with a meeting in Lahore in 1963.

At the time of the 1965 war, staff in Philadelphia reported
that two hundred Pakistanis had participated in international
seminars in the United States, Europe, and Asia and over
forty in conferences for diplomats and leaders.[6] The number
of Indian participants was not compiled at the time, but
would have been somewhat higher.

Quaker Action in the Crisis

With this background of experience it is not surprising that
Friends heard the news of August and September 1965 with
great consternation. They feared the renewal of the terrible
days of partition, when fighting between religious communities took a deadly toll in human spirit and life. They realized
how drastically even a short war would set back the plans for
village development in both countries. They saw the barriers
of communication across the borders rising higher than ever.

Such thoughts and feelings brought forth a major concern
in the Meeting for Sufferings in London of September 3,
1965. Although it is hard to identify any specific decisions at
this meeting, the airing of views stimulated later action by
staff and committees. An India-Pakistan subgroup of the

6. Minutes, International Conferences and Seminars Program Committee, AFSC, 27 September 1965 (AFSC Archives), p. 7.

Peace and International Relations Committee, one of the regular committees of London Yearly Meeting, was formed and met first on September 14. The group included several members with wide experience on the subcontinent, and Horace G. Alexander was chairman. Meeting frequently during the next five months, the group sent emissaries to confer with the Commonwealth Office, the British Foreign Office, and the high commissioners of India and Pakistan, arranged meetings with experts to discuss the issues, and made recommendations to the Peace Committee.

On the other side of the Atlantic, the staff and committees of the American Friends Service Committee in Philadelphia were also studying the crisis and deciding what action should be taken. Figuring prominently in the deliberations were urgent messages from field staff, especially those from Warren Ashby, then director of the Conference and Seminar program based in New Delhi. Warren Ashby was in Pakistan from August 23 to September 3 to obtain clearance for Pakistani participation in a conference of Asian leaders planned for Nepal from September 22 to 30. A promise of clearance was obtained from Pakistan's Ministry of Foreign Affairs, but not long afterward the accelerating war forced the cancellation of the conference. Ashby reported back to the AFSC that a main cause of war was the struggle of national identity in each country. Moving back and forth between the two nations, he had become acutely aware of the distortions, delusions, and falsifications with which each nation looked at the other. In describing this mirror-image phenomenon, Ashby presented a composite speech which, he said, could issue from spokesmen of either side:

> What else could we do but defend our homeland when it is attacked without warning by an enemy set on our destruction? Because of the spirit and heroism of our jawans [young soldiers] we won against vastly superior

forces. Now we are completely behind our leaders, united and determined as never before. We do not want this thing settled until *they* see that aggression does not pay, until *they* accept our existence, until *they* stop their lies and attempts to destroy us. For eighteen years they have been up to their mischief and we have been patient. But we will take their nonsense no longer, They are building up their forces and getting ready to attack us again. This time we will be prepared.[7]

Warren Ashby suggested that a valuable exercise for the conciliator was to identify the items not mentioned on each side. On the debate as to which side was the aggressor he wrote:

What is it that I have never heard a single Pakistani mention? I have never heard one of them mention the infiltrators; when I mention the subject the belief is usually expressed that they weren't infiltrators and this is asserted despite the fact that General Nimmo's [United Nations] report is perfectly clear. What is it that I have never heard any Indians mention with the exception of those who want to make an accommodation on Kashmir? . . . I have not heard any mention that it was the Indian army that was the first army to cross a cease-fire line and that it was the Indian army that was the first to cross the boundary into what is universally recognized as another sovereign nation.[8]

The Idea and Purpose of a "Mission"
The first allusion to a possible Quaker mission came up spontaneously in the September 3 Meeting for Sufferings

7. Staff Report "Between Pakistan and India," 1 November 1965, AFSC Archives.
8. Report of November 1965, AFSC Archives.

mentioned above. John Dennithorne asked for a Quaker mission to India and Pakistan at the earliest possible moment:

> Such a mission would invite the leaders of these nations to realize that this political problem could be solved only by raising the spiritual awareness of their peoples and of themselves. The principle of "holding by letting go" was the principle to be held out to them and it was appropriate that Friends as "a spiritual people" should do this.[9]

When reduced to cold print in the minutes, such a message, arising from the prayerful spirit of the meeting, took on the semblance of "spiritual imperialism," although the speaker would be the first to deny any such intention. There were Quakers in India who took this message as an indication of a "holier than thou" attitude. One of them wrote a letter in the October 8, 1965 edition of *The Friend,* a publication of London Yearly Meeting, explaining why India could not possibly "let go" of Kashmir and criticizing meddlers who came on dramatic missions but did not know the Indian scene.

With such criticisms in mind, subsequent thinking about a mission was low key and more politically sophisticated, although the original inspiration was never missing. Across the Atlantic there was a reluctance to use the label *mission* because of the inflated connotation from diplomatic usage, as well as the confusion arising from the term's reiigious usage. The words *team* or *visit* were preferred, but eventually the group itself chose *mission,* following the practice of the Quaker group that went to East and West Germany in 1963.

The first purpose of a visit suggested on September 28 by the London-based India-Pakistan Group was to listen to both sides and report back so that home constituencies would be better informed. Leslie Cross was picked to go to India, because of his experience there dating back to 1942. It was

9. Report in *The Friend,* 10 September 1965, p. 1082.

suggested that Roger Wilson and Adam Curle visit Pakistan, since both had recent experience in that country. The importance of the conciliatory aspect of the mission was first stressed in a letter from Roger Wilson to Adam Curle written on October 11, 1965: "The essence of the operation is that if Friends go they should be able to say that their opposite numbers are engaged in a similar effort to understand the other side of the frontier."[10] The Philadelphia response was highly favorable to the idea of a Quaker visit and the suggested team members, but asked why all the participants should not constitute one team and visit both sides, if travel could be arranged, in order to enhance the conciliatory possibilities. The precedent of the "journey through a wall" in Berlin in 1963 was influential.

The board of directors of the AFSC at its October meeting in Philadelphia created the Pakistan-India Advisory Group as an American counterpart, bringing together individuals well versed in the affairs of the subcontinent. It included two State Department officials, a high official in the World Bank, three professors, and a foundation director, all Quakers acting in a private capacity.

At the first meeting on October 20, 1965, the Pakistan-India Advisory Group worked over a statement of purpose and gave full support to the visit of at least two, preferably three, persons to both countries. Excerpts from the minutes show the care in the discussion and the desire to avoid pretense:

> The primary purpose of a visit should be to listen sensitively in a quiet and unobtrusive way, in order to learn and understand what is going on in the minds of Pakistanis and Indians. This attitude would reflect the friendliness to the people of both countries, and a profound concern that they not follow down the road of mutual

10. Friends House Archives, London.

destruction. The approach then would be one of listening, but with questions to present. Much thought would need to be given to the right questions. Our questions would probably not relate to the central political issue. For example, questions involving the joint interests of the people of both nations, which are very important, are not being asked any more. One of the most important objectives would be slowly to create situations where such questions of mutuality can be raised, in order to legitimize the very function of asking them. These might relate to water resources and uses, exchange of persons, cultural relations and other such. Success in obtaining attention to such mutual problems and approaches would be a marked achievement. While the immediate situation is urgent, any plans of Friends should be developed on the assumption that we have time to do what is right to do. While contacts with high-level government people have value, there was a feeling that it is especially important to have conversations with middle-level people, in private situations which would not embarrass them.[11]

The statement of purpose was modified several times with the intent of expressing in the fewest words possible modest, but not-too-limited expectations. The formulation agreed to on both sides of the Atlantic was summarized in the final report of the team:

First, the members of the mission were simply to inform themselves on the situation so that they might carry back to Friends and others concerned a rather clearer picture of a complex and dangerous situation than might be available from the press. Second, they were to see if there were any helpful roles they could play in this situation.

11. "Report of the Pakistan-India Advisory Group Meeting," 20 October 1965, AFSC Archives.

Third, the mission was to concern itself with ways in which Quaker activities could be best directed towards the development of better relations between India and Pakistan and towards making a more effective contribution to the needs of the countries themselves.[12]

Although not intended for publication, the statement was to be used as the basis for an oral presentation explaining the purpose of the mission to the governments and individuals the team would see.

It was clear from the beginning that the advice and consent of government officials was necessary, so staff and committee members in London and Washington sought out embassy officials. A Pakistani diplomat in the United States who favored a visit by Friends to Pakistan in principle cautioned the committee in October to wait for a more propitious time and to select persons acceptable to his government. An officer in the Indian Embassy in Washington said that such a visit of British and American Quakers would be warmly received in India. Their good offices, he thought, might even usefully convey ideas that governments could not put into more official channels.

Selection of the team was carried out by telephone and letters across the Atlantic. The committees in London tended to stress as a qualification the strength of Quaker background, while the committees in Philadelphia stressed knowledge and experience on the subcontinent. Consensus was readily achieved, however, since both sides recognized the importance of all these qualities. Leslie Cross was a unanimous choice. He had gone to India in 1942 with the Friends Ambulance Unit in relief and welfare work and stayed on with other organizations through partition until 1950. He was chairman of the Asia Committee of the Friends Sercice

12. "Report of the Pakistan-India Mission," February 1966, AFSC Archives.

Council and worked as manager of several charitable trust funds. Roger Wilson was unable to go, but Adam Curle was available. Though not long a member of the Society of Friends, Adam Curle, director of the Center for Studies in Education and Development at Harvard University, had wide experience in Pakistan, having served as an advisor on social affairs to the Pakistan government from 1956 to 1959 and as a consultant on education from 1963 to 1964. Since both Leslie Cross and Adam Curle were British, an intensive effort was mounted by staff in Philadelphia to find an American. This resulted in the selection of Joseph W. Elder, associate professor in the departments of Sociology and Indian Studies of the University of Wisconsin. Somewhat junior to the other two, he nevertheless had five years of experience in India in the 1950s, knew Urdu and Hindi, had written many articles on Indian village and religious life, and had been an active Friend for many years.

Before the second meeting of the Pakistan-India Advisory Group in Washington, December 21, 1965, arrangements and schedules had been roughed out for a team visit starting in mid-January. The group supplied the team members, two of whom were present at the meeting, with many suggestions on procedure and substantive issues, but avoided restrictive instructions. Prominent in the deliberations was the plan of moving back and forth between the two countries with the aim of strengthening the moderates on both sides who might work toward a solution. The team was asked to work closely with the resident Quaker staff in the two countries and to bring back recommendations for ongoing work in the future.

Work of the Quaker Mission

The timing of the Quaker mission was the result of practical requirements rather than either clairvoyance or a scientific assessment of the phases of crisis. January 17 was the first date that all three team members could meet in London to begin the trip. As it turned out this was probably the most propitious time for a visit.

The intense fighting of August and September had been followed by a lull, leaving the Indian army at the gates of Lahore and the Pakistani army bracing for siege and counter-attack. The strenuous efforts of the United Nations secretary-general, U Thant, led to the passage of a cease-fire resolution in the Security Council on September 22. The resolution was accepted by both sides, but the situation remained highly inflamed. Patriotism and hatred of the enemy had been whipped up to a fever pitch. The climax was to have been the assault on Lahore for the Indians and a last ditch defense of Lahore for the Pakistanis. At that point suddenly the governments and armies called a halt.

The reaction of the people was one of great frustration, as if the catharsis of victory or defeat was snatched from them at the climactic point. In Karachi on September 21, 30,000 students and others took to the streets, attacking Indian, United States, United Nations, and other embassies and offices. The reaction against the peace was not as violent in India, just as the war was not as close to the people, but a fiery debate in the lower house on September 24 indicated that feelings were still running high against Pakistan. Debates in the Security Council failed to produce any progress on agreement for the withdrawal of troops. Then, in late November, India and Pakistan announced they had accepted the Soviet Union's offer to conduct talks at Tashkent. This led to the Tashkent Declaration of January 10, 1966, a nine-point agreement to restore relations, withdraw armed forces, repatriate prisoners, and end hostile propaganda.

Although the central issue of the war, the status of Kashmir, was not settled at Tashkent, the basis for a cooling-off period had been established. The time was ripe for the intervention of an unofficial, unpublicized third party to strengthen the forces of moderation on each side and to promote thinking on the terms of a longer-lasting peace. As far as is known, the Quaker group was the first and only attempt of this kind by an unofficial party.

The itinerary of the team of three involved a week in Pakistan, a week in India, and then a return visit to each state for a week and a half. A final week in Pakistan for writing and conferring brought the total to six weeks. Pakistan was put first on the agenda because of the tendency of the people in Pakistan to feel they received less attention from the West than India.

In analyzing the role of the team as an intervening party it will be helpful to follow the discussion of "The Identity of the Third Party" in Oran Young's book, *The Intermediaries*.[13] Although his treatment applies primarily to official intervention by governmental bodies whose activities are officially acknowledged by the parties in conflict, his categories are nevertheless useful in analyzing the Quaker operation in which the intervenors were self-invited and entirely unofficial.

Establishment of Confidence

The first necessity for a third-party entering into conciliation is the establishment of confidence, and the basic qualities needed to establish and maintain credibility, according to Oran Young, are impartiality and independence.

A third party must be seen by the protagonists as not favoring either side. The Quaker team members were willing to assess the pros and cons of each side's position, and if they started with any preconceptions of an easy or one-sided solution, they soon learned better. Impartiality, however, implies an aloofness or indifference that does not adequately describe

13. Oran R. Young, *The Intermediaries: Third Parties in International Crises* (Princeton, N.J.: Princeton University Press, 1967), chap. 3.

the Quaker approach. A more accurate though paradoxical description might be "balanced partiality"; that is, they listened sympathetically to each side, trying to put themselves in the other party's place. The evidence is clear that they were perceived as sympathetic listeners on both sides. A good indication of this balanced partiality is the wording of the mission report. Under the headings "The Pakistan Viewpoint" and "The Indian Viewpoint," the team carefully worded the historical facts and judgments as an insider on each side would, rather than as an outside observer. Readers of the report on both sides later expressed satisfaction with the way the Quakers had described their side of the situation, although they raised grave doubts about the statement setting forth the other side's view.

Another aspect of balanced partiality is the Quaker concern for all people involved in a situation. The Quaker team emphasized the need to maximize the gains that might accrue to both sides through a settlement. Time and again on both sides they raised questions about the burden of the arms race and the futility of military means, as shown by the recent fighting. The history of Quaker services in humanitarian relief and development helped to give weight to their passionate advocacy of peace.

In an exercise of "partiality to each side," there is the danger of grossly misleading a discussion partner into thinking that he has convinced the Quakers of the justice of his plea. How does the sympathetic listener preserve his integrity in his own eyes and in the eyes of the advocate? Roland Warren's answer to this question has been explored in chapter 2. A great deal depends on the nonverbal communication of the conciliator as well as the words he uses. The Quaker tradition of speaking the truth can be helpful, but nothing can replace a personal quality of transparent honesty, which does not necessarily come with membership in the Society of Friends.

The team members underscored their balanced partiality by

reminding their discussion partners that they were hearing different views on the other side, where they would be returning. The fact that all three were involved in the interviews on both sides was also important.

It is frequently easier for a nongovernmental group with no political power to establish independence than a governmental one. Because the Quakers have a reputation, deserved or not, for internationalism and peace-mindness, little explaining on this score was needed. A question of this kind came up only in relation to the nationality of the team members, and it was fortunate that the team was composed of individuals from both Britain and the United States. At that time, Pakistan was inflamed against the United States and India against Britain. Thus, the first entrée was made easier on several occasions because the Pakistanis felt freer to talk with the British and the Indians with the American. In one interview, an Indian pointedly talked only to the American after strongly criticizing British policy.

Other Resources for a Conciliatory Role

Oran Young speaks of "ascribed resources," resources attributed to the conciliator by the parties through circumstances of history and prior contact, rather than resources intrinsically possessed or acquired. Under this heading he lists "salience, respect and continuity." The Quaker team did not have salience as widely recognized mediators in many conflict situations. However, as the result of Quaker Conferences for Diplomats in thirteen prior years, there were people in the foreign office of each country who knew about the Quaker organization and even some who had participated in conferences. The conference program also provided the resource of respect, especially the type that Young calls "affectual respect"—the feeling that the third party will give a fair hearing and be warmly motivated toward the protagonists. As for continuity, Quaker efforts in the immediate past did not involve direct conciliation between highly placed officials, but there was continuity in facilitating communication between the two countries in various seminars and in continuing contact in London, Washington, and at the United Nations with representatives of the two countries. Behind these recent activities of the Quakers lay the work prior to 1950 of the India Conciliation Group, which added a further dimension of these resources. An analysis of the forty-nine interviews reported in the team's journal shows that the India Conciliation Group was the most important source of prior contacts on the Indian side, while the Quaker conferences was more important on the Pakistani side.

Personal Qualifications

Knowledge of political-military affairs and economic and cultural aspects of a dispute are all very important for an intermediary. On this score the team had extensive firsthand experience in India and Pakistan and keen acumen in political analysis. Each member brought different talents whose sum was impressive. Although such a private effort could not match the resources of a governmental enterprise in which researchers would supply background papers on every aspect of the situation, nevertheless, the committees and staff in the United States and Britain and the staff in the field provided significant assistance. The team added to its knowledge of the situation by talking with nineteen well-informed observers in the two countries, including a French journalist, a British High Commission officer, a Harvard University advisor to the Pakistan government, and a United Nations resident representative. Gathering information in the field is easier for an unofficial team, whose activities usually go completely unnoticed by the public; an official conciliator must be constantly cautious about whom he sees lest he set off rumors that would hamper his neutral position.

In this Quaker enterprise the personal qualifications of

individual conciliators were enhanced by the team approach. The three members were quite different and yet complemented each other in remarkable ways. Leslie Cross, the elder statesman, had a special understanding of the problems facing those in power. Adam Curle and Joseph Elder, on the other hand, both believed that any political figure should do more for peace. On the dispute's central issue, Adam Curle had a strong sympathy for the Pakistani search for national identity that sought "liberation" for the Muslims of Kashmir, and Joe Elder had experienced quite directly the village flare-ups between Indians of Muslim and Hindu communities that were continually ignited by the Pakistani press. The team's range of ages was valuable in relating to a variety of discussion partners. Adam Curle would present the case to the younger, brasher, and more skeptical; Leslie Cross would do the honors with the older, more senior people.

With such differences one might expect tension, but there is unanimous testimony from team members and observers that there was no sense of rivalry or jealousy in their relations, no jockeying for position in the interviews, no pride of paternity in an idea or a phrase, and no post-mortem criticisms. This harmony of teamwork arose largely from a common dedication to an important job and from a sense of the group's strong support in the two home committees. It is also clear that none of the three required large ego satisfaction from this exercise. They did not have a future reputation at stake, a book to write, or an individual hypothesis to prove.

The three men lived closely together for six weeks and spent a considerable portion of their long days discussing the mission. Before any important meeting they would consider their approach, the issues to be raised, and sometimes which one would pose a particular question. They also considered how the meeting related to those held in the past or planned for the future. They exploited their differences, recognizing that each could do certain tasks better. In the preparatory sessions for important interviews, Adam Curle stressed the importance of role playing. He would typically play the part of the person to be interviewed, challenging the team members on the purpose for their visit, misinterpreting statements made, and finding suspicious undertones in the phrasing of questions. In addition to being fun, these exercises helped the participants to avoid mistakes in the real interviews and to gain greater understanding of the full dimensions of feeling and logic of the persons whose role they represented. In one preparatory session they had a meeting for worship. As Joseph Elder described it in a letter written on November 30, 1972:

> Our most serious meeting came, I believe, when we learned that we were going to be able to see Ayub Khan. We decided that we would have a three-person silent meeting for worship to prepare ourselves for whatever we would encounter. The meeting was one of the most moving I have ever participated in—in Leslie's room I recall, with each of us sharing our own sense of inadequacy at what we were trying to do, and yet each of us sensing something like a "Quaker legacy" that we had been drawing on throughout the trip that provided a power well beyond what any of us individually possessed.[14]

This description of the Quaker emissaries and their operations must of necessity be based on the one-sided testimony of the team members and close associates on the staff. Exactly what the Pakistanis and Indians thought of them is unknown, but there is one bit of evidence. The following year a Quaker couple saw nearly all of the people the team interviewed, and in not one case was there a negative reaction about the purpose and functioning of the team; in most cases

14. AFSC Archives.

the reaction was strongly positive. The mission report sent to all those interviewed and dealing with highly controversial issues was well received, bringing strong but friendly criticism from only a few individuals.

The Process of Conciliation

Going with only modest expectations, the team found their role progressing from gathering information, to serving as a channel of communication across the lines, to giving their own assessments on certain aspects of the situation, and finally to proposing tentative and modest measures that might help bring peace.

The importance of listening was indicated by the degree to which the team was used as an audience. Time and again after the team members introduced themselves and their purpose, the person they were talking to would list the many grievances against the other side. After a while team members could predict the selection of facts and history that would be given. This was particularly true on the Pakistani side, where there was a great sense of grievance and injustice. Although eventually totally familiar with these recitals, the team members felt it was necessary to listen, nod their heads dutifully, and occasionally raise some pointed questions.

Listening was the main feature of the team's activity during the first week in Pakistan, but following this, on the first trip to India, the team found there was interest in what was being said "on the other side." During later visits to Pakistan and India the function of reporting back and forth grew. It is hard to estimate the value of this communication function, but it is clear that each side had been limited to one-sided reporting in its own partisan journals, and, with the objective channels shut off, the team was able to bring reports that were news. These reports were eagerly solicited and accepted as accurate by both sides, and the team was seen as reporting not its own views but the views of the other side. As an example of this reporting, we single out the matter of aggression highlighted earlier by Warren Ashby. It was easy for the team to point out that each side was firmly convinced that the other was the aggressor and to detail which events in the sequence of attacks and counterattacks were singled out by each side. For some this kind of information was a moment of awakening: "You mean they are saying the same thing we are?" It must be said, however, that some reacted by saying that it was merely an indication of the depravity of the other side that they would commit such bald aggression and then justify it as "self-defense." Thus, the report reinforced the prejudices of some.

In many cases the message carrying was personal, since some knew the persons on the other side to whom the team had talked or would talk. In one case the team talked with two brothers, each highly placed on his side of the border. The team tried to enhance the feeling that common problems could be dealt with by sensible and open-minded persons on both sides.

As time went on the team members were asked more and more quietly what they themselves thought. Thus, the next level of functioning was conveying their own assessments of the situation. They sedulously avoided taking sides on the interpretation of history and confined themselves to conclusions regarding present and future. On this score their message to Indian leaders was that Ayub Khan was the most moderate leader Pakistan was likely to have and that he was having a hard time convincing the people that the Tashkent Declaration was anything but a complete defeat. Since Tashkent provided no settlement for the Kashmir issue, the objective of the fighting was, in Pakistani eyes, lost. The team also reported in India that the Pakistani public believed they had won the war, stopped the Indian army in its tracks, and shown great restraint in not going on to capture all of Kashmir. The Quaker team reported the snubs that President

Ayub Khan had received, the defection of his own protégé, Foreign Minister Z. A. Bhutto, and the trap in which the Pakistan Information Service found itself in trying to modify the results of its own prior exaggerations and the biased reporting of the government-controlled press.

In talking to Pakistanis the team emphasized the difficulties Indira Gandhi faced in the rising clamor of the extreme rightist Jan Sangh party, which thought Tashkent was a sellout. While Mrs. Gandhi could ignore this extremist minority, she could not ignore the same strong views when they infected her own Congress party. The Quakers reported that the death of Prime Minister Lal Bahadur Shastri just after the signing of the agreement in Tashkent was widely considered as the only thing that prevented widespread protests against the signing of the agreement.

The process of evaluation moved naturally into the next stage, proposing or transmitting measures for ameliorating the situation. The team used great ingenuity in making proposals, all the way from very small steps for improving the climate, such as a cricket match between the two countries, to major steps for resolving the Kashmir dispute. Some of the proposals were their own; some were suggested to them. The mission report lists the various ideas. A highly placed Indian official, for instance, suggested that Pakistan participate in the Gandhi centenary to be celebrated in 1969. This idea was tried out on a former Gandhian in Pakistan who was vice-chancellor of a university. His answer was that the idea was unwise, since Gandhi had opposed partition and was unpopular in Pakistan. Moreover, he suggested any such step would be impossible until India made a major move toward conciliation on the Kashmir issue. On the Pakistani side the suggestion was made that a reduction in the Indian arms budget, which had quadrupled since 1962, would be seen as a major sign of relaxation. When this message was conveyed to a highly placed Indian the matter was seriously considered, but the threat of China was used to explain the high military budget.

Many specific proposals for resolving the major issue came to the team from foreign observers and parties in the dispute. But the team soon saw that none was likely to be considered in the near future, and they did not try to develop a comprehensive formula for settlement. Tashkent brought an uneasy truce that was not popular on either side. In India, Kashmir was seen as an integral part of the Union. Indians were willing to discuss other issues with Pakistan, but not Kashmir. In Pakistan, the leaders insisted that India carry through its earlier agreement to a plebiscite. In their view no other issues were worth discussing. Faced with these rigidities the team tried to probe for possible means to soften positions. Was there any way in which the situation could be defused and cooled off enough so that some settlement of Kashmir involving consultation with Pakistan could be considered in the future? As they labored with this they came to formulate what they privately labelled "The Question." In talking with the vice-president of India it was first phrased in this way:

> Should we tell the Pakistanis that the cease-fire line was the international line; there was no more point raising the issue; or should we say that if they simply let up the pressure for five or ten years the status of Kashmir might change?[15]

In later interviews this question was raised again and again in various forms.

On the Indian side, although the usual answer was that the status of Kashmir in the Indian Union was not negotiable, at high levels of government the answer was more conciliatory. For the present, it was indicated, the issue was closed. Pressure and threats from Pakistan would be of no avail, but if

15. "Journal of India-Pakistan Mission," Friends House Archives, p. 20.

there was a long enough period of peace and if India could count on Pakistan not to commit aggression, then it might be possible at some future time to consider some mutual arrangements for Kashmir.

In posing "The Question" on the Pakistan side the team explored unilateral steps and promises that might be made by India to improve the climate and encourage the Pakistanis to wait patiently for a later resolution of the Kashmir issue. One question often asked was, "If you were Indira Gandhi, what would you do?" The usual uncompromising answer of governmental as well as unofficial leaders was that no promises or gestures on other issues would count if India made no moves on Kashmir. The least Mrs. Gandhi could do, they said, was to have the issue of Kashmir discussed at a ministers' meeting. At high levels of responsibility in Pakistan, however, there was an openness to conciliatory signals from the other side, and a series of unilateral actions that would help restore confidence was suggested for the Indian side. It was suggested that India refrain from any further steps to integrate Kashmir into the Indian constitutional and legal framework, provide decent treatment for people displaced by the war, and reduce the grossly inflated military budget.

On the team's return visit to India, the suggestions brought back were seriously considered, and reasons were given why most of them could not be implemented. Returning to Pakistan, the team conveyed Indian reactions to the various proposals to the government. At this point the team members believed they had done all they could and that further messages would be better channeled through official avenues.

Summary of the Team's Operation

As one reviews the activity of listening, message carrying, assessing, and proposing, one is impressed by the perseverance and ingenuity of the Quaker go-betweens, who kept up hope in a situation that was almost completely blocked. As one probe after another ended in disappointment, they saw that neither side was in a position to move. There was no break-through in the stalemate because even minimal proposals were unacceptable at the time. Yet one can discern real value in the total effort. Most clearly evident is the support given to the position of moderates on each side. The team interpreted the practical reasons behind seemingly irrational statements of opposing leaders and explained the phenomenon of in-flamed and uninformed public opinion on both sides. Most important, they helped to change the perceptions of the op-posing leaders by demonstrating to each side that their counterparts were also reasonable and well-meaning people, motivated by similar ideas and pressures. Although at the time the process of changing perceptions was ineffective with the extremists, the important job was to strengthen the voices of moderation and support the truce against the strong forces of extremism on both sides.

In this case the Quaker effort was only a minute part of the total picture. The major operating forces were beyond the influence of the Quakers. The great powers, especially the United States and the Soviet Union, for their own reasons did not want strife. The leaders of the Pakistani and Indian armies were more realistic about the chances of success in renewed fighting than the newspaper writers and readers. On the political scene, although Tashkent was a burden for both heads of government, renewed war was not viewed as a way out. Serious economic, political, and minority problems in each country put a premium on each retaining an outside enemy, but at the same time inhibited the renewal of armed conflict, which would only have made matters worse. So although the Quaker mission was unsuccessful in assisting any major breakthrough, by aiding the cooling-off process it did play a more important role than was anticipated.

The Mission Report and Follow-Up

The team spent a final weekend working together to hammer out a report, Joe Elder doing the historical part, Adam Curle the nonhistorical, and Leslie Cross the story of Quaker work. The report gave, in concise form, the background of Quaker work on the subcontinent, a sketch of the two national viewpoints, and an account of the team's functioning. It ended with a conclusion which put the burden on the nation in possession of the prized part of Kashmir to make a conciliatory step. This controversial suggestion was made in these carefully guarded words:

> But if in the years to come India, which in the eyes of the world is still an India of Gandhi, finds it both possible and wise, acting from a position of strength, to be magnanimous in spite of recent events, the future of both India and Pakistan may be brighter than now seems possible.[16]

After a minimum of editing in London and Philadelphia, the report was approved as a confidential document. The London Committee thought the British public needed such balanced information about the situation and hoped that it would be published as a pamphlet. Philadelphia committees thought such a pamphlet would not find widespread use in the United States and might put the Quakers on record on controversial points and thus harm the continuing effort of conciliation which the report itself recommended. Decision was delayed until recommendations in the supplement of the report could be carried out.

The mission strongly recommended in the supplement that a Quaker representative be appointed to spend equal time in Pakistan and India carrying on such conciliatory work as

16. "Report of the Pakistan-India Mission," February 1966, AFSC Archives, p. 15.

might be possible through visitation and arranging international seminars. Following this recommendation the assignment of an experienced Quaker couple, Harold Snyder, on leave from the Washington International Affairs Seminars, and Betty, his wife, to carry on this role provided a happy solution to part of the question of how to use the report. The Snyders followed up the work of the mission by going back to those interviewed and presenting copies of the report for reactions.

On the Pakistan side the report was taken seriously. Comments from officials from the president down were favorable, though not without criticism of some "errors." In unofficial circles the report was warmly received and several people urged that it be published. On the Indian side the report was welcomed in official and unofficial circles, but less carefully scrutinized. In one case a high official took the report to task for "biased reporting." He seemed to get his whole impression from the concluding paragraph, which called for a generous gesture by India.

In the spring of 1967, Harold Snyder gave approval from the field for publishing the report, and a mimeographed issue, no longer confidential, was produced in London but received little circulation. The Snyders continued with the work of communicating across the lines of the two countries and helped organize three international conferences in which Indians and Pakistanis of senior rank and responsibility participated.

Since history, as of this writing (1978), has already moved through a second war between the two nations, the reader may ask what the Quakers were doing at the time of the civil war in East Pakistan in 1971 and the intervention of India. The answer is long and complicated and too near at hand for adequate study. Suffice it to say that when and if the story is written it is likely to reveal contrasts of assumption and analysis, which made any concerted Quaker effort difficult.

There was no clear opening for a renewal of the Quaker "mission" approach. Humanitarian interest, however, continued strong and led to early relief work in the new country of Bangladesh.

Chapter Four

The Nigerian Civil War of 1967-70

During the Nigerian Civil War of 1967-70, one of the most devastating in recent African history, the Quakers felt that the best contribution they could make to relieve the suffering was to seek an end to the war through a negotiated settlement. As the war dragged on, however, direct relief operations were initiated, leading to projects of rehabilitation.

Throughout the thirty months, a team of three men, John Volkmar, Adam Curle, and Walter Martin, stood ready to undertake missions of conciliation, usually in pairs, depending on who was most available. These three men became well known in top governmental circles in Lagos and in the various improvised capitals of the secessionists, who called their country "Biafra."[1] Their efforts were enhanced by frequent visits to the representatives of Nigeria and Biafra in the world crossroads of New York, Washington, London, Paris, Geneva, and Lisbon. They consulted closely with the personnel of the two multinational organizations most involved in making peace and attended the Kampala talks of May 23-31 arranged by the Secretariat of the Commonwealth and the Addis

1. During the war the name "Biafra" was unacceptable in Nigeria, and its use still betokens in some minds partisanship to the rebel side. The use in this writing is designed for convenience, since there was such an entity, and not as any judgment of the historical events that eliminated that entity.

Ababa talks of June 1968 arranged by the Consultative Committee of the Organization of African Unity. They were called in to consult with officials of Britain and the United States as these two great powers tried to find a role in making peace, and they advised a number of private organizations and individuals on their peace initiatives. Four times during the course of the war members of the team made the hazardous trip into Biafra; seven times they held consultations with General Gowon in Lagos.

After the first year of the war the Quakers also undertook a relief program; the two were closely correlated, and the head of the relief mission in Lagos, Kale Williams, also helped in the last conciliatory efforts. Quaker Service personnel were working on both sides, and in all their work and relationships they attempted to show that they worked for the welfare of the people, not to further the war aims of either party.

In the complicated actions and reactions involving the two belligerent parties, internal factions within each party, several foreign powers, international agencies and a number of private organizations, all engaged in different phases of the war and in negotiations and relief, the Quaker enterprise was a small footnote. In enlarging that footnote to fill many pages there is an inevitable distortion, making the Quaker effort appear more important than it was. Thus, throughout the chapter we will try to remind the reader of the larger picture.

The Crisis of Unity in Nigeria

We will not dwell on the long train of events that led to the secession of one region of Nigeria in the summer of 1967. Many good historical studies are available.[2] It is necessary,

2. See John Hatch, *Nigeria, Seeds of Disaster* (Chicago: Henry Regnery Co., 1970); John P. Mackintosh, *Nigerian Government and Poli-*

however, to outline the three-region geographical-political structure that set the stage for the power struggle in the new state, and which was a major factor tending to produce rivalry and secession rather than a cohesive nation.

When the Nigerian Federation gained its independence from Britain in October 1960, after a period of planned devolution, it was a country divided into three areas: the large Northern Region and, south of this, the Western and Eastern Regions. There was also the small Federal District around the capital city of Lagos. This governmental structure of strong regions under weak central authority, which had its origins in the colonial history of the late 1800s and 1900s, was bound to accentuate the conflict for power between the three large ethnic groups that prevailed in each of the regions.

These three groups had quite divergent languages, customs, value systems, and political-economic structures. The North, by far the largest and most populous, was dominated by the Muslim feudal patterns of the 14 million Hausa-Fulani; the West, by the part-Christian, part-Muslim, part-animist urban culture of the 13 million Yorubas; and the East, by the 8 million largely Christian Ibos, living in traditionally autonomous village clusters.[3] Party politics in the newly forming democ-

tics: Prelude to the Revolution (Evanston, Ill.: Northwestern University Press, 1966); James O'Connell, "Political Integration; The Nigerian Case," in Arthur Hazlewood, ed., African Integration and Disintegration: Case Studies in Economic and Political Union, Oxford University Institute of Economics and Statistics and Royal Institute of International Affairs (London: Oxford University Press, 1967); Joseph Okpaku, ed., Nigeria, Dilemma of Nationhood (Westport, Conn.: Greenwood, 1972); S. K. Painter-Brick, Nigerian Politics and Military Rule: Prelude to Civil War, published for the Institute of Commonwealth Studies (London: The Athlone Press, 1970); and Walter Schwarz, Nigeria (New York: Praeger, 1968).

3. Population figures are only approximate, being subject to controversy. One of the most bitter seeds of dissension was the census of 1963, which was said to inflate the figures of Northern population in order to justify Northern majorities in the central seats of power.

racy tended to mirror the geographic, ethnic contours. In each region well-organized parties developed that promoted the interests of that region and its major ethnic group. The over two hundred minor ethnic groups, constituting almost half the population, could only look to the majority parties for representation and the perquisites of power.

In the days before independence some thoughtful Nigerian analysts of different ethnic groups saw trouble ahead and favored further divisions to break up the concentration of power and to give minorities a larger role in the regional and federal governments. The active political leaders of the major groups, however, accepted the colonial legacy and set out to organize power in each region and then to control the central government through coalitions. In the West, Chief Obafemi Awolowo, a Yoruba, organized the Action Group. In the North, the Northern Peoples Congress (NPC) was formed around the political and religious leader of the Hausa-Fulanis, Sir Ahmado Bello. Nnamadi Azikiwe, an Ibo, tried to make the National Council of Nigeria and Cameroun (NCNC) a national party, but its strength was largely in the East. Each party controlled the legislature in its region and the regional representation in the Federal parliament.

As independence approached there was intense rivalry over the control of federal power, which would include such matters as foreign affairs, defense, higher education, customs, posts, and highways. The elections of 1959 brought an uneasy coalition of the Eastern NCNC and the Northern NPC which controlled 216 seats in the Federal House of Representatives to 73 for the Action Group. When independence came on October 1, 1960, Nnamadi Azikiwe, an Ibo, was governor-general, and Abubakar Tafawa Balewa, a Hausa, was prime minister.

The next five years brought one crisis after another in the institutions of the newly formed democracy. Internal rivalry among the Yorubas in the Western Region stemming from a long history of clan feuds were now accentuated as the stakes of power became greater and Northern and Eastern leaders entered the arena to extend their control. The Action Group soon broke up into factions, and in 1962 a tumultuous fight in the Western legislature over the question of which rival leader was the legitimate prime minister caused the Federal government to declare a state of emergency and take over the regional government. Before long Chief Akintola, the Yoruba leader backed by the Northern party, was installed as regional prime minister, replacing Chief Awolowo's henchman, and Awolowo himself was accused of treason and condemned to prison. At this time a small new region was carved out of the Yoruba West by going through the constitutional process of securing the majority vote of two out of three regional legislatures, the Federal legislature, and the people of the area through referendum. Creation of the Mid-West Region, with its mixture of Yoruba, Ibo, Edo, Bini, and other peoples, was a move in the direction of reducing ethnic group politics, but it was too small a step to affect the tripartite power struggle.

Party power was intimately connected with the first national census of population, which would decide the proportion of representatives from each region in the national legislature. Each area tried to run up the totals, and after the rejection of the first census in 1962 and much controversy over the procedures of the second census, the final figures showed an inflated total of 55.7 million people, 30 million in the North. Over many protests the census was confirmed by the Northern dominated Federal government in 1964. Shortly thereafter the coalition of NPC and NCNC broke up, each party seeking new alliances and trying to get a foothold in other regions. At the time of the elections at the end of 1964, a potential beginning of national two-party politics was created in two loose aggregations of parties, but under the facade of the National Alliance and the Progressive

Alliance, the NPC and the NCNC were hard at work extending the rival power of the North and the East. The ensuing election of December 30, 1964 was accompanied by wide-scale violence, intimidation, and voting frauds. The Eastern Region boycotted the polls entirely, and in the other regions the National Alliance won easily. President Azikiwe, under pressure from Ibos and others to declare the election invalid, finally followed the constitutional mandate in accepting the elections and reappointing Tafawa Balewa as prime minister.

Regional elections in the Western Region in November 1965 brought a new high of violence and voting frauds as Eastern and Northern forces tried to gain control of the West. Again the faction backed by the Easterners lost out. The electoral process was at the point of breaking down amid boycotts, riots, and ballot frauds. To this was added wide-spread disillusion with the whole democratic process as the people saw their elected officials and certain families getting rich through land-grabs, payoffs, and other crude or refined methods of gaining private advantage at the expense of the public. The stage was set for a coup of army officers who thought of themselves as the final guardians of the national interest.

The Slide Toward War
On January 15, 1966, a reform-minded group of younger army officers, mostly Ibo, assassinated Prime Minister Balewa, Ahmado Bello, the powerful Northern leader, and Chief Akintola, the Yoruba prime minister of the Western Region who had been supported by the North. The rebels aimed to take over all regional and national power, but prompt action by army leaders quelled the mutiny and installed Major General Aguiyi-Ironsi, an Ibo but not one of the plotters, as head of the military government. Ironsi proceeded to abolish political parties and legislatures in the federal capital and in the regions. There was a general acceptance in the country for

the strong army measures to clean up corruption, and at first there was a sense of relief in the North that the rebellion had been quelled. Ironsi, who had served with distinction in the UN Congo operation, where he had seen an African country tearing itself apart, sought to create a strong unitary state by decrees, promulgated in May, which reduced the regional governments to administrative districts. Consternation grew in the North. The assassination of the major Northern leaders in January now appeared part of a plot by the Ibos to take over the whole country, which Ironsi was seen to be carrying out. Peaceful demonstrations in the North against the centralizing decrees turned into major riots against the Ibos living in that area. Over the years thousands of Ibos and other southeastern people had migrated to the North, where many held key posts as merchants and civil servants.

A countercoup in July by a coalition of Northern officers swept Ironsi from the scene and installed young Lieutenant-Colonel Jakubu Gowon, a Northerner but of a minority ethnic group, as supreme commander. Gowon reinstituted the federal structure and set about to try to bind the nation together. He gained the cooperation of the West, but was unable to dampen the fires of hatred in the North against the southeastern peoples, fueled by a century of prejudice and friction and sparked by reports of mob action against Northerners in the Eastern Region. In October, for the first time, army soldiers joined civilian mobs in burning, looting, and killing in the major cities of the North. About ten thousand Ibos and other Southeastern peoples were killed, and 1.5 million fled to the southeast, each with tales of rape, torture, and massacre.[4]

4. The number of dead and fleeing have been variously quoted by propagandists and officials. John De St. Jorre, the English journalist, has made a careful estimate, based on the best available information. See *The Brother's War: Biafra and Nigeria* (Boston: Houghton Mifflin, 1972), p. 87n and p. 412.

The terror of October gave an irresistible thrust to the move for secession, which politicians and intellectuals were already promoting on economic, cultural, and political grounds. It seemed clear to the Ibo people that they could no longer expect protection in the Federal Union. The military governor, Lieutenant Colonel Chukwuemeka Odumegwu Ojukwo, at first a reluctant secessionist, became the leader of the movement.

As relations between the Eastern Region and Lagos deteriorated, outsiders attempted to mediate. In January the Ghanaian head of state, General Ankrah, succeeded in arranging a meeting of the four military governors and the head of the Federal government, Gowon, in Aburi. Ojukwu came to the meeting with a carefully planned agenda and a series of resolutions tending to loosen the bonds of Federal control. The other officers, expecting to renew communication in the clubby atmosphere of old school contacts and then talk about an agenda, were taken by surprise. Gowon, who had spoken strongly for a unitary state in November, found himself accepting Ojukwu's formula, which allowed each state considerable autonomy. Ultimate authority was given to a Supreme Military Council, of which Gowon was to be chief, but the requirement of a unanimous decision left power in the hands of any one state.

No sooner had the governors returned home than the process of interpreting the Aburi agreement led to even worse misunderstanding. Ojukwu tried to please the strong secessionists in his state by pointing to the degree of independence given each state, while, in contrast, in Lagos senior civil servants tried to implement the agreement so as to retain a unitary state with a degree of central control.

Political leaders in the North and West had talked seriously of secession at one time or another before and after independence. Earlier the strongest leadership for independence and unitary state had come from the East, with Nnamadi

Azikiwe as the figure closest to being a national hero. But when the Ibo leaders lost the political power struggle and the Ibo people felt their very existence threatened in the union, the talk of secession in the provincial capital of Enugu and the University at Nsukka grew like a blazing forest fire.

Quaker Conciliatory Efforts

Shortly before Nigeria became an independent nation in October 1960, a concern arose among Philadelphia Quakers to send a representative to the largest and potentially most important West Africa country. Before 1960 there was no organized Quaker program in West Africa, although individual Friends, especially from Britain, had held various government and teaching posts and a Quaker meeting had been organized in Ghana. In 1960, Paul and Priscilla Blanshard went to Nigeria as the first Quaker international affairs representatives with an open-ended assignment and only a vague idea of what they might do. The reports they sent back to Philadelphia emphasized the great variety of languages, nations, and sub-nations comprising the amalgamation which the British colonial administration had put together as Nigeria. Early on they saw the internal stresses caused by this diversity and the rivalry among the three dominant ethnic groups. In December 1960, Paul Blanshard wrote "A Proposal for Strengthening Nigerian Unity," a plea for a Quaker-sponsored cultural relations program to reduce tensions and create understanding among ethnic groups.

Although the Philadelphia committee expected that Paul Blanshard's contribution in Nigeria would grow out of his communication skills in radio and television, as it turned out, he was most successful in developing work camps, a long-standing Quaker activity in other parts of the world. Building on previous experiences of Nigerians in Ghanaian and European work camps, in 1961 Blanshard helped to organize the first international work camp in Nigeria. Twenty-four volunteers, twelve from West Africa and twelve from the United States and Europe, built a youth center at Ibadan. As a result of this effort a Nigerian work camp association was organized, and in 1962 the American Friends Service Committee sent John and Ann Salyer to assist the Nigerians in organizing national work camps. A major emphasis was strengthening Nigerian leadership for a youth movement to cut across tribal lines.

Another Quaker program grew out of the requests of West Africans who had participated in the student seminars and diplomat conferences described in chapter 1. African leaders, called in to advise the Quaker committees, asked that the new program's focus be on the barriers of language and culture imposed by contrasting French and British educational and cultural systems. The conferences for West Africa, they thought, should bring together new and potential leaders of English- and French-oriented countries to find African solutions for African problems. Accordingly, a Quaker office was established in Lomé, Togo, in 1963, and the staff began its visits to sixteen West African countries from Mauritania to Gabon. The bilingual program, *Dialogue Internationaux en Afrique Occidental,* or International Dialogues in West Africa, gained momentum rapidly. By the outbreak of the Nigerian Civil War, there had been six major sessions involving 146 persons, 25 of whom were Nigerians from all sections of the country. The friction within each country was a frequent preoccupation of the French-speaking and English-speaking African participants.

Prewar Quaker Mission to Nigeria, 1967
The staff members in Lomé were well aware of the tensions in Nigeria. They knew Dr. Eni Njoku, an Ibo, who was ousted as vice-chancellor of the University of Lagos in 1965 to make

way for a Yoruba, Dr. Samuel O. Beobaku, whom they also knew. They followed closely the events of the January 1966 coup and the countercoup of July. In December 1966, John Volkmar, the head of International Dialogues in West Africa, reported that the slaughter of thousands of Ibos in the North in May and October had led the people of the East, most of whom were Ibo, to fear for their future in a federated Nigeria. Two million Ibos, it was believed, had fled to the Eastern Region, adding to the grave economic problems of that area. "Fear," Volkmar wrote, "is the main stumbling block to reconciling Nigeria's problems." A great deal needed to be done, he thought, to improve communication between the areas and to break down prejudice, but this was a task for Nigerians themselves. The dialogues could contribute by inviting Nigerians from all four regions to international seminars outside Nigeria.

At the same time that Volkmar was considering action in the field, Adam Curle, from his post at Harvard, was thinking of ways in which his conciliation experience with the India-Pakistan Quaker Mission in early 1966 might be put to use in Nigeria. Professor Curle had previously spent three years in Ghana as head of the Education Department of the University of Ghana and through the Harvard Center for Education and Development he was associated in assisting a model public school at Aiyetoro, Western Nigeria. Walter Martin, the third member of the Quaker team, had joined the Quaker United Nations Office after ten years of experience in Quaker reconstruction and reconciliation in Kenya. Martin arranged a meeting for himself and Adam Curle with Ambassador J. T. F. Iyalla, Nigeria's deputy permanent representative to the United Nations, who had been the first Nigerian at a Quaker Conference for Diplomats.

The meeting on January 4, 1967 was marked by a cordial and candid exchange. Adam Curle outlined his concern for the problems of Nigeria and asked if Quakers might be used as channels of communication between different parts of the country. The deputy representative expressed interest, but cautioned that Nigerians, so recently independent, were sensitive about outside meddling. He welcomed the idea that Curle, who was planning to visit Nigeria on school business, might take soundings on a personal, unofficial basis in the various regions.

After suitable clearances with committees in Philadelphia and in London, Adam Curle, joined by John Volkmar, visited four Nigerian regions and the Federal District during four weeks in April and May. Their purpose, similar to previous missions, was to express a concern, listen attentively, and find ways of helping through conciliation or relief.

The Quaker team found ready access to key people and held long and frank discussions. Surprisingly, a large number of persons they met knew of the Society of Friends, and some had been involved in Quaker programs. Of the seventy-eight persons for whom there are brief interview reports, thirty-five had prior Quaker exposure; twenty-seven had been in touch with one of the organized programs such as seminars in the United States or dialogues in West Africa; eight had known Quakers in other connections, usually while students in North America or Britain. Adam Curle's connections in education and development were an asset in many situations.

The team reported that tensions were high. Although no one wanted Nigeria to break up, such a disaster might occur, and the failure of unifying forces in this largest of African states might augur similar rifts in other new nations of Africa. The East was prepared to secede, they wrote, if there was no guarantee that authority would be decentralized so that the more populous North could not dominate.

Even at the eleventh hour the report was still hopeful that civil war might be averted. In contrast to the situation in India and Pakistan, where Adam Curle had found very little organized activity for peace on his visit in early 1966, he and John Volkmar found many organizations interested in peace in Nigeria. The mission recommended, therefore, that a Quaker representative be sent to Nigeria to help in coordinating the work of the various groups promoting peace and understanding. This and other recommendations were rendered obsolete by Ojukwu's act of secession a week after the team left.

Although this visit had no effect in lessening the violent confrontation, it gave the Quakers a balanced understanding of the total situation and established a firm base for conciliation. Because of their overall knowledge, helped by the reporting of Curle and Volkmar, the Quaker organizations did not yield to the pro-Biafra sentiments that swept the churches of Europe and North America. Through their contacts on this trip the team established a firm base for good offices over the ensuing two and one half years. In the East they had been cordially received by Lieutenant Colonel Ojukwu, and they had seen most of the key people later involved in negotiating and in presenting the secessionist cause in the Western world. They did not see the head of the Federal government in Lagos, Lieutenant Colonel Gowon, but their contacts with his principal secretary, Hamzat Ahmadu, an alumnus of a European seminar, and with Dr. Okoi Arikpo, who became commissioner of external affairs, were very helpful in later endeavors. In the North, where they had the fewest contacts, they found that word of their mission had preceded them, and the top civil servants were very apologetic that Lieutenant Colonel Hassan Katsina, the military governor, was away. Other top-ranking officials met with the Quaker team.[5]

5. Adam Curle and John Volkmar, "Report on Mission to Nigeria, April/May 1967," AFSC Archives.

The Outbreak of War

Cognizant of increasing signs of defiance from Enugu, the Eastern capital, Gowon worked toward the establishment of a twelve-state system, which he saw as the best possible long-term solution to the problem that had long haunted Nigeria and as an immediate means of consolidating support in the rest of the country. Hausa-Fulani leaders, under pressure from many minorities, agreed to split the vast Northern Region into six states. The Yorubas in the West were left with their state almost intact. The Mid-West Region, with its mixed population, was unchanged. The Eastern Region was split into three parts: East Central State, predominantly Ibo, Rivers State, and Southeastern State, predominantly non-Ibo. Lieutenant Colonel Ojukwu pronounced the plan unacceptable and unconstitutional and, on May 30, 1967, issued a declaration of secession, establishing the Republic of Biafra outside the Nigerian Federation.

Still hoping for an agreement, on July 1 Gowon, now promoted to major general, proposed a six-point plan to avoid a clash. These points were interpreted by the secessionists as a call to surrender, and their preparations for war continued. Federal troups massed in the North for what was planned as a quick march to Enugu to suppress the rebellion. On July 6 shots were exchanged and the war began. Although Federal troops succeeded in taking Enugu and occupying one half of the declared territory of Biafra in the first four months of the war, Biafran resistance and the offensive in the Mid-West which brought Biafran forces within a hundred miles of Lagos in August promised a prolonged war.

First Conciliation Trip

With the coming of war, the Quakers contacted high-level representatives of both sides in New York and London. Walter Martin, in his function as a member of the Quaker staff at the United Nations, had expressed to Ambassador

Iyalla, deputy permanent representative, the Quaker concern for the tragic situation and offered to help with conciliatory work or relief. On October 20, Iyalla brought the commissioner of external affairs, Dr. Okoi Arikpo, to Quaker House in New York for a meeting with Walter Martin and William Huntington, director of the Quaker United Nations Office. The Nigerians expressed confidence that the war would be over soon and suggested that the Quakers pass along a message to the other side. If Ojukwu and his immediate associates abdicated, the Federal government would grant amnesty to all other rebels; there would be no reprisals or executions; General Gowon would restrain the troops from occupying the East; and an Ibo would be appointed to administer the East Central State.

Quaker staff members decided that the errand suggested by the foreign minister hardly conformed to the role of a neutral mediator. It seemed to the Quakers that their first move should be to support the mediation of the Consultative Committee already set up by the Organization of African Unity, at its annual summit conference at Kinshasa, Congo, September 11, 1967. This committee, composed of the heads of state of Ethiopia, Niger, Cameroon, Ghana, Congo, and Liberia, was asked to try to make peace within a "context of preserving the unity and territorial integrity of Nigeria." The Quakers sought out members of the OAU staff in New York and learned of the difficulties in getting the heads of state together. The Consultative Committee finally met in Lagos in November and issued a statement calling on the secessionists to accept the Federal offer of peace. They made no move to visit the rebel-held territory, and Ojukwu, the leader of the rebellion, ignored the message that General Ankrah of Ghana tried to send him.

Not long after this meeting, John Volkmar was in Niamey, the capital of Niger, to talk about the dialogues program. He told the president, Hamani Diori, of his trip to Nigeria with

Adam Curle in April and May and the talk with Dr. Arikpo in New York in October. He asked President Diori what hope there was for conciliation through the OAU Consultative Committee, of which Diori was a member. President Diori reported his great disappointment in the widely publicized Lagos meeting of November, which he felt had been used not for reconciliation but for marshaling the support of the other heads of state to Nigeria's side. The African heads of state, all threatened with possible secession in their own countries, had little interest in reconciliation. They could not even talk to Ojukwu, since Biafra had no official status in international relations. Diori thought the Quakers, concerned but without official inhibitions, might do better. He proposed a secret meeting of lower-level officials for a step-by-step search for areas of agreement.

President Diori's proposal, when considered in Philadelphia, seemed like a small contribution that might be appropriate for the Quakers, given their long conference experience. Since the Nigerian government insisted that the conflict was an internal police affair, official bodies, whether national or international, were inhibited from taking steps that might imply tacit recognition of Biafra as an independent entity. Thus, an unofficial, nonpolitical group might arrange talks that would prepare the way for more formal discussions.

Committee authorization and clearance for visits to both sides were secured in Philadelphia. At a meeting of the staff on January 17, the objectives were discussed with Adam Curle. While Curle tended to think of a meeting for high-level conciliation, staff tended to think of a lower-level meeting like the seminars in West Africa. All agreed, however, on "proceeding as the way opened," in the time-honored Quaker phraseology. The Quaker organizations would offer to set up a meeting for the parties and would also provide a chairman and observers if desired. The Quaker position of relating openly to both sides was made clear from the beginning, and representatives of the Federal government and Biafra in New York agreed to the visit on this basis. Adam Curle and John Volkmar were selected to go.

By a fortunate coincidence, when Adam Curle arrived in Lomé, Togo, to confer with John Volkmar, William Barton, the general secretary of Friends Service Council, was also there. As a result, the London office could enter into the planning from the beginning. Close collaboration across the Atlantic continued throughout the enterprise. Britain, through its historic and current links with Nigeria, had a more important role in relation to the conflict than the United States, so London was a frequent checkpoint on the way to and from Lagos and Biafra.

This trip to Nigeria had a more focused purpose than the prewar one. The Quaker representatives' objective, though clearer, was difficult to achieve and required careful thinking on procedure. They obviously needed to reach top people on each side; if they divulged too much at lower levels, however, their proposal might be sidetracked by opponents of any talks. An early interview with Major General Gowon, they believed, was the key to the whole trip. Since they had not seen him on the first trip, they sought the counsel of various individuals as to the best approach. They received contradictory suggestions, leading to several false leads.

Hamzat Ahmadu, principal secretary and an old friend of the Quakers, had a direct line to the general, so it seemed logical to request an interview through him. Although much thought went into designing a letter that would raise interest without being too explicit, the letter did not open the door. When there was no response, they sought out Edwin Ogbu, the permanent secretary in the Ministry of External Affairs, who was said to be a particularly understanding person close to Gowon. For the first time they confided to him the main purpose of their visit. Familiar with Quaker Conferences for Diplomats, the permanent secretary thought the proposal for a meeting worth considering. Overriding all opposition, he arranged a meeting for February 3.

Curle and Volkmar, preparing for the interview, used the role-playing technique that Curle had found valuable on the mission to India. They took turns putting themselves in the position of Gowon and anticipating what objections he might raise. They wrote out a nine-point proposal for an open-agenda meeting of persons appointed by each side. The suggested meeting would be without policy-making authority, but might lead to others at higher levels. Points 8 and 9 showed the Quaker sensitivity to the Federal understanding of the struggle:

> 8. The present troubles are an internal concern of Nigeria, and we have no intention of exaggerating the very small part we might possibly play. We can, however, draw on the long experience of Quakers in comparable situations and establish conditions in which the points at issue were considered calmly and constructively.
>
> 9. We are aware that initiatives of this sort have been used by the other side for propaganda purposes and shall therefore be very reticent concerning any positive suggestions that the Federal Government might make with regard to such talks.[6]

The general's unpretentious, warm, and straightforward manner made them feel at ease immediately. Adam Curle's introduction told of his May 1967 trip with John Volkmar and of his work with the Pakistan-India Quaker Mission. Gowon responded that he had studied about the Quakers in school and knew of their concern for justice and peace. The general gave the government's position at length, emphasizing the guilt of the rebels. He then carefully went through the Quaker proposal and expressed skepticism about the idea of

6. Memorandum of 2 February 1968, AFSC Archives.

an unpublicized meeting. The many attempts to get the parties together, he explained, had failed. When the Commonwealth Secretariat had arranged for meetings in London in October and November 1967, the rebels had not shown up. As the ninth point suggested, rebel propaganda had misconstrued his overtures for peace, and he was afraid the Quaker effort would receive the same treatment. He would not oppose their going to the other side if they were willing to take the risk, but he was fearful for their safety, which he could not guarantee. Adam Curle said that both he and John Volkmar had been under fire in the past and were willing to take the risk. Gowon said he was willing to have such a meeting, and that team members could tell Colonel Ojukwu that as soon as a cease-fire was agreed upon, he would stop his troops' advances and bring in a third party to police the lines. As the team later learned, this last concession was new and significant, since it was a tacit admission that the war was more than an internal affair. Gowon also said he would be very interested in their report from the other side.[7]

Their week in Lagos provided an opportunity to assess the public mood in the capital city. Curle and Volkmar were unpleasantly struck by the war mentality that had seized almost everyone. As outsiders they could see that the Biafrans had some justification for their stand, despite the compelling logic of the Nigerian case. Everyone in Lagos, however, had forgotten that the Biafrans had a case at all. The less extreme blamed what they thought were the "insensate ambitions of Ojukwu" and his "criminal clique"; the more extreme blamed "the whole corrupt and treacherous Ibo race, who wanted to dominate all sections of Nigeria." There was a universal ten-

7. For authoritative discussion of the negotiation process based on interviews with the principals and relevant documents, see John J. Stremlau, *The International Politics of the Nigerian Civil War 1967–1970* (Princeton, N.J.: Princeton University Press, 1977).

dency to minimize the ability of the "rebels" to maintain a viable state and hold out against the Federal army.

After the encouraging visit with Major General Gowon, John Volkmar returned to his program duties in Lomé, while Adam Curle in London learned all he could about the negotiating situation, pending action from Biafra on his visa application. He made contact with Biafran leaders in London, Paris, and Geneva and explored with Duncan Wood, director of the Geneva Quaker Center, the possibility of a site in Switzerland for Quaker-sponsored talks. He conferred with persons in the Commonwealth Secretariat who had been trying to arrange talks for some time. They listened eagerly to Curle's firsthand report of Federal openness to a third-party policing force. He learned of other peace initiatives, such as that of the World Council of Churches and the general secretary of the Presbyterian Church of Canada, both of which were rebuffed by the Federal side.

In the meantime in New York the Nigerian representative to the United Nations called on the Quaker staff to say that he had received positive reports from Lagos on the Quaker visit and proposal. He emphasized that point 8 of the Quaker proposal gave an acceptable frame of reference, since it stressed that the troubles were an internal problem of Nigeria. He was pleased that the team had explained their plan to so few people, since they were operating in an extremely sensitive area.

After a month of waiting, visa clearance came from Biafran authorities. Adam Curle and Walter Martin, who was asked to go because of John Volkmar's illness, left Lisbon March 4. This first entrance into war-torn Biafra was less hazardous than later trips, since the commercial airport of Port Harcourt was still under Biafran control. On arrival from the Portugese island of Sao Tomé, they were warmly greeted by Sir Louis Mbanefo, chief justice of Biafra. Although Sir Louis was busy with a delegation from the British Council of

Churches, he took time the next day to hear the Quaker team members explain their confidential mission. He promised to arrange a meeting with the head of state, Lieutenant Colonel Ojukwu.

On Saturday, March 9, the two Quakers were taken by car from their residence in Aba to the temporary capital of Umuahia, where they met Ojukwu, a powerfully built, bearded man, quiet and serious. Adam Curle explained the purpose of their visit and told of the meeting with Gowon in Lagos. Ojukwu listened carefully and studied the memorandum about a proposed meeting. He said that the idea was acceptable in principle. He said he wanted peace; war was senseless and unnecessary. The Biafrans, he said, were more united than ever and intent on defending themselves against the threat of genocide. Talks without preconditions should be held as soon as possible. Although he saw nothing new in the position of the other side, he said the auspices of a nongovernmental, nonpolitical organization might make the other side more willing to accept talks. He was perplexed, he said, as to who really held the power in Lagos and hearkened back to what he considered the betrayal of the Aburi agreement by Gowon, under the influence of "shadowy figures." It was very difficult to negotiate, he said, with someone who agreed one day and changed his mind the next. Nevertheless, he was glad to have the Quakers carry back the message that there should be secret talks without preconditions as soon as possible on neutral ground. A cease-fire would be a help, but he would not insist on it as a precondition to talks. There was no point, he thought, in talks at a low level; representatives would need to have the full confidence of the real leaders on each side. It would be important, he thought, to have the Quakers there as honest brokers.

Curle and Martin did not press the colonel on the Biafran attitude toward the peace terms that had been announced repeatedly from Lagos. It was clear that he was in no mood to concede much. The Quakers felt that at this early stage their role was not to try to find common points in the opposing positions but merely to offer an unofficial setting for talks. They were aware that when policy positions were so far apart any talks were likely to be inconclusive, and yet such talks seemed the only hope of reducing the barriers of suspicion and exploring the possibility of compromise.

The prospects for a meeting seemed bright at this point, and the two team members were able to report to Gowon on March 18, only a week after they left Biafra. The wartime exigencies and the hostility of West African countries to Portugal required that they travel back to Lisbon and London before they could get to Lagos. The Nigerian Head of state was accompanied by his foreign minister, Dr. Arikpo, and the head of the navy, Admiral Wey. Adam Curle reported that although Ojukwu had reacted favorably to the Quaker proposal of a secret meeting in a neutral place, he also thought that a meeting would serve no purpose unless senior people were involved at cabinet or permanent secretary level, and that there should be no preconditions for talks. No publicity was given to the visit, the Quakers reported, an indication that the Biafrans might be serious in wanting talks. A channel for return communication to Ojukwu through his delegate in London had been established.

Thanking the team members, Major General Gowon said he was deeply touched by their willingness to risk their lives and their diligence in coming back to see him, which other mediating groups had failed to do. No publicity of the visit from the rebels was a good sign, he thought. Although he was anxious to end the war, he stated two preconditions: the rebels must renounce secession and must accept the twelve-state division. This state system, he added, might itself be modified later. If these conditions were met, there could be an immediate cease-fire and talks could begin.

Gowon expressed fear that Ojukwu would use an agendaless

meeting to repeat his performance at Aburi, where his detailed and well-thought-out memorandum had taken the others by surprise. Dr. Arikpo also quizzed Curle and Martin about Ojukwu's ideas for an agenda and was not satisfied when all the Quakers could say was that Ojukwu's concern was to end the war quickly through negotiations if possible. The team members were asked to report back to Ojukwu, emphasizing the two preconditions for talks.

Curle and Martin left the meeting with mixed feelings of disappointment and hope. The interest of top leaders on each side in talks indicated that the initiative was being taken seriously, but it was evident that the eagerness for open-ended talks from the Biafran side accentuated suspicion and led to a reiteration of preconditions from the Lagos side. It was important to follow through with a report to Ojukwu and with further talks with others involved in mediation whom Gowon had mentioned. In the likely event that Ojukwu would not accept the preconditions, the Quaker initiative might be to suggest a meeting to examine the implications of preconditions.

During this first period of intervention and assessment the team members concluded that the war was likely to be long and drawn out, and that it would involve terrible suffering on the part of civilians, particularly in the diminishing territory of Biafra, already crowded with refugees. While the positions of the two sides were inflexibly opposed, changes in many factors might alter the bargaining positions and make negotiations more possible. An effort to change each side's perceptions of the other might be of value, since distortions caused by propaganda and suspicion greatly accentuated the already wide gap in their positions.

To improve perceptions on each side, the Quakers took pains to report their general observations. The Quaker team reported in Lagos, after their visit to Biafra, saying that while there were severe shortages of protein foods and medicines in

Biafra, the people were not as badly affected as many reports indicated. There was a shortage of many goods, but others, such as gasoline, were not even rationed. In general the morale was high, and contrary to the common assumption on the Nigerian side, they found broad support for Ojukwu, and not just from the Ibos. The fear of genocide was firmly implanted in people's minds, and the Quaker effort to explain that genocide was not the intent of the Federal government was ineffective as long as the aerial bombardment and the food blockade continued. Ojukwu was a charismatic leader who represented the hope to escape annihilation through an independent nation.[8]

Returning to London in mid-March the two Quaker representatives delivered a letter to the Biafran representative, to be forwarded by telex, reporting the Federal reaction. The Quaker message was evidently ignored, for it was two months later that a polite but unresponsive reply was received.

Negotiations under the Commonwealth Secretariat
Soon after the Quaker visit the Biafran leader showed that his major interest was not negotiation but recognition from other states and the consequent support for morale and arms which it might bring. At the end of March the former president of Nigeria, Dr. Nnamdi Azikiwe, the most widely known and respected Ibo, was sent by Ojukwu on a tour of five African capitals to ask the heads of state to recognize his government and to prevail on Nigeria to declare a cease-fire and to accept peace talks without preconditions. The first recognition following this mission came on April 13, 1968 from President Nyerere of Tanzania, who said that he was convinced that the

8. In an interview with John Stremlau after the war Gowon noted that the Quaker contacts were helpful. Stremlau, *The International Politics of the Nigerian Civil War 1967-1970*, p. 283n.

unity of Nigeria was too far broken by pogroms and military invasion to be healed and further war would only make matters worse. Recognition by Gabon, Zambia, and Ivory Coast followed in May. Hopes were high in the Biafran capital that other nations would follow, but the OAU's nonrecognition policy held firm in the rest of Africa and the world.[9]

The Federal government countered with diplomatic and military offensives. Commissioner of External Affairs Arikpo denied that the Nigerian government had imposed preconditions on talks, but said that the purpose of talks would be to convince the "rebels" they had much to gain by staying in a united Nigeria. The Federal position was portrayed as eminently reasonable; all the "rebels" had to do was to accept a united Nigeria with the new twelve-state administrative structure and all would be forgiven. On the military side the Federal armies were advancing in the northeast and pressing hard on Port Harcourt in the south.

The Commonwealth Secretariat, based in London, but legally a separate entity from the British government, had tried from the beginning to bring the parties together for talks. Now that each side was trying to appear conciliatory before the international public, Arnold Smith, the general secretary, a Canadian, sought again to bring the parties together. The Biafrans were suspicious of the Commonwealth Secretariat, thinking it was under the thumb of Britain, whose policy at the time was solidly tied to the Federal government. But Commonwealth auspices were more acceptable than the Organization of African Unity, and in late April the announcement came that the Biafrans had agreed on preliminary talks in London to plan a major parley in some African capital.

In Philadelphia, the American Friends Service Committee's

9. There was one strange exception: Duvalier, the ruler of Haiti, proclaimed recognition of Biafra in March 1969.

Board Committee on Africa, meeting May 3, 1968, urged that a representative go to London to be in touch with both sides and try to help in the search for a peaceful solution. By this time the plight of refugees in the war zones was being dramatically portrayed in the Western press. The committee thought everything possible should be done to promote negotiations and to avert the likely increase of suffering as more and more of the population was pressed into the Ibo heartland.

Walter Martin, sent to London as the representative of the Quaker service bodies, had long talks with the chief negotiators on the Biafran side, Sir Louis Mbanefo, chief justice, and Dr. Eni Njoku, former head of the University at Nsukka, and a shorter talk with Nigeria's senior representative, Chief Anthony Enahoro, minister of communications. Although he made several suggestions aimed at resolving points of impasse, Martin's major contribution may have been in trying to reassure the Biafrans as to the neutrality of the Commonwealth Secretariat. These talks were only preliminary, but there were stubborn disagreements on the locus of the proposed conference, the chairman, the agenda, and even the date. When plans were finally agreed on for a conference to be held at Kampala, Uganda, starting May 23, it was evident that the central issues of the conflict would not be easily resolved and conciliatory services were all the more important.

As a result of his intercession, Martin gained the confidence of all parties for Quaker participation in the next stage. His recommendation that a Quaker delegation be sent to Kampala was supported in Philadelphia and London, and Adam Curle and his wife, Anne, were selected. A letter from staff in Philadelphia stressed the low-keyed Quaker approach: "It must be understood of course that our role in this whole process is a very humble one. We do not presume to be acting as major negotiators in any way. We are merely hoping to put our relationship of confidence to good use on both sides."[10] A similar letter alerted leaders of the East Africa Yearly Meeting in Nairobi, the largest Quaker group in the world, that British and American Quakers were trying to help in the Nigerian civil war.

At the meeting in the Parliament Building of Uganda's capital, the press was present in force, and the major spokesmen, Chief Anthony Enahoro and Sir Louis Mbanefo, talked more to the world audience than to each other. After some agreement on procedural questions, the Biafrans sought to focus the debate on a cease-fire. Sir Louis insisted that the killing of innocent victims must stop immediately if there were to be any further negotiations. On May 28, after a delay of three days, Chief Enahoro gave the Federal government's answer at a plenary session. Among the twelve points in his response were a cease-fire twelve hours after the "rebels" renounced secession and laid down their arms, Ibo jurisdiction in Ibo East Central State, and amnesty to the "rebels." Sir Louis Mbanefo responded that the twelve points were not a serious approach to cease fire negotiations, but a naked demand for surrender.

Private talks were continued the next day with a small group, and Arnold Smith remarked to Adam Curle that he thought they were making some headway. Enahoro had indicated a somewhat more flexible position: a new Nigerian union, with the implication that the integrity of Biafra (or East Central State) would be safeguarded. Arnold Smith drafted some notes that the Biafran second-in-command, Eni Njoku, seemed to accept. But these hopeful signs were cut off sharply in a plenary session called by the Biafrans, against Arnold Smith's strong advice, for the morning of May 31. In

10. Letter from Secretary, International Affairs Division, 23 May 1968, AFSC Archives.

a hard-line speech, which evidently came straight from Ojukwu, Sir Louis said he saw no useful purpose in continuing the talks while the fighting continued and lives were being lost. The Nigerian response to the cease-fire proposal, he said, showed that they were unwilling to negotiate and only wanted surrender. This the Biafrans could not accept.

Arnold Smith endeavored to salvage the talks both by talking to the parties directly and through messages to the Biafrans carried by Adam Curle. When his efforts were unsuccessful, he and the Curles discussed what had gone wrong in the proceedings. Smith tended to blame the inexperience and ineptness of the Biafrans as well as their apocalyptic mood. Curle found the Biafran leaders alternating between excessive optimism and intense despair. He also felt the Federal representatives were rigid in interpreting their objective of one Nigeria.

Another role which Curle was developing cautiously was that of proposing possible terms of settlement. He showed Njoku a paper written by Harvard professor Carl Friedrich, an internationally known expert on federal systems, which suggested a constitutional settlement to the problem of Biafra along the lines of the relation of Puerto Rico to the United States. Curle gave copies of the paper to members of each delegation as well as to the Commonwealth Secretariat. Njoku thought such a pattern might be acceptable to Biafra. Arnold Smith was guardedly optimistic. The Nigerian representatives gave no comment. The natural optimism of the conciliator was expressed at this time by Curle's statement: "We have to strive to get over the idea to both sides that it is possible in terms of constitutional precedent to have a form of association which satisfies 90% of what both sides want."[11]

Among the last to leave Kampala, Adam and Anne Curle took a plane to Lagos on June 7. They talked to a number of

11. Letter of 1 June 1968, from Kampala, AFSC Archives.

people and arranged a meeting with Gowon. On Monday, June 10, General Gowon greeted Adam Curle and gave his opinion that the talks had failed because Ojukwu "and his gang," encouraged by Zambian recognition, were not serious in seeking peace. Without disagreeing, Curle explained the variation in mood of the Biafran leaders between exuberance and despair, neither of which was conducive to negotiation. He proposed to return to Biafra in order to encourage a more practical and reasonable approach by the top policy makers and to suggest again a low-level unofficial meeting. Gowon supported the idea. Curle also raised tentatively the matter of constitutional arrangements somewhat along the lines of Carl Friedrich's ideas, which might satisfy the secessionists.

Peace Talks in Addis Ababa

In London, Curle talked with Sir Louis Mbanefo about another Quaker visit to Biafra. Sir Louis thought that such a visit would be unnecessary if there was a cease-fire in the near future. Biafran hopes, unrealistic as they were, were dashed by the June 24 communiqué of General Gowon and Lord Shepherd, special representative sent by the British cabinet to Lagos: "no cease-fire without concessions." The counter terms, "cease-fire before any concessions or talks," were reiterated by Ojukwu in a speech to his Joint Consultative Assembly on June 30.

In the meantime the Federal forces had scored a major military success, capturing Port Harcourt and thus completing the blockade of Biafra by sea. With the rising tide of suffering and the horrible prediction of the death of millions, it was difficult for any government to avoid making some move to end the tragedy. African states particularly felt the need to deal responsibly with this African problem, and since the Commonwealth initiative had failed, the way was open again to the Organization of African Unity.

The president of Niger, Hamani Diori, arranged for a meeting of the Consultative Committee in his own capital of Niamey. General Gowon addressed this group on July 16, and Lieutenant Colonel Ojukwu flew in on July 19 on the personal plane of the president of the Ivory Coast. After these publicized appearances, in private sessions between Allison Ayida of Nigeria and Eni Njoku of Biafra considerable progress was made toward agreement on a "mercy corridor" for relief and on conditions for further negotiations to be held in Addis Ababa, Ethiopia, under the chairmanship of Emperor Haile Selassie. Once again hopes were raised that the tragic war might be ended.

The Quaker team members had not tried to get to Niamey, but thought it important to go to Addis Ababa. John and Joanne Volkmar arrived from Lomé the weekend of August 3-4 as the Nigerian and Biafran delegates were assembling. The Volkmars stayed at the hotel where the Biafran delegation led by Dr. Eni Njoku was housed. Adam Curle came four days later and stayed in the same hotel as the Federal delegation led by Chief Anthony Enahoro.

John Volkmar reported in a letter that the general atmosphere of the talks was one of propaganda warfare rather than of conciliation. The Nigerians had come to celebrate their hoped-for victory. The Biafran position was enunciated by Ojukwu himself in a brilliant two-and-one-half-hour oration designed to justify Biafran independence to the conferees and the world. Adam Curle was perturbed by the formality of the proceedings in Africa Hall, with the delegations addressing each other across empty space and with the emperor as a formidable though not mediatory chairman. The meetings were a depressing succession of statements and counterstatements, with each side seeking to score points through personal attacks or leaks to the press. Subtle elements of flexibility put forth in several speeches from each side were lost in the clamor of debate. The destructive glare of publicity and tight security made it difficult for the

Quaker team members to make quiet, private contacts. In contrast to Kampala, there were few openings for contact with the organizers of the conference, the OAU secretariat and the Ethiopian government.

There had been no modification of the sticking points since Kampala. The position of the Federal side was strengthened by events on the battlefield, since only three major cities (Owerri, Aba, and Umuahia) remained in Biafran hands. The Biafrans, taking their lead from Ojukwu, were determined and obdurate. Their courage was bolstered by the promise of French military supplies following the French cabinet's statements of July 31 calling for a resolution of the conflict on a basis of the right to self-determination.

Among the observers at the conference the question was not which side would win, but whether the Biafrans would continue warfare indefinitely with a strong guerrilla force. Continued fighting, the reasoning went, might provoke internal strains in Nigeria to the point of explosive and general chaos. The Nigerian spokesmen, on the other hand, predicted that once the main centers of population were occupied, the Ibos would see the folly of further resistance and then would be won over by the moderation and clemency of the Federal government. The Quaker team members, impressed with Biafran morale, compounded both of fear and hope, were inclined to think that a disastrous guerrilla struggle would continue. Estimating that moves toward peace would not be made in Addis Ababa, the Volkmars and Curle decided to go to Lagos to discuss this eventuality with Gowon. They realized that they would be presenting more of their own point of view than before, but they felt they should speak out as tactfully as possible, even at the risk of offending the Nigerian leader.

An even more pressing reason for going to Lagos came out of a session with Njoku. On the eve of their departure, the chief Biafran negotiator spelled out in private the terms the

Biafran government would be willing to accept, but would not state openly for fear of appearing to weaken. Njoku maintained that his government was willing to become part of a Nigerian union; the concept of sovereignty, more a symbol of defiance than a political necessity, could be diluted to the point where it was much less objectionable to Nigeria. Dr. Njoku said they were willing to be flexible on matters such as cease-fire lines, actual boundaries of the eventual state, composition of a peacekeeping force, and even on the name of the state. The inference here was that the emotion-laden word "Biafra" could be discarded. On only two points would they insist strongly: an army under Biafran control within the cease-fire boundaries, and international standing for the resultant state.

On August 14, in Lagos, Curle and Volkmar gave General Gowon copies of a paper they had drawn up describing Dr. Njoku's proposals, and they gave their own suggestions on ways of meeting the two points on which the Biafrans insisted. The army, they said, could be a militia or homeguard, armed only with defensive weapons. As for international standing, perhaps this could be met with membership on international or regional commissions. Gowon questioned the degree to which Njoku represented Ojukwu and the Biafran hard-liners. The response of the Quakers was that Dr. Njoku had spoken openly of the items about which he would need to persuade others, and in any case, the only way to test his influence and reliability was to respond in a positive, though tentative way.

Apologizing for their temerity, the team members went on to express their hopes for a negotiated settlement to avoid the possible extension of the war into guerrilla activity. General Gowon answered that his men knew how to deal with guerillas, and that without a good supply line from the outside, such guerrilla activity could not last long. At the end of the meeting General Gowon thanked Curle and Volkmar and said he would study carefully what they told him and might call on them to speak to other officials.

As the Quakers were leaving the Dodan Barracks, the head-quarters of the military government, a group of senior field commanders was gathering for a meeting that the press high-lighted as an important military consultation. This grim portent indicated that it was probably too late to prevent the final military drive. John Volkmar stayed in Lagos in case any follow-up was needed, and Adam Curle went to London and then to the United States to see whether anything might be done to salvage the Addis Ababa talks.

It was later learned that the Quaker report had aroused a controversy in the inner councils of Lagos; some maintained that significant concessions were being offered, others that there was little new. The hawks prevailed, and on August 16 Volkmar was called in so that the head of the secretariat for the military government, Mr. H. A. Ejueyitichie, and Hamzat Ahmadu, Gowon's principal secretary, could inform the Quakers that the decision had been made to pursue the war into the heart of the East Central State. In a discouraged let-ter to the other Quaker conciliators, Volkmar wrote that hopes for a negotiated peace were slim.

On August 24, after another meeting with his commanders, General Gowon announced "the final push." The talks at Addis Ababa were still in session but seemed more and more futile. The Quakers turned their attention to relief operations, and John Volkmar spent the rest of August 1968 in Lagos providing a liaison headquarters for the Quaker Mission of Inquiry sent to investigate relief needs.

The Proposal for a Quaker-Sponsored Meeting Renewed
The next episode in the Quaker conciliatory effort involved a complicated series of trips by the three members between September 1 and October 30, 1968. John Volkmar conferred with President Hamani Diori of Niger twice in Niamey and

once in Paris. He also visited the OAU Heads of State Conference in Algiers. Team members made two trips to Biafra and Lagos.

The initial impetus for this series of visits came from inquiries made by Walter Martin and Adam Curle at the United Nations, where the idea developed that an initiative by the secretary-general might be appropriate, since the OAU-sponsored Addis Ababa talks were winding down to an ineffectual conclusion. Although U Thant, the secretary-general, had throughout emphasized that the initiative for peacemaking should come from the Africans and the OAU, reliable sources confirmed that he would be willing to offer his good offices if a strong invitation came from African leaders. He had already taken an initiative on the relief problem by appointing Nils-Goran Gussing as his personal representative to Nigeria to assist in relief and humanitarian activities for the civilian victims of the war. Walter Martin learned that President Kenneth Kaunda of Zambia would propose such an initiative to Secretary-General Thant at the upcoming OAU Heads of State meeting in Algeria. If President Diori's voice could be added, it would greatly increase the chance of favorable action, since Diori was an influential member of the OAU Consultative Committee, chairman of OCAM (Afro-Malagasy Common Organization), and highly respected by U Thant.

On September 9, John Volkmar in Niamey, Niger, urged President Hamani Diori's support for an initiative by U Thant in Algiers. Diori was willing to undertake this, but he did not think the Federal government would allow it. He strongly urged the Quakers to continue their own efforts to sponsor an unpublicized meeting, as he had proposed the previous December.

The atmosphere of the September 13 OAU summit meeting at Algiers was not conducive to peace initiatives. The French policy, tilting toward Biafra, led to strong accusations of French imperialism. The Algerian government, resolutely pro-

Nigerian, was ready to obstruct any Biafran representation. U Thant was not able to offer any new initiative. President Kaunda was sharply rebuffed. Volkmar was refused observer status and was unable to contact President Diori. Quaker neutrality had no place in this atmosphere, and Volkmar's attempts to deliver reports giving the Biafran point of view on the Addis Ababa talks tended to identify him with the Biafran side. The OAU Heads of State passed a resolution supporting Nigeria as strongly as the Kinshasa resolution of the year before, although it did call for general amnesty for the rebels.

One possible way out of the growing impasse was the Diori idea of a Quaker-sponsored meeting. It seemed a forlorn hope, but the Quakers felt they should make every attempt to stop the fighting and killing. The next step was another trip to Biafra to explore further the Njoku proposals, which were still being debated in Lagos. An important added purpose was to take money for relief, which the Quaker service exploratory team, after their August trip, said was greatly needed.

On September 19, Adam Curle and Walter Martin were in Sao Tomé hoping to board one of the relief planes organized by Church Aid that were flying by night into Biafra. The first flight they were on turned back because of engine trouble, but the second managed to get up to 18,000 feet to avoid antiaircraft fire and then descend by a steep spiral to land on the Uli airstrip, which was only lighted at the last minute. Father McGlade, a missionary to Nigeria for twenty-six years and the organizer of distribution for Caritas, drove them to the seminary at Awoamania. He told them that Biafra now measured only sixty by thirty miles. The Federal troops were advancing, and Owerri had fallen. The week before Oguta had been lost and the Uli airstrip was under shellfire, but in a counterattack led by Ojukwu the town was retaken.

During their brief stay of twenty-seven hours in Biafra, Martin and Curle found many Biafrans hoping for a quick end to the fighting. A tough and bitter group, though, was determined to fight to the last and to continue with guerrilla action when field forces could no longer be organized. The likelihood of imminent military collapse meant that dollars would be all the more important, and the Quakers left most of the $55,000 in cash they had brought with the head of Caritas relief, Bishop Whelan of Owerri.

They saw Mr. Onyegbola in Umuahia, who listened carefully to their proposal for a meeting arranged by Quakers and said he would convey it to Lieutenant Colonel Ojukwu. The colonel was probably too busy at the front, he said, to see them, but he would deputize someone to speak with authority. Later that day they met Dr. Sylvanus Cookey, commissioner of commerce and industry and a trusted lieutenant of Ojukwu. Cookey expressed interest in the proposed meeting and said that Biafran missions abroad would be alerted so arrangements could be easily made. He stressed, as Ojukwu had in March, that delegations must be high level.

Their twofold mission accomplished, Curle and Martin managed to get on a Red Cross plane flying to the Spanish island of Fernando Po. From there they went to Douala, Cameroon, where it was agreed that Walter Martin would go directly to Lagos and Adam Curle would go to London to alert Friends of the possibility of a conference and to discuss the proposal with Arnold Smith and a British government representative.

Arriving in Lagos on the morning of September 23, Walter Martin reported directly to Dr. Okoi Arikpo; he was interested in Martin's account and arranged a meeting with General Gowon on September 26. John Volkmar came from Lomé to join Martin, and the two were ushered into a large conference room where they found nine persons seated on one side of a large oval table. General Gowon greeted them warmly and introduced them to his colleagues, Dr. Arikpo; Brigadier Ekpo, Chief of Staff; Chief Anthony Enahoro,

Minister of Information and senior negotiator, at the London, Kampala, and Addis Ababa talks; Allison Ayida, Deputy negotiator; P. Adiodu, Permanent Secretary in the Ministry for Industry; H. A. Ejueyitichie, Secretary to the Federal Military Government; Anthony Enahoro, Jr.; and Hamzat Ahmadu. Volkmar and Martin sat on the opposite side of the oval table and recounted their recent activities. John Volkmar spoke of his meetings with Hamani Diori, of his talks with Biafrans in Paris, and of his visit to Algiers; Walter Martin spoke of the visit of himself and Adam Curle to "rebel-held territory."

General Gowon responded with appreciation for what they had done, but expressed disappointment that they had not seen Ojukwu. Gowon questioned the Quaker team closely on the sincerity of the Biafran desire for meaningful talks. The Quaker team said they thought the Biafran leaders were more despondent and realistic, probably because of their military defeats and their diplomatic setbacks at Algiers. Gowon asked whether the other side had made any preconditions for talks under Quaker auspices. Walter Martin replied that they had stressed only their desire for delegates with full power and a venue in a neutral country such as Italy or Austria.

Gowon then turned to conditions within the "rebel" territory. Walter Martin in his reply stressed three points. First, he and Curle had seen bombed-out hospitals and markets. They had tried to explain the bombings as unintentional mistakes, but there was no doubt that the people felt that nonmilitary targets were being deliberately bombed, adding credibility to their leader's warning of genocide. Second, on the more positive side, in the recent "liberation" of Oguta by Federal forces there had been no vindictive killing, and as a result, the fears of the local people were greatly lessened. Third, though the mass of the people seemed exhausted and anxious to get back to normal life, all the evidence pointed to continued guerrilla activity if military defeat came.

General Gowon ended the meeting by again warmly thanking the two and by saying that his government would further consider the Quaker offer to sponsor an unpublicized meeting, along with similar suggestions from other quarters. He asked the Quakers to remain in Lagos for a few days to receive the answer.

That same afternoon, Martin and Volkmar talked at length with Sir David Hunt, the United Kingdom high commissioner, and Lord Shepherd, the special delegate sent by Prime Minister Wilson to assess the possibilities of negotiations. They agreed that a settlement would be of more value to the Federal government than "total military victory," since it would avoid the likelihood of protracted guerrilla warfare and a Biafran government-in-exile. The British representative insisted that there was no evidence that the Biafrans were serious about negotiating within the terms of "one Nigeria." The Quaker conciliators could not be specific, but could only point to the general mood and the statements that Njoku had made to Volkmar and Curle in Addis Ababa.

Two days later, on Saturday September 28, Hamzat Ahmadu gave the Quaker delegates Gowon's answer. The Federal government was still not convinced that the Biafrans were sincere about negotiations. Ojukwu's speech to his Consultative Assembly on September 25, in which he said they would fight on with guerrilla activity if necessary, was not reassuring. The government was aware that some top Biafran leaders who had counselled Ojukwu to negotiate would be coming out of Biafra. Would the Quakers be willing to meet them, gauge the atmosphere in Biafra and the attitude of the top leaders, and report back? Martin and Volkmar agreed to do so.

Walter Martin went to Lisbon, where he had long talks with Dr. Eni Njoku and Dr. Okoro. He felt reassured that the points Njoku had made to Adam Curle and John Volkmar in Addis Ababa were those of his government and not just personal opinions. Martin drafted a paper proposing a meeting of the two sides and went over it thoroughly with the Biafran representatives. Points 7 and 8 presented the basis for agreement:

> 7. Both sides recognize that the objective is a united Nigeria and their discussions will work towards this. There is no gainsaying the hostility, mistrust and bitterness engendered perhaps over a long time, but which have deepened immeasurably during the period of warfare, and it is likely that special measures will have to be agreed on to cover a transitional stage until the objective is fully attained.
>
> 8. The issue thus appears to be the maximum of freedom and autonomy that is compatible with the ultimate objective of a united Nigeria and that is adequate to restore confidence and a sense of security to the population of the war areas.[12]

In the meantime John Volkmar had flown to London on September 30 on the same plane with Lord Shepherd and Dr. Arikpo. Shortly after his arrival in London, Lord Shepherd announced that he had been approached by several Biafran leaders in Europe who had indicated to him that Biafra was ready to talk of surrender. This public declaration was a major blow to any hopes for quiet talks. The next morning when Volkmar went to see the Biafran representative in London he found him upset over Lord Shepherd's talk of Biafran surrender. Nevertheless, he thought Ojukwu wanted to have talks, and he agreed to send a telex to Umuahia asking his government to name someone to discuss with a Federal counterpart in Europe the details of a possible meeting under Quaker sponsorship. He would undertake this himself only if designated by his government.

12. Memorandum of 9 October 1968, AFSC Archives.

In several meetings during the week with officers of the Commonwealth Secretariat, it was confirmed that they had been approached by Biafrans to see if Lord Shepherd could arrange peace talks with the Federal government in the context of "one Nigeria." Now that Lord Shepherd had spoken out so rashly, even using the word "surrender," the initiative of the Commonwealth Secretariat was ended. Perhaps the Quakers could still arrange something.

In Paris, John Volkmar found the Biafran representative, Raph Uwechue, whom he had come to know quite well, totally despairing of the war effort and the lack of any response from his government to the need to negotiate. Several leaders, including himself, Uwechue reported, had drafted a recommendation to Ojukwu that he seek terms that would give up secession, but guarantee the security of the Ibo people. They each received a telegram a few days later telling them to return immediately to Biafra or resign in seven days. Raph Uwechue showed Volkmar a three-page telex he had sent to Ojukwu refusing to return and saying in essence that His Excellency was immoral in continuing the war.[13]

On Monday, October 7, Martin and Volkmar went over their draft proposal of a meeting with Chief Enahoro in London, who made suggestions for revision. Then, on Tuesday word came that the Biafran government wanted to see the Quakers in Biafra. Hoping to assess the readiness of the Biafrans for talks within the framework of "one Nigeria," Martin and Volkmar departed from Lisbon for Sao Tomé. On the same plane were several Biafran officials who had been mentioned by Raph Uwechue as being under suspicion because of their advice to Ojukwu to seek a settlement. When the Quaker delegation arrived from Sao Tomé at the Uli air-

13. In December Uwechue resigned his Paris post and in March 1969 published his book proposing peace terms: *Reflections on the Nigerian Civil War: A Call for Realism* (London: International Publishers, 1969).

strip, they were taken in an official car to a remote guest house at an agricultural college five or six miles from Umuahia.

A preliminary meeting with Dr. Sylvanus Cookey and Dr. Eni Njoku gave them a chance to report on their activities and present their memorandum. They stressed the importance of seeing Lieutenant Colonel Ojukwu if they were to be taken seriously on their return to Lagos. The next evening, Monday, October 14, they had a meeting with seven major Biafran figures. Sir Louis Mbanefo, chief justice, presiding; Dr. Eni Njoku, senior Biafran representative at Addis Ababa; N. U. Akpan, chief secretary; C. Kogbara, Representative in London; S. Cookey, Special Commissioner for State House Affairs; Matthew Mbu, Commissioner for Foreign Affairs; Dr. Michael Okpara, Political Advisor to the Head of State. Sir Louis opened the proceedings by expressing appreciation for their visit. Biafra, he said had always been anxious for a negotiated settlement, but Lagos had shown no interest. The Nigerian leaders wanted a total military victory, he continued, and the launching of the "final offensive" while the Addis Ababa talks were in progress was proof of this. He went on to condemn the United States and the United Kingdom for not bringing the war to a halt and stated that the purpose of Lord Shepherd's recent visit to Lagos was to bring about the total surrender of Biafra.

Sir Louis then apologized for his attack on absent parties, saying, "You see, you are the closest we can get to Lagos." This gave the Quaker negotiators the opportunity to bring attention to the document that they had worked over with Biafran leaders and with Chief Enahoro. The initial six paragraphs dealing with place, time, privacy, and informality of the meeting were acceptable, but the Biafrans were insistent on two points to reopen negotiations: a cease-fire during the period of talks; and no agreement in advance to the concept of "one Nigeria."

Walter Martin commented that it was very unlikely that the Federal government would accept these two points. The "one Nigeria" idea was vital to Lagos, and if the Biafrans accepted this *en principe,* the Quaker team members would be willing to impress on the Nigerians the need for a cease-fire. The Biafrans spoke with one voice against this possible compromise. After an hour and a half, the meeting ended with expressions of appreciation for what the Quakers were doing and a promise to see if a meeting with Colonel Ojukwu could be arranged.

Walter Martin and John Volkmar were disappointed that the Biafran line had hardened considerably in comparison with talks which they had had outside Biafra and in Biafra on the last trip two weeks earlier. They conjectured that the supply of arms from France was having an effect. Morale was certainly higher. It appeared that the Quakers had been called to Biafra to witness a show of solidarity, and it seemed the hard line of Dr. Cookey and Sir Louis Mbanefo was as much directed to the other Biafrans present as to the Quakers.

It was noteworthy that no private conversations were possible and that all contacts with Biafran leaders were in formal meetings. This was again an indication that all the spokesmen were moving cautiously to avoid an impression of differing voices. That no meeting with Colonel Ojukwu took place could also be interpreted as an attempt to play down his central position and to emphasize that all were in agreement.

Although there had been no breakthrough on a formula for peace talks, the Quaker team members felt it important to report back to Lagos. Arriving on Saturday, October 19, they had a meeting with Gowon on Monday in the company of Mr. Ejueyitichie, permanent secretary of the Federal Military Government, and Mr. Baba Gana, the new permanent secretary in the Ministry of External Affairs. The conversation covered the same ground, but this time they reported the hardened position of the Biafrans. Gowon agreed with them that there was no room to maneuver. He explained that in response to the OAU Heads of State appeal, Nigeria was prepared to grant amnesty to all Biafrans except Ojukwu. When Volkmar raised the problem of bombing hospitals and marketplaces, Gowon indicated that he had given strict instructions some time ago for accurate bombing of military installations only, but perhaps the time had come to reissue the order.

However close the parties seemed to talks at one brief period, there now seemed no possibility of peace negotiations.

Conciliatory Efforts
in the Period from October 1968 to October 1969

The Biafran Republic seemed close to collapse when Adam Curle and Walter Martin visited it at the end of September 1968. But the Biafrans were able to reequip their forces with military aid from France and check the Federal advance. Umuahia, the last major Biafran city, held out and was still the capital. The Uli airstrip was functioning for night flights of relief supplies, and according to rumors military supplies were coming in from Gabon, either to Uli or to a secret airstrip. The Federal lines were overextended and a stalemate ensued. In February 1969, General Gowon made his first visit to the front to try to improve the coordination of the three divisional commanders. A renewed attack in the spring of 1969 led to the fall of Umuahia in late April, but at the same time the Biafrans recaptured Owerri and moved their capital to that city. The Biafrans even hit back with a mini air force drawn together by the Swedish count Carl Gustav von Rosen.

The general condition of stalemate in the field of battle during 1969 brought the issue of relief to the fore and gave strong motivation for various efforts to bring about a negotiated settlement. For the Quaker team of conciliators this was a period of careful monitoring of other conciliation efforts, helping where appropriate, and watching for any opportunity that might open. Contacts with both Nigerians and Biafrans were maintained in the United States and Britain, with offers to help if desired.

The American Friends Service Committee in the winter and spring of 1968-69 lent support to two non-Quaker initiatives: one by a Harvard professor who sought to apply in the civil war negotiating techniques he had tested in other conflicts, another by a United States congressman who was hopeful of getting agreement on a new airstrip for relief supplies that would not threaten the military positions of either side. Neither of these approaches was successful. The Quaker organizers were content to facilitate these initiatives through consultation and financing without exerting any substantive control. They took the risk of compromising their own credibility, reasoning that their own efforts were at a standstill, and others might be able to do better.

In their own counsels the Quaker conciliators turned again to the OAU Consultative Committee as the most likely official sponsor for peace talks. As the instrument of African states, all with dissident minorities, the committee was inevitably slanted toward Nigerian hopes for unity. The Nigerian government constantly emphasized that the OAU was the main vehicle for negotiation, while the Biafrans were just as insistent that the committee could not be a proper mediating body. An obvious way to improve the Consultative Committee was to enlarge it by including one or more states that recognized Biafra.

An unsuccessful meeting of the OAU Consultative Committee in Monrovia, Liberia, in April 1969, with the heads of state listening first to one side and then to the other, underlined the need for some enlargement of the committee. John Volkmar went to Lagos on May 14 to try out this idea and was told in the utmost confidence that secret talks were going on directly between representatives of the two sides some place in Europe. Volkmar sent word to Philadelphia and London that any new initiative should be suspended until it was seen what would happen. By the end of June there were brief comments in the press about the talks that had taken place in Geneva. As far as can be judged without access to government documents, these negotiations were as unsuccessful as all the others. Meanwhile the war ground on.

Quaker Relief

While the Quaker conciliation efforts continued, worsening famine in Biafra necessitated special attention. It was widely reported that there were 5 million additional mouths to feed in the Ibo heartland, 2 million refugees who returned to Biafra after the pogroms in the North in 1966 and 3 million displaced from areas occupied by the Federal forces. Estimates of likely civilian deaths from hunger and disease ran into the millions. These reports were exaggerated, but the truth was bad enough. The story of suffering in Biafra was spread around the world by a professional press service engaged by the Biafrans in Geneva and by reports from the scene by relief workers and journalists. The Nigerian blockade was depicted as part of a concerted campaign of genocide against the Ibo people. A government statement issued from Umuahia, December 29, 1968, said:

> Nigeria's leaders have openly stated that starvation is a legitimate weapon of war. . . . The entire people of Biafra are fighting a war of survival, a war in which, if Nigeria obtains complete mastery, would result in the extermination of the whole Biafran people.[14]

14. Anthony H. M. Kirk-Greene, *Crisis and Conflict in Nigeria: A Documentary Sourcebook* (London, Oxford University Press, 1971), vol. 2, pp. 342–43.

While the Federal Military Government adamantly defended the blockade as a necessary war measure, official policy was to minimize civilian suffering, since all the people were Nigerians and would soon be back in a united Nigeria. Occasional statements by Radio Kaduna in the North or independent voices in the government saying "starve out the rebels" went against this official policy, but the continuing intransigence of Ojukwu and his close advisors gave support to the hard-line position.

Repeated attempts by the International Committee of the Red Cross, the Commonwealth Secretariat, the Organization of African Unity, and various governments and private individuals to negotiate free passage of civilian relief goods by road, sea, or air led to one failure after another. The restrictions the Federal government imposed, such as inspection of cargo and limitation of route and time of flight, were unacceptable to the Biafran authorities. The Quaker conciliators followed these negotiations closely with special assistance from Duncan Wood, who was in touch with the Geneva headquarters of the International Committee of the Red Cross. When the major impasse seemed to be over inspection of cargo, the Quakers offered to provide a neutral, unofficial inspection service, but the suggestion did not help resolve the puzzle. Each side accused the other of holding the lives of millions of people as hostage to the needs of the military. While carrying on negotiations for recognized daytime routes, the International Committee of the Red Cross continued to fly in large amounts of relief supplies by night from the Spanish island of Fernando Po. At great expense and risk, major amounts were also flown in from Portuguese Sao Tomé for private organizations, notably Oxfam, the World Council of Churches, and Caritas, by the coordinating agency, Joint Church Aid.

On the first Quaker visit before the war started, Adam Curle and John Volkmar had strongly recommended that the

Friends organizations provide relief for refugees who had fled to eastern Nigeria from the North. After their second trip to the same area, they again reported in some detail on conditions there. At that time (March 1968) the main problem was lack of medicines, vitamins, and protein-rich foods, rather than actual starvation.

At the same May 3 committee meeting of AFSC that urged conciliation missions to London and Kampala, an exploratory mission to investigate the opportunities and possibilities of relief in the Federal Republic and in Biafra was also recommended. As a result, a three-man Mission of Inquiry Regarding War Relief Needs was sent to Nigeria and Biafra from July to September of 1968.

The Quaker representatives were cordially received and given every help by the Federal authorities. They visited the main areas of reoccupation on the Federal side and with Federal approval made a flying tour of Biafra from August 27 to 31. Their assessment of the confused situation, pointing to serious needs but counteracting exaggerated reports, was sought by the Africa subcommittee of the Senate Foreign Relations Committee and the media. On the basis of their reports the board of AFSC gave approval to the staff to raise funds and appoint personnel for combined medical and relief teams to work on both sides of the battle lines.

The implementation of plans was subject to many delays, and not until January 1969 was the first team sent to work in Biafra, where the Quakers joined with the Mennonite Central Committee in the operation of a hospital at Abiriba. On the Federal side, in the reoccupied territories the first medical relief operation of Quaker Service was established at Ikot Usen, Southeastern State, in March 1969. This area, close to the southern war front, had about 80,000 refugees in a total population of 170,000. The Quaker-Mennonite Service in Biafra had to move several times because of the changing war zone. Toward the end of the war additional

programs on the Federal side were being started in the Asaba-
Ibusa area of Mid-West State, and at Awgu in the northern
part of the former Biafra.

Political Hazards of Relief Work

Any relief operation carried out in the midst of civil war has
potentially strong political and military implications and may
well jeopardize the neutral role necessary for conciliatory
work. In the Nigerian situation, where the blockade was a
major part of Federal military strategy, the suffering was almost entirely on the Biafran side. The large number of
disease-threatened, hungry refugees was in the diminishing
areas of Biafra, and these people could only be helped by airlifts over the Nigerian blockade.

The first member of the Quaker Mission of Inquiry happened to arrive in Lagos in July of 1968, just at the time
when Gowon called in all relief agency representatives to
warn them of political interference in Nigerian affairs. He
singled out two organizations for special reprimand: Oxfam
of Britain, for having used biased, prorebel appeals in British
newspapers, and Caritas, for reportedly sending relief supplies
on the same aircraft illegally flying arms to the rebels.

The Quakers sought an evenhanded approach by offering
aid on both sides, and this was appreciated by the Federal
officials, although it was not really a balancing act, since the
relief work on the Federal side was largely for Biafran
refugees in Federal-occupied areas. The risk of offending
Nigerian officials was compounded by the need to make
broad dramatic appeals for financial support. These difficulties were highlighted in three separate incidents, two involving publicity in the United States and one involving personnel in the field.

In October 1968, a mimeographed report of the AFSC
titled "General Situation in Nigeria/Biafra" was strongly
criticized by J. T. F. Iyalla, now ambassador in Washington,

to whom it was sent. A major complaint was the use of the word "Biafra," which to the Nigerians meant recognition of the rebellious group. Furthermore, reference to deficiencies of Federal relief in occupied areas were taken as unfair condemnation of the Nigerian government. A third complaint was that in certain phrases the Quakers were exaggerating the suffering, just as, the ambassador felt, the Biafran Press Agency and the pro-Biafran relief organizations had been doing. In informal conversations the ambassador expressed worry that the paper might strengthen the hands of the hardliners in Lagos who were opposed to Quaker conciliatory efforts and opposed to relief. The matter was smoothed over with a promise from the AFSC to watch carefully the wording of all releases and to limit publicity, seeking funds as much as possible on a private basis.

This promise presented the publicity department of the Service Committee with an impossible task. Although some picture of the organization's work had to be portrayed to the public to raise the considerable funds needed, there were severe restrictions on painting the picture. After the ambassador's complaint a complete moratorium was imposed on all publicity. Planned speeches at the AFSC annual meeting were canceled, and regional offices in the United States were asked not to issue any news releases, since the word "Biafra" was unacceptable to the Nigerians and any substitute was an outrage to the Biafrans. Responding to the subsequent dismay of fund raisers and relief organizers, the Philadelphia office issued another in-house memorandum in December proposing a policy of "muted publicity" which would, as much as possible, try to avoid three pitfalls: naming Biafra, criticizing the Nigerian government relief efforts, and exaggerating the deprivations of the war.

The second publicity-related crisis came in the spring of 1969 when the Quakers had already begun a hospital and relief program in Abiriba, Biafra, and had sent a medical relief team to the Southeastern State of the Federation. The Quaker fundraising was lagging for both the medical relief work in Quang Ngai, South Vietnam, and in Nigeria/Biafra. Emotionally gripping firsthand reports of extreme suffering came in February from field staff in the two areas. These became the inspiration of a three-quarter-page advertisement in the Sunday *New York Times,* April 27. At the top was the caption "An Appeal by the American Friends Service Committee; Two Wars–Two Letters." In parallel columns excerpts from the letters were printed—one from Abiriba, Biafra, one from Quang Ngai, Vietnam—vividly depicting the efforts of doctors and nurses to rescue the living from the dead in truckloads of women and children removed from bombed areas. Between the two columns was a picture of a jagged hole in the midst of which was the caption, quoted from one of the letters, "Looking Through a Hole into Hell."

The text did not explain the source of bombing in either case and made no accusations. A note at the bottom signed by Gilbert White, chairman of AFSC, was intended to allay any suspicions of political bias: "Our work is directed to the victims of war without regard for geography or politics. We believe that all sides share responsibility for war's tragedy; we know that all sides suffer from it." But the reader of the advertisement was likely to know that nearly all the bombing in the Nigerian war was from the Federal side using MIGs supplied by the Soviet Union and piloted by Egyptians.

Kale Williams, the field director, wrote from Lagos that he understood the reasoning and feeling behind the advertisement, but added, "One can predict that the reaction here will be that this is another example of the selective reporting which gives the impression that only one side is at fault in the war. I think this criticism of the international press is well founded and I am troubled that our first publication is open to the same criticism."

Nothing was heard from Nigerian sources for three months.

Williams was running into great delays in getting visas for new personnel, import permits, and residence permits, but there had been delays before from red tape. On July 10, 1969, Williams sought out a high government official who had all along been friendly to the Quaker efforts. The officer in Lagos mentioned the advertisement, but spoke in detail only when pressed by Williams. The anger was so deep and intense, the official said, that no one in the government had spoken to Williams about it: "If an African berates you and takes you to task for an injury it is a sign that he still wants to continue the relationship, but if he is hurt very deeply, he will say nothing." The objections to the advertisement, the Nigerian official said, arose from the graphic description of the results of bombing just as the Nigerians were receiving what they regarded as unjustified criticism of their bombing policy and from the inclusion in the text of "Biafra" as a sovereign entity on a par with Vietnam and Nigeria. The anger of Nigerian officials was all the greater, he reported, because they had trusted the Quakers more than any other agency. Several persons in the Executive Committee and the Supreme Military Council had proposed that the Quakers should be thrown out. He and others argued against this and had been accused of being pro-Quaker and pro-American.

Kale Williams explained that the publicity was not against Nigeria, but against war in general, and mentioned the chairman's statement, which made clear that the letters did not support one side or the other in the conflicts. The official said he had used this argument himself, but his associates were not convinced. He asked Kale Williams to warn his colleagues in Philadelphia that further publicity of this sort might be disastrous to the position of the moderates within the government. The atmosphere of the interview was not hostile, and the official ended on a note of gratitude for all that the Quakers were doing in both relief and diplomatic fields.

Reaction in Lagos to the advertisement was serious enough to be included in a personal letter from General Gowon responding to Volkmar's farewell letter of May 20, in which he said he was leaving his post in Lomé to go to the Quaker United Nations Program. In his letter of July 3, Gowon expressed his gratitude to Volkmar and his colleagues for their attempts to find a peaceful solution and went on to mention an "unfortunate tendency which has become increasingly evident in an aspect of the activities of the American Friends Service Committee." The letter hearkened back to the incident in October 1968 and expressed dismay at the *New York Times* advertisement. It ended with the hope that these incidents would not endanger future cooperation and the "very fruitful work which the Quakers have been doing in this country both in relief and in other aspects."

A third incident showing the political hazards of relief work occurred in the field, where an able Canadian doctor was declared by the Federal military commander of the area to be "unsafe for use in liberated areas." The Quaker doctor had been overheard in a private conversation asking about the reality of a genocidal threat to Ibos. This was a sensitive topic, particularly for that military commander, who had been accused of cruelty. On hearing the story he concluded that the doctor was pro-Biafra. Disclaimers by the doctor and efforts by the Quaker director with Federal authorities in Lagos could not get approval for the physician to go back to work in the field, and after a frustrating wait, he returned to Canada.

Final Conciliation Mission, October–November 1969

In the spring and summer of 1969, the problem of relief administration caused the Philadelphia and London headquarters to favor a top-level consultation in Lagos. When

Kale Williams, field director, sought a meeting with Gowon on September 26 to talk over these matters, the general's secretary reassured Williams that the problems in the relief operation were being ironed out and could be discussed with the rehabilitation commissioner. Then the official added that General Gowon had always been appreciative of the Quaker efforts, and "If John thinks it would be useful to sample the political climate on both sides, we would be glad to talk with him." Adam Curle was quickly recruited to join John Volkmar, and they were both in Lagos with Kale Williams by October 5, 1969.

While waiting for their meeting with Gowon, the three men talked to a number of well-informed people and learned much about the internal conditions in Nigeria that would be important to report to Biafran leaders as arguments for peace. Gowon, though having difficulties in the Western State, was firmly in command. The North was not the dominant force that the Biafrans suspected; in fact, the six Northern states formed in 1967, far from being a monolithic block, were developing their own identities and rivalries. The chief influences on Gowon were moderate, and the warm reception accorded to former Nigerian president Dr. Azikiwe in August when he disavowed the rebellion and came to Nigeria suggested a general friendliness for the Ibos and a desire for a new start.

On October 10, 1969, General Gowon greeted the three Quaker representatives as cordially as ever. He emphasized again that his government did not want to "conquer the Ibos," and that he was waging a limited war, waiting at each stage for any opportunity to engage in what he called "meaningful talks." This phrase meant, of course, talks within the framework of the OAU resolution passed at the beginning of the war in September 1967, reiterated at Algiers in September 1968, and just recently repeated at Addis Ababa. There had been a slight change of wording in the new OAU resolution which appealed to "the parties in the civil war to agree to negotiations intended to preserve the unity of Nigeria," rather than appealing to "the secessionist leaders to cooperate with Federal authorities in order to restore peace and unity in Nigeria." When asked whether the Quakers could take this as a slight softening of position, Gowon neither admitted nor denied it, a response the Quakers took as tacit approval of their interpretation. The full meaning of the phrase "preserve the unity of Nigeria" was still uncertain, but might be a basis of negotiation.

The Quaker delegation was further encouraged by General Gowon's reply to a question about Raph Uwechue's new book, *Reflections on the Nigerian Civil War,* which was on the general's desk. He said it was a useful first step, though instead of Uwechue's proposed six states, there would have to be at least twelve. Uwechue's emphasis on security rather than sovereignty for the Ibo people was quite congruent with federal aims. Gowon said that all along he had wanted a settlement that would ensure their security, but some of the measures proposed to safeguard security, such as an independent army and diplomatic missions in other states, would in effect nullify his principle aim of one Nigeria. His emphasis on these two points were reminiscent of the report of the Quakers to him in August 1968, when they discussed the same issues insisted upon by the Biafrans.

General Gowon had a specific message for the Quaker team to carry; they were to suggest to Ojukwu that if he agreed to "meaningful talks" he should express his willingness in a letter to one of "his friends," meaning the head of state of one of the nations that had recognized Biafra.

In evaluating this interchange, the three team members found a slender hope. Perhaps the depleted state of their resources and the reduction of area under control to onetenth of the original Biafra would make the Biafrans more amenable to talk of a Nigerian union. The high degree of suspicion between the parties, however, made agreement on any formula of words difficult. This time the team never got to Biafra. The three-team members got as far as Sao Tomé by using a chartered plane from Douala in Cameroon, but unable to get clearance for either a Biafran or Church Aid plane to the Uli airstrip, they had to return to Douala. The next best thing was to present their message in a memorandum at the Biafran offices in London and New York.

On October 17, two days after their arrival in London, they saw the announcement in the press that President Bongo of Gabon had received a note from General Ojukwu[15] saying that he was prepared to enter into a further round of talks. The Quaker message carrying was evidently one of several channels being used by the Nigerians. The unfortunate publicity leaked in Gabon led to further charges and counter-charges between the two contestants and did not help to bring talks.

When Kale Williams, back in Lagos, reported to a high official in the Commission of External Affairs on November 5, he was treated to a full account of the very confused situation that had developed. A letter sent from Ojukwu to the prime minister of Sierra Leone, rather than Gabon, had seemed to constitute an acceptable bases for starting talks, but Ojukwu's speech on November 1, and differing voices from Biafran representatives in Geneva, London, and Owerri, made the Federal government unsure whether there was any change in the Biafran position. The Nigerian official approved of Williams's plan to go to Biafra to visit the Quaker relief operations, but also hoped that he might discover what the current thinking of the other side was. He said that the Nigerian side was ready for talks arranged by the OAU without preconditions, but would not agree to a prior cease-fire.

15. Ojukwu was declared general of the People's Army in May 1969 by the Consultative Assembly of Biafra.

With this encouragement, Williams was able to carry out the mission of direct conversation in Biafra which the team of three could not accomplish. Not long after arriving on November 11, Kale Williams arranged to talk with two high officials concerning the Biafran position on talks. He found that the Biafrans were ready to join in meaningful talks "without preconditions." By this they understood that the Biafrans would come to the talks believing that they were independent, and that the Nigerian representatives would come believing that they were all part of one Nigeria. They had made this position clear, the spokesman said, and had been waiting for some time for a formal response from Lagos. Since the OAU was committed to a precondition, the Biafrans had asked for a written assurance from officials of the OAU that the proposed talks were without preconditions. Ojukwu's recent speeches, the Biafran spokesman said, were intended primarily for an internal audience and were consistent with their understanding that they would be entering talks while upholding their present position.

As to the confusion of statements about sovereignty and security that had come out of Geneva and London in October, the official asserted that the security of the Ibo people was the primary commitment of the government. Heretofore they had been convinced that full sovereignty was the only guarantee, but now they were prepared to consider alternatives. Neither of the two men, in separate interviews, specified a cease-fire as a prerequisite to beginning talks, though both spoke of the difficulty of conducting successful talks while bombs were dropping.

Williams was encouraged by the change in position, but he was discouraged by the deep suspicions that made each side see the actions of the other as calculated moves to gain military or politcial advantage. "This reinforcing cycle of mutual distrust," he reported, "is itself the greatest barrier to beginning talks and to finding mutually acceptable solutions to the crisis."

Kale Williams traveled over much of the remaining Biafra during his four-day visit. The Quaker-Mennonite Service team was supervising fifteen sick bays and one improvised hospital in an area bounded by the Cross River on the east and the Imo River on the west. High-protein foods brought in nightly by the Joint Church Aid airlift were distributed to supple- ment the local root crops grown in every cultivatable plot of land. Ibo tenacity and improvisation were still very much in evidence.

As a whole, Williams found the general relief effort failed to maintain as clear a separation as desirable between civilian and military operations. Because of the great shortage of transport, trucks carrying the identification of relief agencies were frequently commandeered by the army and used for transporting armed soldiers and ammunition to the front. Some food was distributed to soldiers in uniform, but Wil- liams was assured that no food was distributed in bulk to army units. The three Quaker-Mennonite Service workers—a doctor, a nurse, and a technician-administrator—were doing a heroic task under difficult circumstances, trying to cover too much territory and without time to work out satisfactory relationships with the government and relief officials.

On his way back to Lagos via London, Williams joined Adam Curle for talks with the head of the Commonwealth Secretariat and the Biafran representative in London. One topic was the possibility of the Commonwealth Secretariat coming back into the picture if the Biafrans refused the auspices of the OAU. In Lagos, on November 21, 1969, Wil- liams reported to an official in the Commission on External Affairs and was glad to learn that the Nigerians had sent a conciliatory response to the Biafran proposals. They ex- pected the terms would be acceptable and that talks would be held without preconditions on December 10 in Addis Ababa under OAU auspices. The objection by the other side to the OAU could be met, the Nigerian official said, since the OAU was only convening the parties and not mediating a solution, and therefore the OAU resolution should be no problem. If these talks should fail to come off, the official said, the Nigerians would have no objections to working through the Commonwealth Secretariat.

The messages given to Kale Williams by the two sides were a clear forecast of the final negotiating debacle in Addis Ababa. Each side was putting forward a position intended to appear reasonable and flexible, yet containing a convenient excuse for not negotiating if their suspicions of the other side's intention seemed confirmed. General Ojukwu sent his economic adviser, Dr. Pius Okigbo, to Addis Ababa with the public statement that the Biafrans were responding to the invitation of Emperor Haile Selassie in his capacity as an African head of state rather than as agent of the OAU. The Nigerians asked the emperor to clarify the auspices of the meeting before committing themselves to coming. Prodded by both sides, the Ethiopian government was forced to declare that the talks were being called by the OAU, whereupon Dr. Okigbo on December 18 announced that the Biafran delegation was leaving. In a speech in Kano on the same day, Gowon said that if secessionist leaders refused peace talks under the OAU mantle, Federal forces would have to pursue "a speedy military solution."

The last futile talks on relief flights also occurred in December. The International Committee of the Red Cross had conducted negotiations with both parties throughout the summer leading up to an agreement signed September 13 between the ICRC and the Nigerian government. Daylight flights subject to Federal inspection would be allowed into Uli airstrip. The Biafran government then said that these terms were different from those they had accepted with the

ICRC on August 1. They could not agree, they said, to Federal inspection and control, as the Federal government would take military advantage of the flights. In early December, when the relief issue came up in one of the perennial debates in the House of Commons on the British policy of sending arms to Nigeria, Gowon gave strong assurances to the British government that the Federal government would stick to its agreement with ICRC and take no military advantage of daylight flights into Uli airport. A spokesman of the State Department on December 10 said the United States hoped the Biafran government would accept the assurances given and agree to daytime flights.[16] The answer from Biafra was that the Nigerian promise would have to be guaranteed by a neutral power, a quite impossible demand, both because of the sensitivities of Nigeria toward foreign intervention and because of the long-established position of the International Red Cross as a neutral guarantor itself.[17]

Still working on the negotiating front after the failure of the OAU in Addis Ababa, Kale Williams exchanged letters at Christmastime with Curle, Martin and Volkmar, probing the possibilities of talks under the Commonwealth Secretariat or even another attempt at Quaker auspices. Volkmar got strong indications from persons he talked to in New York that the hawks clearly held the upper hand in Lagos. On November 17, the Nigerian chief of staff had announced the final offensive. Such an announcement had been made many times before, but this time the army was operating under more unified command and the Soviet Union had supplied high-precision 122 mm guns in its ongoing effort to win favor in this largest of African states.

16. The *Times* (London), 11 December 1969, p. 1.

17. According to Stremlau, Ojukwu steadily refused to accept daytime flights because he needed the cover of night relief flights to protect the clandestine arms shuttle. (*The International Politics of the Nigerian Civil War 1967-1970*, p. 246.)

The End of the War

The end came more rapidly than anyone anticipated. A forced move of the Quaker-Mennonite Service team in late December west of the Imo River was caused by the advance of the First and Third Division of Federal forces from the north and south on the Umuahia-Aba road, cutting off the Eastern sector, the largest food-producing area. The road from Onitsha to Enugu in the north was cleared by the Second Division, leaving the Uli airstrip open to attack. When Ojukwu rushed forces to defend Uli, Owerri came under attack from the Third Marine Command Division. Suddenly it was all over.

On January 10, General Ojukwu announced that he was traveling out of Biafra for a short time "in search of peace." As he boarded the last flight out of Uli airstrip, he offered to give up sovereignty for security, a formula that might have succeeded when proposed more than a year earlier by Dr. Azikiwe, Raph Uwechue, and others.

Lieutenant Colonel Philip Effiong, left in command by Ojukwu, instructed his men on January 12 to lay down their arms. General Gowon accepted the surrender and ordered that all measures be taken to effect a peaceful transfer without any vindictiveness. He saluted the soldiers who had fought so bravely on the other side as "victims of Ojukwu's vicious propaganda and the machinations of certain foreign governments" and welcomed all the people back as brothers.[18] Instead of declaring a day of victory, he declared three days of prayer. The story of General Gowon embracing Colonel Effiong, published all over the land, was the symbol of reconciliation.

The reality of amnesty and reconciliation in the postwar

18. Broadcast at midnight, January 12, 1970 (Kirk-Greene, *Crisis,* vol. 2, p. 452).

period went a long way to corroborate the policies that General Gowon had enunciated all along. From the beginning of the war in July 1967 he had issued an *Operational Code of Conduct for the Nigerian Army* to all men in uniform. This code demanded the highest conduct in dealing with civilians, surrendering soldiers, and property in war areas. Nigerian forces must show the whole world, the code stated, that they could follow the Geneva Conventions explicitly, because they were not fighting a foreign enemy but only subduing a rebellion of Ojukwu and his clique and bringing back their Ibo brothers into the unity of the nation.[19]

One of the many repeated announcements of this policy was given June 30, 1969, in the statement on relief by Chief Enaboro, minister of public information, who justified his government's willingness to allow supplies to go through the blockade to civilian victims. "The Federal Government realizes that it is necessary to demonstrate to the Ibo that Federal forces are not fighting them as people . . . and that after the current war Nigerians intend to live in peaceful and equal compatriotism with their Ibo brothers."[20]

While ugly incidents had been perpetrated by Federal soldiers, especially in the early days, the international observer team, called in by General Gowon in September 1968 in an unprecedented action to monitor the Federal troops, confirmed the high degree of restraint. Pro-Biafra voices dismissed the reports of this team as one-sided and limited in scope, but the reports gradually won confidence in the non-committed world.

It is remarkable that the Ibo claim of genocide gained such wide acceptance throughout the world. Stemming as it did largely from prewar incidents of mob violence but broadcast as a fact of current Nigerian policy by a remarkably proficient

19. Ibid., vol. 1, p. 456.
20. Ibid., vol. 2, pp. 406-07.

Biafran propaganda bureau in Geneva, this charge of genocide became the ground for rescue operations of all kinds, from relief to military. The exaggerated response of major elements of the world press to the conclusion of the war was a final tribute to the pertinacity of the accusation. There were dire predictions of millions of refugees dying for lack of food and of a bloodbath perpetrated on the rebellious leaders.

The Nigerian government on its side did little to allay the suspicions of the foreign press. The government insisted that it would handle the situation in its own way, largely with its own resources. It would accept no aid from the four countries it claimed were identified with the Biafran side nor from the largest organizations involved in the illegal airlift. It refused to keep the Uli airstrip open and refused offers of massive airlifts from the United States and Britain. As Gowon himself said, "We must get rid of Uli, get it out of our minds. It has been used too much in international politics."[21] Thus, seven thousand tons of food were stranded at Sao Tomé while millions were reported hungry and many starving in Owerri.

There was little news from the recent battle areas, and the restrictions on visits by correspondents made everyone suspicious. A special government tour to rectify this was mishandled in a way to make matters worse. After a week of waiting, about eighty correspondents went to the airport early January 19, where they were promised passage to Port Harcourt and the battle area of Owerri. The first of three planes took off early, circled back, and was taken over by a party of finely dressed African men and women who were going to the wedding of the military governor of Rivers State. Seven hours later two planes took most of the sweltering, angry correspondents, but only after they had staged a demonstration marching single file towards General Gowon,

21. Interview in *New York Times,* 23 January 1970.

who had come to the airport to meet UN General Secretary U Thant. The reports from Owerri stressed the devastation and suffering, and the correspondents were subject to more delays on the way back to Lagos.

The Quaker organizations had the advantage of a remarkable firsthand look at the situation from the trip that the field director, his son, and two representatives of the Friends Service Council, London, made from Lagos through most of Eastern Nigeria during the two weeks from January 5 to 20, when the last fighting and surrender took place.

After visiting the site of a rehabilitation project that the Quakers were undertaking in the villages of Asaba and Ibusa in Mid-West State, the group of four ferried across the Niger River to Onitsha on January 8. Sounds of distant artillery fire were heard as they passed through the devastated city, but they drove the forty-eight miles to Enugu without difficulty on a road liberated only four days before. They were the second nonmilitary vehicle on the road. South of Enugu they visited the newly installed Quaker medical-relief team at Awgu. Driving down the road through Umuahia and south, where the first breakthrough of the Federal forces occurred in late December, they joined their Quaker Service colleagues at Ikot Usen, Southeastern State, in taking care of new refugees. At a prison camp nearby, they observed a group of five hundred Biafran soldiers, in nominal detention, well fed and cared for, with only three armed guards and sometimes none at all. They were at the Quaker Service house when news of Ojukwu's flight on January 10 and Colonel Effiong's surrender on January 12 came through. On January 13, they went with part of the service team to start a program of medical-nutritional work in Arochuku, a group of villages with a population of around seventy thousand in one of the most deprived areas of the Eastern wing of Biafra. They reported suffering and serious deprivation in that area, but not mass starvation.

Kale Williams and his party then made their way back to Lagos by the same route. They were in Enugu on Janaury 19 and reported that the change in ten days was unbelievable. The population had almost tripled. The streets were jammed with cars of returning Ibos, who were registering with the East Central State government and going back to work. The road to Onitsha was crowded with cars, nearly all bearing Biafran license plates. Back in Lagos they reported that conditions in former Biafran territory were bad, but not as reported in the international press. They had not visited Owerri, the most congested area and the scene of the last battles, but soon had reports from Andrew Clark, head of the relief team in Southeastern State, who was called to Owerri to help the Nigerian Red Cross set up a food distribution system.

The resolution of the Nigerian government to take things into their own hands and ban agencies they felt had been pro-Biafran, such as the World Council of Churches and Caritas, was understandable, Andrew Clark reported, though it meant increased suffering. He wrote that difficulties were tremendous, with a limited relief staff, quite strange to the area, trying to handle so many refugees. Relief supplies were coming in much too slowly by truck, and they could have used a Western airlift. But in view of two years of Nigerian hostility toward foreign-organized relief, Clark understood and accepted the need to be patient.

Summarizing the general impressions of Quaker workers, Kale Williams reported:

> There is some severe malnutrition and many people are showing the effects of long periods with inadequate diets, but there was no evidence of large numbers of people faced with imminent starvation. Medical and relief teams from the Nigerian Red Cross and other voluntary agencies have moved promptly into the area formerly held by Biafra, and have incorporated the supplies and workers

of relief agencies working on that side of the conflict. There is a great movement of people as those who have been displaced return to their own homes, but there has been no new uprooting of civilian populations.

The general amnesty declared by the Federal Government has been given effect. Former Biafran civilians, soldiers and policemen are moving freely and many of them had resumed their jobs under Federal auspices in the first week.

There have been no reports of reprisals or misuse of weapons by Federal troops occupying the liberated areas and lives of civilians and surrendered soldiers have been protected.[22]

To complete the Quaker conciliation enterprise, both Adam Curle and John Volkmar were sent into Nigeria to observe the postwar situation and offer any further conciliatory help that might be appropriate. Arriving in Lagos January 16, Curle found that Kale Williams was already touring the country, so it was best to pursue "a policy of masterly inaction."[23] Using his time while waiting to assess the mood in Lagos, he reported to the service bodies that the Nigerians were emotionally sensitive about foreign intervention, deeply resentful of the groups that had helped Biafra, and inclined to reject any offers of assistance made in such a way as to suggest that the Nigerians could not solve their own problems. Government officials insisted that reconciliation must be a Nigerian affair. Foreign relief had supported the rebels; now Nigerian generosity must welcome them back. Rather than importuning officials with offers of help, it was better to wait until the Nigerian government set up a new administra-

22. "Observations on the End of a War," 21 January 1970, AFSC Archives, p. 1.
23. "Report on Visit to Nigeria," 16–23 January 1970, AFSC Archives.

tive arrangement for rehabilitation, which was in process. Williams, returning on January 20, confirmed the impression that Curle had gained in Lagos that the Federal government was acting with humanity and good sense. The two decided that they had no good reason to seek a talk with General Gowon and instead sent a letter expressing their respect and admiration.

John Volkmar spent a week in February visiting Lagos, Enugu, and Ibadan. He reported on the remarkable incidents of reconciliation, such as Hamzat Ahmadu entertaining his Biafran counterpart, Mr. Onyegbola. One Nigerian explained the phenomenon:

> You Europeans will never be able to understand what has happened. If you knew the extended family system you'd know what is going on. For three years we have had a quarrel in the family and for three years the other members of the family have been vainly searching for a solution. Now that one member had defeated the other, the whole family is rejoicing and expressing their joy in being reunited again and are trying to forget the past.[24]

In the universities, Volkmar found much animosity. The University of Ibadan was receiving returned Ibo staff coolly, and the students coming back to the University of Nigeria at Nsukka felt insecure about the future. Renewing his contacts among students and professors, Volkmar made suggestions for reestablishing communication across the lines through exchange of letters, visits, or joint work camps.

Weaknesses in the Nigerian Federation present from the beginning in the power struggle of the three largest ethnic groups brought the extremity of civil war. The Federal victory in the battlefield strongly reinforced the center, but there were still many forces of separation and discontent.

24. John Volkmar, "Trip Report," 24 February 1970, AFSC Archives.

Quaker workers saw the disparity between the North and South in education, wealth, and other matters as a major source of future weakness, and therefore a medical assistance program was instituted in the North in addition to programs in Mid-West and East Central States. This balance in assistance programs was acceptable to the Nigerians, and the Quaker work continued for two years after the war. The dialogues continued to draw individuals from various parts of Nigeria, but the kind of "internal reconciliation program" proposed in 1961 by Paul Blanshard was now seen more clearly than ever as a task for Nigerians and not appropriate for an outside organization.

Summary and Evaluation

Was Negotiation Possible?

Was a negotiated settlement at any time possible or advisable? Certainly the hawks in Lagos said all along that military defeat of the rebellion was the only solution and all efforts to talk of terms were not only futile but contrary to the goal of national unity. Several historians in retrospect point to the gap in the war aims of the two sides and say that negotiations were never a serious possibility and talk about talks was only used by each side to woo international support. For example, John De St. Jorre, a balanced and responsible reporter, says, "Neither side was prepared to moderate its mutually irreconcilable demands and each as events proved was prepared to fight it out to the bitter end."[25] This is easy to say after the

25. *The Brother's War*, p. 302. See also: Kirk-Greene, *Crisis*, vol. 2, p. 45 and passim; Sir Cecil Rex Niven, *The War of Nigerian Unity 1967-70* (Tolowa, N.J.: Rowman and Littlefield, 1971), p. 143; Frederick Forsyth, *The Biafra Story* (Baltimore: Penguin, 1969), chap. 12; Suzanne Cronje, *The World and Nigeria; the Diplomatic History of the Biafran War, 1967-70* (London: Sedgewick and Jackson, 1972), p. 319; and

fact, but let us review the phases of negotiation briefly to see whether there were not some real possibilities of a settlement.

The first efforts at peacemaking by the Commonwealth Secretariat in October 1967 and the OAU in November were premature. They came at a time of great enthusiasm for Biafran independence on the one side and hopes for quickly crushing the rebellion on the other. It was at this time that the Quakers did not respond to a Nigerian suggestion that they convey terms of surrender to the other side, a move that would certainly have jeopardized any future role as inter-mediaries.

In February and March 1968 when the Quakers did become involved in direct intervention, the Federal armies had re-duced the breakaway state to the Ibo homeland, with only Port Harcourt left as a point of contact by sea or land with the outside world. Gowon predicted in his 1968 New Year's message that the war would be over by the end of March. When the Quakers visited him on February 3 he was skeptical about talks but willing to have the Quaker team sound out the other side. When they returned to him on March 19 with the report of their meeting with Ojukwu, it was clear that the promised deadline for ending the war would not be met, and it seems likely that the Quaker report contributed to a new understanding in Lagos of the unity and determination of the Biafrans. Gowon showed more interest in talks and was glad to have the Quakers promoting negotiation along with several other groups. But talks, he said, had to be on the basis of two preconditions: renouncing secession and accepting the twelve-state system. In the Biafran view, this amounted to surrender, and they were far from ready to give up at that point.

Stremlau, *The International Politics of the Nigerian Civil War 1967-70*, passim. But see, per contra, Hatch, *Nigeria*, p. 291 and Nbeyong Udo Akpan, *The Struggle for Secession, 1966-70, A Personal Account of the Nigerian Civil War* (London: F. Cass, 1972), chap. 11.

There ensued the Biafran political activity to gain recognition and supplies and the military activity of the Nigerians to cut off Port Harcourt in the south. Each side was pushing for a stronger position, and the climate was not conducive to negotiations. Yet the series of talks through the period from May to August moving from London to Kampala, Niamey to Addis Ababa had potential at the time and seem futile only in retrospect.

The Quakers played an auxiliary role to the Commonwealth Secretariat and OAU in this period, the most noteworthy part being their transmittal of a message from Dr. Eni Njoku to Lagos in August. Evidence that the Biafrans were thinking of major concessions at that time comes from Mr. Nbeyong Udo Akpan, chief of the Biafran Civil Service, who was one of the negotiating team in Addis Ababa in August 1968. He reports that Ojukwu was confident that the meeting would end the war, since he would offer to Gowon concessions, including the acceptance of Nigerian unity and confederation along the lines of the Aburi agreement.[26] As we have seen, Ojukwu's opening speech, a long history of past abuses, did not sound at all conciliatory, and Enahoro's response was equally uncompromising. Nevertheless, there were elements of a possible solution, and in the light of Akpan's report and later events the message that Dr. Eni Njoku, the chief remaining Biafran negotiator, asked the Quakers to take to Lagos was a genuine feeler.

The indication that the Biafrans were willing to consider autonomy within a loose union made an impression and was seriously considered in Lagos, though it had the defect of not coming from Ojukwu himself. But it was too late to strengthen the peace party against the war party, which was clamoring to get the armies rolling before Biafra could be re-

26. Akpan, *The Struggle for Secession,* chap. 11.

armed by France. Thus, Gowon announced the "last push" on August 24, 1968.

Perhaps the greatest possibility for peace was in the last days of September 1968, when the Biafran position in the battlefield was seriously threatened and French aid had not yet materialized. It was at this time that the Quakers carried on a major initiative, going back to Biafra twice and to Lagos three times. On September 19 in Biafra there was great interest in talking to Nigerian representatives. The report of this in Lagos received the full hearing by nine government officers on September 25. By that time, however, the Nigerians had heard of the split in Biafran leadership they had been looking for all along. Several Biafran leaders abroad, including Dr. Azikiwe and Raph Uwechue, listening to overtures from the other side, began to see that the Ibos might gain security by giving up sovereignty, whereas if they continued to seek independent nationhood, they courted complete defeat. The Nigerians suspected that these persons did not represent Ojukwu and his hard-liners. The Quakers were asked to go back to Biafra, and on the second visit they found military and civilian morale much improved. Reinforced by French arms and financing, the Biafran leaders closed ranks under Ojukwu and raised again the banner of sovereignty as a necessity for security.

Stalemate and talk of talks followed for the next year. The last Quaker political involvement in October 1969 was at a time when there again seemed considerable hope that a final push by Federal forces could be avoided. From the stage when each side was stating preconditions for talks while claiming no preconditions, there was a shift to the realistic formula that each side would come with its own preconditions, or as the Biafran spokesman put it to Kale Williams, the Biafrans would come believing they were independent, and the Nigerians would come believing that Biafrans were part of one Nigeria. But by the time Williams reported this softening position back in Lagos on November 21, the momentum for a final military victory was already well developed and the Federal government was not interested in the December Addis Ababa meeting unless it meant surrender.

Undoubtedly, the odds against a negotiated settlement were high at all times, and yet the factors contributing to a softening or hardening of each party's position were complex and highly variable. Any one of the factors, such as internal factionalism, particularly within the Federation, degree of foreign support, economic resources, military position of the armies, or determination and solidarity of leadership, might at some point have altered the course of negotiations toward settlement. Conciliators should be as realistic as possible, but must also have enough optimism to pursue the possible, even if not probable, goal. The Quakers shared this kind of optimism with many other individuals and groups who were striving to find a means of ending the war and the huge suffering entailed. On two or three occasions there were substantial reasons for optimism.

Credibility of the Quaker Team

The success of the Quaker team in gaining access to political leaders on both sides was more a matter of "personal qualifications" than "ascribed resources," to use Oran Young's categories (chapter 3). In distinction from the situation in Germany and the India-Pakistan subcontinent, there was little general knowledge of Quakers in West Africa. That influential persons had come to know individual Quakers through participating in Quaker programs, however, did ensure a welcome for John Volkmar and Adam Curle on their first visit in May 1967.

The willingness of officials to talk frankly and openly was largely a personal matter. It was John Volkmar that Mr. Ahmadu would talk to at any hour of the day or night, not any Quaker. Adam Curle had contacts from academic circles. Continuity in the team of conciliators was important, though it was found possible to extend this confidence to associates, first to Walter Martin and then Kale Williams.

The personality of the participants was also important: their friendly, low-keyed approach and their understanding of African dignity and resentment of white domination. Their willingness to take risks for no personal gain impressed the Nigerian leaders, who thought that anyone going into the rebel enclave must be dedicated. On the Biafran side the leaders had had personal contact with the Quakers, and since their cause depended a great deal on support from the outside, they welcomed the Quaker intervention in conciliation or relief. While the Quakers as a whole did not have a public reputation as peace negotiators, Adam Curle's references to his work on the Quaker India-Pakistan Mission added weight to his initial presentation. Although Nigerians and Biafrans were at times inflamed against Great Britain, the United States, or both, the fact that the team had both British and American members was not as important as it had been in the Pakistan-India situation.

Initially the personal resources of the participants was most important, but as the operation continued, the organization as such became a prominent factor. In the middle of 1968, it was "the Quakers" who were welcomed on both sides in a Mission of Inquiry into Relief Needs. This organizational and individual confidence in the Quakers remained high to the end of the war, despite the strain on the Federal side caused by the two incidents of relief publicity that we have recounted.

An important element was that the Quakers were able to keep their conciliatory efforts out of the limelight. It is surprising that given the degree of involvement of the Quaker team at all stages of negotiation and the press's avid interest in all information, there was only one minor leak. An item in

the *Times* on November 8, 1968, which reported on the
failure of parties to negotiate, mentioned incidentally that
two informal contacts in Umuahia, "one of them a Quaker
delegation," reported that Ojukwu was adamant against
negotiation. Walter Martin wrote a letter to the Biafran
representative in New York denying that any of his colleagues had spoken to the press or had reported to anyone
in those terms. The explanation was accepted and not mentioned further. The Quakers themselves were guilty of a slight
lapse when *The Friend* in London, December 13, 1968,
reporting on a session of the Meeting for Sufferings, included the reference to a confidential report on efforts of
Friends representatives to bring about negotiations. Walter
Martin took the persons responsible sternly to task, saying,
"Not only the details of our peace activities, but the fact that
we are active at all, were confidential."

While maintaining a closed door to the press, and to a large
extent to their own constituency, the Quakers inspired confidence by the openness of their reporting of their own activities to the officials of the two sides. At each major interview session they gave a rundown on all the various people
on both sides with whom they had spoken. Neither side
seemed worried that Quaker intermediaries would report
confidential information, nor did either side seek to elicit
such information from the team members.

The Quakers put their credibility under some jeopardy
when they undertook to sponsor two non-Quaker efforts in
the spring of 1969. The reason and circumstances of the temporary and loose alliances have already been noted. The advice of a Nigerian official at the United Nations, which they
did not follow, was probably sound. In December 1968 he
asserted that the Quaker role was known, understood, and
appreciated by the Federal government, but the motivation
of certain other persons was unknown. Thus, the Quakers
might be misunderstood if they were linked up with proposals

they could not fully support from their own convictions. This judgment was confirmed at the close of the war when in a private conversation Nigerian authorities criticized the Quakers for having abetted the efforts of other parties whose neutrality the officials questioned.

The Process of Conciliation

The conciliatory functions performed by the Quaker team moved through stages similar to those identified in the two previous studies, from listening in order to understand each side, to communicating the reality and perceptions of the other side, to analyzing the situation and making proposals for solution. An additional activity important from the beginning was the effort to get representatives of the parties together to talk directly about the issues.

The listening process was successful for the listeners. They learned the two points of view thoroughly and on several occasions said they were thankful not to have to adjudicate the dispute since it was so hard to choose between the sides. Again their attitude was one of "balanced partiality" rather than impartiality.

The effectiveness of the Quaker interpreters in changing perceptions of the parties in conflict is impossible to measure, but some things can be said. The Quaker influence was one of several supporting a policy in Lagos aimed toward negotiating peace. Although such a settlement was not achieved, the military victory was followed by a magnanimity toward the defeated rebels hardly paralleled in recent history.[27] The flight of Ojukwu made it easier to sustain the view that the

---

27. See John De St. Jorre, *The Brothers' War*: "The most outstanding feature of the end of the war was the remarkable atmosphere of reconciliation, especially at the top levels, but also lower down . . . . 'There will be no Nuremburg Trials here,' Gowon promised shortly after the collapse and the spirit behind his statement went right down the line" (p. 407).

secession had all along been the work of him and a small clique. The restraining hand of General Gowon and the doves in Lagos was clearly evident in the peace terms that resulted, with no vindictive trials or executions of rebel leaders and pardon for rebel civil servants and reinstatement in their former jobs. One qualified observer said he thought the remarkably peaceful end to hostilities was in part due to the way in which the Quakers had constantly tried to straighten out perceptions distorted by fear and anger.

On the other side the Quaker team failed to make much of an impression on Ojukwu. They did not see him after the first two visits, when the Quaker delegation was primarily listening rather than reporting or suggesting. Thus, they did not have any opportunity to discuss with him directly the facts that might help correct such Biafran illusions as genocide, Northern domination, or imminent defection of the Western State. These themes recurred again and again in Ojukwu's public speeches. The Quakers had some influence on associates of the general. For example, in a conversation with John Volkmar in February 1969, Raph Uwechue, Biafran representative in Paris, testified that his realization that there were people like the Quaker team who had no vested interest in the war, but for humanitarian reasons were making every effort to help bring it to an end, helped him rethink his own position and decide to protest to Ojukwu and then resign. But there was not much possibility of an indirect influence on Ojukwu, since even close associates who had traveled out of Biafra were unable to change his mind.

In carrying messages, making proposals, and entering the negotiating process itself, the Quaker team moved into a more central role than in the German or India-Pakistan conflicts. They were, for example, asked to carry specific messages and sound out specific proposals from one side to the other on a more sustained basis than the previous examples. The Quakers were far from being the only intermediaries, and General

Gowon implied as much in several talks he had with the team members, but he seemed happy to use the Quakers as one of the agencies available for seeking negotiations.

At several points the Quakers suggested proposals of unilateral action to each side, such as pauses in bombing, daytime relief flights, and a halt to propaganda in order to create a better climate for negotiations. When the possibility of talks was blocked by preconditions set by first one side and then the other, the Quaker spokesmen proposed a preliminary discussion of the implications of preconditions. They even developed a framework of settlement based on a paper by Professor Friedrich aimed at synthesizing the goal of Nigerian unity on the one side and the goal of autonomy and security for the Biafrans on the other. Of several alternatives, such as Uwechue's six-state proposal and Sir Louis Mbanefo's return to four states, the Curle-Friedrich formulation had the advantage of leaving the twelve-state system intact, provided that Biafra would give up its unrealistic claims to Rivers and Southeastern States. None of these possibilities could be explored, however, until representatives from each side sat down together to talk. A major part of the Quaker effort was aimed at bringing this about.

The Quaker offer to provide a setting for talks was a potentially significant form of third-party intervention, although rather unrealistic. The Quakers stumbled into this role by simply trying to get people together for informal, unofficial sharing of views on the well-established pattern of the Quaker seminars. They realized that in a polarized situation, where "traitors" are imprisoned or executed, leading citizens of one side cannot afford to meet their opposite numbers in a group situation, no matter how secret, unless sanctioned by their government, but they did not realize that only responsible officials as Ojukwu specified would get such approval. Thus, a simple plan of a seminar across the lines proposed by President Diori was transformed into the idea of a major conference more appropriately sponsored by official bodies like the Commonwealth Secretariat and the OAU. Yet the Quakers were encouraged in September 1968 and again in October 1969 to come back again with their proposal for quiet talks. They went so far as to draw up a paper outlining the circumstances of such a meeting, which was worked over by the representatives of each side. The spokesmen of the two sides did not rule out the possibility of such a meeting, and yet they probably did not take it seriously. The attitude of the Nigerians on several occasions was that an unofficial meeting under the Quaker auspices was acceptable, but if it was to be semiofficial, as the Biafrans insisted, then the sponsor should be the OAU. In looking back the proposal seemed more important as a convenient talking point than as a viable proposition. It justified the movement between opposing forces, which was valuable on other accounts.

Assistance to Official Negotiations
Official talks under official auspices were at all times the goal of the Quaker intermediaries. The proposed seminar under Quaker auspices was intended to pave the way for more official sessions. Thus, the Quaker team members devoted a great deal of thought to the most appropriate and acceptable auspices for talks. On the one hand, they tried to persuade the parties to accept the proffer of mediation, whether it was the Commonwealth Secretariat or the Committee of the Organization of African Unity; on the other hand, they sought to help those bodies improve their position as intermediaries, the one by a visit of its officials to Biafra, the other by a change of composition to include African states sympathetic to Biafra. They also probed the possibilities of United Nations good offices.

When the parties did agree to official talks, the Quakers were on hand to give assistance. The high point of this Quaker role was the work of Adam and Anne Curle at the Commonwealth Secretariat Meetings at Kampala in May 1968. Curle explained the complementary relation of unofficial to official efforts: "It is not our role to arrange a conference such as this. . . . But there is a lot of persuasion, clarification, message carrying, listening, defusing, honest brokering, encouraging, and liaison with the Commonwealth Secretariat to be done."[28] Even at the very end, in December 1969, when the OAU-sponsored meeting in Addis Ababa failed, the Quakers were talking with the parties about going back to the Commonwealth Secretariat.

Use of Political Pressure in Conciliation

A prime tenet of Quaker conciliators was to abstain from bringing political pressure to bear and to make the most of their lack of political power. As we have seen, the credibility of the Quaker conciliation was based on its nonpolitical nature, its inability to call down sanctions of any kind. This enabled the team workers to be accepted and listened to as human beings of integrity by both sides. The lack of political power by the Quakers, who are a very small sect with little influence and less resources, was made into a general principle of "private diplomacy" by Adam Curle in his book *Making Peace*. "What is intrinsic to private diplomacy is its absolute separation from political interest and hence its potentiality to permit an open and relaxed relationship between human beings."[29] This does not mean, of course, that political power is unimportant for official intermediaries. In some cases it may be a prime requisite for success.

An instance in which the Quakers came close to violating this tenet is instructive. When the war and negotiations were

28. Letter from Kampala, 1 June 1968, AFSC Archives.
29. Adam Curle, *Making Peace* (London: Tavistock Publications, 1970), p. 239. A valuable discussion of the whole process of third-party conciliation based largely on his Nigerian experience is included in chapter 19.

bogged down in stalemate in the winter of 1968–69 and thousands of Biafran civilians were dying, Adam Curle, casting about in desperation, proposed bringing the United States in as an uncommitted neutral force which might be able to bring the parties together. With a Harvard associate he gave a memorandum to contacts in the State Department and in the White House, outlining why the United States should seek an arms limitation agreement by the three major supplying powers and invite the two sides to declare a ceasefire and enter into talks. "The role seen for the United States is not that of an intervenor, but rather a peacemaker and generous bringer of aid to a suffering people, affected by the war on both sides of the firing line."[30]

Since Biafran policy all along had sought to internationalize the quarrel, while Nigerian policy insisted on its domestic nature, the effort to secure United States good offices was bound to seem one-sided. By July, Adam Curle counseled against any further Quaker involvement along this line, since he saw clearly that though intended as an impartial move, it had developed into an effort to bring United States pressure on Nigeria in favor of Biafra.

Practical Aspects of Conciliatory Activity

The Quaker participants were firmly convinced of the importance of more than one person on each errand of conciliation. The needs for sharing were great indeed. The work alternated between long periods of tedium, discouragement, and confusion and bouts of excitement, exhilaration, and tension. Members of a mission could help each other keep a calm perspective, whether playing cards to while away an inordinate waiting period or a quick glance of reinforcement in a tense interview. Closely tied to this emotional and psycho-

---

30. "Possibilities of a Nigerian Settlement," confidential document, 11 April 1969, AFSC Archives.

logical support was the benefit of more than one mind in analyzing tangled issues, preparing to maximize the brief time of an interview, or figuring out the next steps. Teamwork implies that individual styles of operating can be harnessed in the group effort. The participants achieved a high degree of compatibility in spite of considerable differences in style and background.

It is unfortunate that all three could not have been together on some of the more important occasions, such as the August 1968 visit with Gowon and the October 1968 visit with eight of Ojukwu's close advisors. One cannot say what difference it might have made, but from the team's own guidelines of operations the effort should have been well worth it.

Lack of sufficient staff support on trips was troublesome. The kind of trips and interviews carried out by team members required an inordinate amount of time for such detailed arrangements as visas and reservations, chartered flights, requesting, confirming, and changing appointments, and all the work of writing proposals, reports, notes, and letters. On the India-Pakistan mission Friends' staff in both Delhi and Karachi could take care of much of the detail. In Nigeria the team members themselves had to do it all.

The home offices could have provided better coordination. The whole operation was begun and continued on an ad hoc basis, which provided flexibility but lacked continuity and close attention. The actual conciliation teams were picked from persons with other responsibilities, although they were prepared to concentrate on the Nigerian Civil War when needed. Coordinating responsibility was carried in the headquarters by several people with other problems on their minds. It would have been helpful to have one person at the home office either in Philadelphia or London spending full time coordinating the whole program. Such a person could have kept abreast of news reports in order to analyze con-

tinually the possibilities of conciliation, maintained a flow
of information among the main protagonists, and helped plan
the actual visits, perhaps participating as an assistant on some
of the trips. Such staffing was proposed by Adam Curle, but
the Quaker organizations, prone to think in terms of slim
budgets, never considered it seriously.

A major limitation to such auxiliary resources of the operation was, of course, financing. Travel under the circumstances
was inordinately expensive, since team members had to take
flights wherever and whenever needed and at times use
chartered planes. Other expenses were minimal, since no
salaries or consultant fees were involved. Funding came mostly from one foundation and at first was on a trip-to-trip basis.
Credibility had to be secured not only with the two conflicting parties, but also with the funding source. Only after
officers of the foundation received firsthand reports was
their initial skepticism overcome, and only toward the end of
the war was a drawing account set up. Grants when they came
were generous enough to cover all expenses and were not as
much a limitation on adequate staff as Quaker parsimony.[31]

Conclusion

One may conclude that the Quakers, in offering to set up an
unofficial meeting, were drawn into a conciliatory role which
they sustained with sensitivity, flexibility and imagination,
and without making mistakes serious enough to detract from
the whole effort. They were only one of several official and
unofficial agencies trying to bring about a settlement. Such a
negotiated solution was not achieved, but the peace terms
resulting after the military solution were imbued with the
spirit of conciliation. The amazingly generous policies of
Gowon and the Federal government were part of a continuing

31. The Ford Foundation supplied the major part of the expenses
($28,510).

policy that favored negotiations from the very beginning. An adamant position against talks would have meant dominance in Lagos of the bitterest anti-Ibo groups with strong leading from the North toward extreme vindictiveness, which might have brought some fulfillment to the Biafran prophecy of genocide. Any contribution to prevent such an eventuality was of utmost importance to relieve suffering and insure a better future for the people. It is in this respect that the Quaker effort, along with many others, can be said to have contributed to success.

Chapter Five

Quaker Conciliation and Peace Research

Although many of the ways of operating outlined in these case studies pertain to other organizational frameworks, this chapter points out certain unusual characteristics of the Quaker approach which give rise to special assets and limitations. We will discuss these special attributes as they fit into the broader picture of third-party intervention, and then consider the question of the kinds of conflict in which the conciliation we have been describing is appropriate and the types where it may be inappropriate.

Quaker Values and Conciliation

Concern

While not ignoring the many factors making for successful intervention in a controversy, the Quakers set great store on the element of concern, the religiously inspired impulse to action. There were many conflict situations in the period from 1960 to 1973 in which the Quaker organizations did not feel called to intervene: the southern Sudan was the site of intense and prolonged conflict,[1] the Kurds were battling

1. The All-Africa Council of Churches and The World Council of Churches played a major role in third-party conciliation, and some

for independence for many years in Iran and Iraq; and there was a disastrous civil war in Indonesia. What led the Quaker organizations to choose to work in one place and not another? The decision was less an objective assessment than a subjective interest on the part of individuals whose past or present involvement led them to feel strongly moved to action. Most of the conflicts of the world were presented by individuals or groups to the Service bodies at one time or another for Quaker action, but only a few brought a response as a result of a Quaker concern. In keeping with the strong emphasis in Quakerism on experience rather than theory or creed, the concern arises directly out of the experience of one or more individuals. A news item in the paper about the massacre of Ibos in Kano may stir sympathy or prayer but will not lead to a concern unless someone because of past experience or deep sensitivity feels involved and responsive to the particular human need. The concern of John Woolman, the supremely conscientious eighteenth-century Quaker, for the degradation of the Negro slaves and the moral plight of the slaveowners arose from his personal experiences with the purchase and sale of human beings in New Jersey. In each of the case studies presented here we have documented the concern of certain Friends who had prior involvement in the situation.

The initial concern is then tested in a group: the monthly or the yearly meeting, as it largely was in the past, or a special committee established for oversight in certain areas of concern. The Indian Affairs Committee of the London Yearly Meeting was such a group and acted as a precursor to the

---

Quakers were involved near the end. See Elfan Rees, "Exercises in Private Diplomacy: Selected Activities of the Commission of the Churches on International Affairs," in Maureen R. Berman and Joseph E. Johnson, eds., *Unofficial Diplomats* (New York: Columbia University Press, 1977).

India Conciliation Group. For ambitious enterprises such as those described in this book, the special committees and programs set up by Quakers for international outreach after the two World Wars were important factors, enabling a constructive, informed, and sustained response to the situation.

It is the genius or plague of the Quaker movement, depending on one's point of view, that there are many approaches, and a concern ignored by one Quaker body may bring inspired support from another. It is even possible for an initiating group to create a newly constituted organization of supporters using the Quaker name, since that name has no copyright restrictions. During the Vietnam War a Quaker Action Group was organized in the United States as a non-tax-exempt agency to carry on nonviolent action against the war effort in a way which the American Friends Service Committee could not do without running the risk of losing tax exemption. An individual may even feel constrained at times to take his concern outside the Society of Friends, as Carl Heath did in forming the India Conciliation Group, both to avoid the possible veto of Friends consensus methods and to include in the conciliatory function a wider association.

However the group process for testing a concern is carried on, it will deal more or less rigorously with the important questions of resources available, prior experience in the conflict area, contacts with responsible decision makers, and in-depth knowledge of the various elements of the controversy. If the concern comes with the backing of "weighty Friends" and gains support, the necessary resources will usually be found from Quaker or non-Quaker contributions. At this point the wisdom of historical study and conflict research should be included in the testing process by the appropriate consultants and committee members. The committees thus play an important role, especially when an enterprise is first launched, in assessing, refining, and analyzing. A good example was the functioning of the Pakistan India Advisory Group of AFSC in the fall of 1965. But committees occasionally initiate. For example, the Meeting for Sufferings in London first broached the idea of a mission to India and Pakistan, and the AFSC's Committee on Africa sent staff to the Commonwealth negotiations in London in May 1968 during the Nigerian Civil War. Thus, organized bodies like the American Friends Service Committee and Friends Service Council with experience in international relations and wide contacts among knowledgeable people are in a better position to carry through a responsible program of this type of conciliation.

The Quaker method has the strength of combining the intensity of individual commitment with the tempering of group process. It has the weakness of being cumbersome and uncertain in application; the concern may be lacking or the committees may take an inordinate time.

One might postulate a more formalized "Quaker Conciliation Service" ready to prevent or allay conflict wherever it might occur in the world. My own estimate is that Quaker conciliation is best left to the more spontaneous reactions of individuals and groups with subsequent gathering in of resources as needed, rather than to a special bureau which might come to operate without the religious conditioning of Quaker "leading." We have attempted to describe this leading in the historical precedents and case studies. It is a combination of sympathy for suffering human beings and practical wisdom as to possibilities, coupled with a religious impulse, a sense that the work is important in the sight of God. None of these elements can be called forth at the sounding of an alarm bell. They depend ultimately on the right type of persons having the call to undertake the conciliation, either from their own experience or laid upon them by the group. The religious leading is both corporate and individual.

This sense of religious leading is closely related to Quaker involvement in practical programs of relief and rehabilitation in various parts of the world. The wide range of Quaker contacts give credibility to their efforts in conciliation. As a Quaker worker said after talking to a high government official in Pakistan: "It was fortunate we could cite to him and others this one tangible service project [urban community organization in Lahore], as Americans organizing political discussion alone are suspect in many Pakistan circles."[2]

The religious incentive guides all aspects of the conciliation process. For example, in the important initial listening process, as one Quaker conciliator has written:

> Because of the fundamental belief of that of God in every man, [the conciliators] treat the people with whom they are talking . . . with respect and attention. They really listen to them and I mean by that that they still the noise and confusion of their own thoughts and emotions and open themselves up completely to what the other person is trying to say, or perhaps feeling without expressing. This kind of listening . . . has a very real effect on the person being listened to. He becomes calmer, himself more receptive and open to ideas.[3]

So also the approach that I have called "balanced partiality"—a sensitivity to all the individuals and groups involved in a dispute—is enhanced for many by the divine prompting that is nourished in periods of quiet waiting upon the light. Here is an expression from a conciliator of his own experience:

> Rather than believe that one of the participants is the aggressor and the other the victim, he should discipline himself to concentrate his sympathies on all those who are suffering as a result of the conflict: the soldiers and civilians who have been killed, wounded, or deprived; the

2. Harold E. Snyder, "Report of Second Visit to Pakistan, December 17, 1966 to January 14, 1967," AFSC Archives.

3. Adam Curle, Letter to the author, 17 August 1976.

statesmen faced by agonizing choices; the children who have lost their fathers; all the people whose lives are being made harder and less happy; the millions whose minds are being twisted by propaganda. From this standpoint it is irrelevant to think of who is right and who is wrong: it is war that is wrong as a means of settling human disputes.[4]

Such intensity of belief and action for the wholeness of mankind may come to humanist, agnostic, or atheist. Quakers may fall far short of it, and yet they feel that they can gain an enhancement of their powers of compassion and a sense of guidance by seeking a higher source in worship. Another Quaker conciliator has said:

Inner peace comes from binding (*religio*) to God. . . . But this inner peace must not lead to inaction. It must be tied with a movement, a necessary unrest, which leads us to action. It is distinguished from the frantic movement of fear and anxiety; it is a movement still bound to God. The greatest mystics, even in their times of ecstasy, felt the need to return to the needs of the world.[5]

The particularities of the Quaker approach to conciliation and the limitation of resources available to Quakers would not hold for a broadly based International Conciliation Bureau, for which I would make a strong case. Such a bureau might have representatives in hot spots of potential conflict all over the world, a research arm ready to bring full knowledge to bear on any conflict, and a panel of experienced conciliators from many different countries ready to intervene when appropriate. Such a bureau might develop the advan-

4. Adam Curle, *Making Peace* (London: Tavistock Publications, 1971), p. 240.
5. Margarethe Lachmund, *Der innere Friede und die notwendige Unruhe* ("Inner Peace and Necessary Unrest") (Bad Pyrmont, Germany: Leonhard Friedrich, 1958), translation by Annette Carlsohn.

tages of credibility, salience, respect, and continuity defined by Oran Young.[6] Quaker insights and leadership could play a part. If well financed, it should be able to offer its services for third-party unofficial conciliation promptly and effectively. It would need to be independent of any national government and of the United Nations in order to act without political inhibitions.

Pacifism

The Quaker testimony against all war can be a bona fide for nonpartisanship in polarized situations. Another expression of this is from the book produced by a Quaker working party on the Middle East conflict:

> We believe, as do many people of other faiths, that the spirit of reconciliation is an ultimate power in human relations and that it can overcome the hatreds aroused by exaggerated nationalism and war. We recognize in our selves, and in all men, dark forces of fear, bitterness and hatred which can drive us toward violence. We may differ among ourselves as to how the forces of destruction may be best contained. However, we acknowledge an inner imperative, linked to the ancient Quaker testimony against war, to affirm our deep conviction that violence almost never brings a permanent solution and rarely produces even a short-term answer for deep and continuing tensions.[7]

The pacifist stand gives the intermediary a certain integrity in circumstances where he must of necessity carry the suspicion of being two-faced in his willingness to listen sympathetically to both sides. At the least it assures the listener that the

6. Oran R. Young, *The Intermediaries* (Princeton, N.J.: Princeton University Press, 1967), chap. 3.

7. American Friends Service Committee, *Search for Peace in the Middle East* (Greenwich, Conn.: Fawcett Publications, 1970), pp. 7–8.

proposed go-between is not intentionally going to help the war effort on the other side. The belief that it is better to suffer than to inflict suffering, which is at the heart of the pacifist position, is a disarming and persuasive element. General Gowon and his associates in Lagos were impressed by the willingness of the Quakers to take the risks of flying to Biafra in the search for peace.

On the negative side, the pacifist position of Quakers might make them suspect for any intervention in a shooting war. Quakers have dreamed of the day when "sometime they'll give a war and nobody will come,"[8] but short of such mass noncooperation, the individual commitment to oppose war becomes irrelevant to the immediate scene when the fighting begins. If leaders in a conflict thought the Quakers came to urge them to lay down their arms, they would not take the intervenors seriously. The Quaker conciliator cannot expect to convince protagonists in the conflict by arguing pacifism. He can make his own position clear, but then put it on the shelf, saying, in effect, to the war leaders on both sides, "I myself believe that all persons are children of God, and I cannot participate in taking the life of another without denying a part of my own soul, though I realize that from your point of view you cannot take this position at this time." A time-honored expression of this comes from the laws of Pennsylvania in the days when Quakers ruled the colony: "the people called Quakers who, though they do not, as the world is now circumstanced, condemn the use of arms in others, yet are principled against it themselves. . . ."[9]

This stand may mean that at times the Quaker intermediary role is accepted, but his arguments to persuade are not, espe-

8. Carl Sandburg, *The People Yes* (New York: Harcourt Brace and Co., 1936), p. 46.

9. Quoted by Sydney D. Bailey, "Some Reflections on the Use of Force," *The Friends' Quarterly* (April 1969), p. 258; from *Minutes of the Provincial Council of Pennsylvania*, vol. 4 (1739), p. 366.

cially when they have to do with degrees of military force or with military action versus negotiation. When John Volkmar on one occasion was trying to convince an official in the Lagos government that a negotiated peace would be best, he was countered with strong arguments for a decisive blow "to subdue the rebellion." The official probably minimized Volkmar's views as conditioned by "sentimental pacifism."

A greater hazard of the pacifist position may arise in a situation of gross inequity where pacifism may become identified with "passivism," the submission to injustice without protest. We will deal with this later under the heading "Conciliation or Confrontation."

Relations of Humanitarian Activity to Conciliation

An important aspect of Quaker conciliation is its long-standing relation to the service of relief and rehabilitation to persons suffering from man-made disasters. Quaker humanitarian work started in the relief of sufferings of its members during the persecutions of the seventeenth century and extended in the eighteenth and nineteenth centuries to other suffering groups "without distinction of race or creed."[10] It is not the quantity or effectiveness of relief that has been important, but rather a manner of giving that reinforces the dignity of the recipient and makes bridges across chasms of enmity.

Quaker relief in the Irish Potato Famine of 1848 was minute compared to that of the British government or other organizations, but it is remembered to this day as aid that was offered without political or religious strings. "The Quakers did not try to convert us," say Irish Catholics of today. While Quakers have undertaken massive relief on occasion, such as the child-feeding in Germany after World War I and the Gaza Strip refugee camps after the Palestinian War of 1948, gen-

10. For a history of Quaker relief, see John Ormerod Greenwood, *Quaker Encounters: Friends and Relief* (York, England: Sessions, 1975).

erally they have left such operations to larger, better financed organizations. The Quaker concern leads them to make a witness to Christian love whether they are going to solve the problem or not. To be sure, the witness must be well designed, intelligently applied, and effectively carried out in order to be a true witness, but the action is considered valid whether a solution results or not. "At least a candle has been lit," say the Quakers, "though the darkness continues."

In most of these relief situations there was an element of bridging across barriers or the evenhandedness that is important in changing perceptions of friend and foe. In Ireland it was a gesture of friendship from Protestant, privileged, British-oriented persons to the oppressed Irish Catholics. In Germany the citizens of conquering nations were offering the bread and soup of fellowship to the conquered foe. In other situations there was the element of compassion for both sides in bitter conflicts. Thus, the Quakers had helped many Jews escaping from nazism in the thirties, and they helped Arab refugees after the war in the Middle East in 1948.

The humanitarian activity of the Quakers has been both a form of conciliation itself and an opening to direct conciliation between the parties. Thus, when thousands of Algerians fled across the border into Morocco at the time of the Algerian War of Liberation from 1955 to 1962, Quaker relief workers in Oujda, Morocco, provided liaison points between leaders of the liberation movement and French officials in Morocco.

We have seen how prior relief work supported the credibility of Quaker representatives both in Germany and in the Indian subcontinent. The years of service showed that the Quaker representatives were not latecomers or unconcerned meddlers. Their appeals for peace to bring an end to suffering had the authority of direct experience.

The Nigerian Civil War was a different case. Quakers had not been involved in relief or rehabilitation programs, but they were in close touch with the situation and saw, as did many others, that the most effective way to avoid massive human suffering was to work for a negotiated end to the war. When suffering became acute and widespread, the Quakers undertook relief operations on both sides as part of their total effort at conciliation.

Other organizations engaged in extensive relief measures in Nigeria and Biafra realized that, important as these were, conciliation was more important. They tended to concentrate their attention on negotiations of "mercy corridors," but time and time again they were confronted with the fact that such avenues of relief could not be agreed upon without a broader settlement. At a meeting of Joint Church Aid in Rome, November 8–9, 1968, there was a realization of the tragic fact that providing food to the Biafrans might prolong the war and thus involve more suffering. The conference gave top priority to securing a negotiated end to the conflict. In July 1969, Walter Martin was called in to advise a group of World Council of Churches and British Council of Churches leaders on how their organizations could better contribute to conciliation. By then, however, these organizations had so jeopardized their neutrality as to be unacceptable to the Nigerian side in any intermediary capacity.

In 1947 the Nobel Peace Prize was awarded jointly to the (British) Friends Service Council and the American Friends Service Committee for the spirit of reconciliation which inspired their relief work rather than for the size and effectiveness of the work. As Gunnar Jahn, chairman of the Nobel Committee, said:

> It is not the extent of their work or its practical form which is most important. . . . It is rather the spirit which animates their work. Theirs is the message of good deeds, the message that men can come into contact with one another in spite of war and in spite of difference of race.

May we believe that here there is a hope of laying a foundation for peace among nations, of building up peace in man himself, so that it becomes impossible to settle disputes by the use of force.

Emphasizing the pacifism of Quakers as their credential for conciliation, Gunnar Jahn ended by quoting the words of Arnulf Overland, Norway's most famous living poet:

> Only those who are unarmed
> Can draw upon inexhaustible resources,
> The spirit alone can be victorious.[11]

Both the pacifist position of the Quakers and their long record of nonsectarian, nonpolitical humanitarian work serve to reinforce their position as an intervenor without any special interests to serve. The Quakers have no arms to sell, no ambition to buy oil. Their position of independence from governmental controls in the United States and Great Britain is carefully guarded. Scrupulous care is taken to insure that the contributions of donors do not influence basic policy. This is not to say that official parties, intervening on a very different basis in disputes, may find the sanctions necessary to reinforce peacemaking in the very implements of oil or arms that the unofficial third-party cannot and should not use.

Indeed, a hazard to Quaker effectiveness in a third-party role comes occasionally from humanitarian zeal rather than special interest. In the Nigerian Civil War, for example, it was not easy to hold to a neutral position in view of the outcries of abused humanity coming from Ibo students scattered in Europe and Africa. Along with many others, Quakers have a strong inclination to see injustices and come to the rescue of an oppressed group. A regional office of the AFSC asked the headquarters whether it should assist in a rally under the

11. Quoted in *The Friend* 105 (December 26, 1947): 1071.

title "International Witness Against Genocide—Fifty years Ago, the Armenians; Twenty-five Years Ago the Jews; Now the Ibo." The answer from Philadelphia, based on a different analysis of the conflict, advised against participation. The letter pointed to the needs of conciliation and suggested that the best way to help the suffering people on both sides was to help bring about a negotiated peace, and this required maintaining contact with both sides.

Another way in which humanitarian zeal may affect conciliation adversely arises from individual cases of alleged injustice. Quakers, because of their reputation, are frequently asked to intercede on behalf of individuals who appear to be wrongfully treated. Such intercession holds grave risks for a third-party role. Special pleading immediately recasts an individual in the role of advocate on one side rather than that of a neutral third party. The Quaker intermediary must assess all aspects of the situation to make as fair a decision as possible.

First comes the question of the facts of injustice. The facts are usually obscure in political cases; even the trial proceedings may not be revealed. The charge of espionage is a particularly difficult one for Quakers to assess, and Quakers have interceded in cases where the grounds turned out to be false. Minimal intercession in the form of discreet inquiries may be wholly appropriate to the third-party role as the mediator seeks to explain the damaging consequences of actions which heighten the hostility and reinforce the prejudices of the other side. It is particularly acceptable from a Quaker intermediary because of the known background of humanitarian work. These inquiries must take into account the effectiveness and practicality of any further pleading. What can be realistically accomplished and by what means? What are others doing? Will protests from some sources only make matters worse? What will be the relative value and effectiveness of private versus public appeals? In the situations where an ongoing work of conciliation is involved the final question is: Can the rapport with the authorities built up over the years bear the weight of direct appeals for justice and clemency, which may imply a challenge to those authorities?

In the German cases, the most that could be done was to make private investigations, which did not bring the ongoing work of conciliation into jeopardy. In some cases, to be sure, it may be important to risk severing all relationships and all possibilities of conciliation for the sake of bearing witness and exposing an injustice. In the difficult process by which home committees and staff assess these unknowns and imponderables the judgment of the field representative should be of prime importance.

Confidentiality in the Third-Party Role

An important advantage of the unofficial conciliator as distinguished from the official one is that the person and/or organization can and should operate outside the public limelight and with the least possible need for public recognition. While every move of the official negotiator is likely to be covered by the press, the unofficial person can move back and forth between the parties with little or no public attention, thus avoiding the inevitable rumors and charges of bias.

This advantage of operating quietly must be constantly guarded, however, from the many temptations to seek publicity or the rewards of recognition. Staff and branch offices of the private organization are curious to know what is going on. There is a need to interpret to constituencies and report to potential contributors, all of which may involve leaks to the public press. The Friends Service bodies are in a better position than most to handle these pressures. Over the years, the Quaker constituency has become used to the fact that certain programs are "hush-hush," although the silence violated Quaker ideas of openness and brought some suspicion and resentment. Funds for these efforts have usually come from private donors rather than public appeals, and the need for confidentiality has been understood. A good example of the pressure for revelation was the instance when the Nigerian conciliation effort was alluded to in a Quaker weekly and called forth a rebuke from the conciliator involved.

Public pronouncements of the kind to which church organizations, and especially Quakers, are prone can be an obstacle to the conciliatory role. In the course of any conflict observers operating at a distance are more likely than field workers to push for policy statements advocating one measure or another to reduce or resolve the conflict. When national policy of home countries is involved, the pressure is all the greater to go on public record. That such public pronouncements are likely to have little effect on policy is not a deterrent to the Quakers, who feel they should proclaim the truth almost whether anyone listens or not.

As an example, in December 1968, the Peace and International Relations Committee of London Friends issued a statement on the Nigerian Civil War asking the British government to take the lead in international action to stop the flow of arms to both sides and to work for a cease-fire with international supervision. This kind of plea could hardly fail to reach consensus in a Quaker assembly, given its predisposition to oppose military conflict. It came at a time when negotiation efforts were at a standstill, and even the Quaker negotiators were casting about for some way that big-power pressure could dampen down the conflict. Thus, the statement may have been justified, but in retrospect one may judge it as ineffectual in its aim and potentially hazardous to the Quaker conciliation. It was a futile proposal, because the Soviet Union was not likely to stop its arms supply to Nigeria on the behest of Britain; nor was De Gaulle likely to respond, since one major motivation in helping Biafra was his hostility to a powerful, united, British-sponsored Nigeria. It might have damaged Quaker relations with one side or the other, particularly Lagos. Fortunately for the conciliation effort, it received no notice outside of Quaker organs and was either overlooked or ignored by the parties in conflict.

The tendency of Quakers to make public judgments on political issues regardless of the consequences must be tempered by a realistic assessment of the consequences to ongoing conciliatory activity.

When a published analysis of a conflict is conceived as part of the conciliatory effort, the matter becomes more complicated, since one part of the effort may hamper another. In the German situation, American Quakers published *Journey Through a Wall,* directed at the part of the conflict situation which was aggravated by American public opinion and policy. The book as a whole was carefully designed to meet the sensitivities of the two sides and to play a constructive role, but the hazards of going into print were underlined by the fact that the cover and the map, which escaped screening, created difficulties for the conciliatory enterprise. Even the carefully edited text brought criticism from both sides. In such a situation the pros and cons of publication have to be balanced carefully. In retrospect one wonders whether the impact on opinion in the United States was sufficient to offset the hazards to the field work. The Quaker representatives were able to restore their credibility, but one important conciliatory enterprise, the Conference of Intellectuals, was lost, probably because of this publication.

A similar case in a conflict not included in our study was the Quaker publication *Search for Peace in the Middle East.*[12] This was directed mainly toward the American public, because of the special relations between the United States and

---

12. American Friends Service Committee, *Search for Peace in the Middle East,* rev. ed. (New York: Fawcett, 1970). For an analysis of the impact of this work see Landrum R. Bolling, "Quaker Work in the Middle East Following the June 1967 War" in Berman and Johnson, eds., *Unofficial Diplomats.*

Israel. Again it was a balanced statement worked over carefully through more than fifteen revisions, discussed at each
stage with Arab and Israeli spokesmen, but this did not fore-
stall the storm of protest that came, particularly from Israeli
officials and American Jewish organizations who felt that the
Quakers' "evenhanded" approach was against them. The results had both positive and negative influences on the total
conciliation effort of the Quakers, and it is too early to tell
whether it was wise to publish it or not, for the conflict and
Quaker efforts continue.

No publicity was sought or public pronouncements made in
the case of the mission to India and Pakistan. Publication of
the team's report to help educate the British public was
debated by the service bodies and postponed until after
thorough field testing, by which time the modest public
report had little effect either on the conciliatory activity or
the public. A newspaper account of the visit of the three
Quakers to President Ayub Khan was unfortunate, but did
not reveal any particulars and caused no stir.

For the individual conciliator there is an additional demand
from the principle of confidentiality: he must not only
renounce publicity; he must also deny himself many elements
of ego satisfaction from his efforts. It takes a certain amount
of brashness and self-confidence to intervene in a complicated, dangerous situation. To keep it up, the conciliator
needs some sense of satisfaction. All this can readily built up
to a feeling that the individual is essential to the resolution of
the conflict, and even that he or she has the solution. Such
feelings are fatal to the kind of unofficial effort we have been
describing, where the parties at conflict are national units
and any solution must be ultimately accepted and sanctioned
by officials who have a much greater personal stake in the
whole affair than any conciliator. Moreover, the authorities
on each side are likely to insist that they can deal only
through officially constituted third parties. Thus, any unof-

ficial intervenor must be careful to play a subordinate and ancillary role, helping the official process where possible, but ready to bow out at any time when the help proffered may be hindering the process or usurping more official functions.

Quakers, as human as any, are quite liable to the sin of self-importance. Yet there are some built-in correctives in the religious underpinnings of teamwork in the field and group assessment at home which operated effectively in the three case studies given.

Officially Unrecognized Parties in a Dispute

A special role that the unofficial third party, whether Quaker or non-Quaker, can play is to facilitate communication of official bodies with parties which do not have an officially recognized status in the dispute and yet are an important factor. Questions of legitimacy in different forms may lead to a major block in any discussions or negotiations, since the very move to communicate by a recognized authority would constitute a concession and a preliminary victory for an unrecognized body. Thus, in the Nigerian Civil War, official bodies like the OAU, the UN, The Commonwealth Secretariat, or governments such as the United States and Great Britain could not visit Biafra or make contact with Ojukwu for fear that in doing so they would confer on the breakaway state a legitimacy to which the Nigerian government insisted it was not entitled. The Quakers, not expected by officials or others to operate under such an inhibition, could be useful in carrying messages, reporting, and assessing. This was a factor in the German situation as long as the alleged illegitimacy of the German Democratic Republic was a strong sticking point in any approaches from the West. In the India-Pakistan War of 1965, the Quaker team might have spent more time investigating the mood and desires of the Kashmiris, who were pawns in the national rivalries. The team's assessment, however, was that the Kashmiris in India would be relatively content with whatever their popular leader, Sheikh Abdullah, advocated. Thus, the team proposed that the Indian government free him from prison.

Case studies of Quaker work in Northern Ireland and the Middle East would show even more important examples of this advantage of the unofficial intermediary. Quakers have been able to make contact with entities such as the Provisional Irish Republican Army and the Palestine Liberation Organization, which are not recognized by one or both official parties to the dispute, but are important factors in any possible settlement. In its published report in 1970, the American Friends Service Committee pointed to the fact, now generally recognized, that no peace would be possible in the Middle East without taking into account the demands of the Palestinians. [13]

Theory and Practice

The new and growing discipline of peace research and conflict analysis has been strong on theory and weak on case studies. [14] These three descriptions of third-party unofficial conciliation in practice are a small contribution compared to what is needed to create firm generalizations and theories. Theorists can gain from practice, and Quaker conciliators and organizers stand to gain from more reading of the work of analysts and theoreticians. Indeed, there is a complex relationship for Quakers between abstract thinking and practical action in the field of peace.

13. Ibid., pp. 71-72.
14. For a good review of the new science, see Michael Nicholson, *Conflict Analysis* (London: English Universities Press, 1970).

Individual Quakers have been in the forefront of the new approaches in peace research, starting with the English Quaker Lewis Fry Richardson, who pioneered in applying the statistical approach to arms races and other causes of war from the end of the First World War to his death in 1953.[15] Many research organizations have important Quaker leadership, such as the Canadian Peace Research Association, The British Conflict Research Society, The Peace Science Society (International), the Conference for Peace Research in History, and the Consortium for Peace Research Education and Development (COPRED). The impetus for organizing the International Peace Research Association came out of a conference of peace researchers at Clarens, Switzerland, in 1963, arranged by the Geneva office of Friends Service Council and American Friends Service Committee. The Chair of Peace Studies at Bradford University resulted from a concerted campaign among British Friends. The first person selected for the chair was Adam Curle, who participated in two of the Quaker efforts described above.

With all this involvement by Quakers in theory and research, one might expect to find a close relationship between Quaker programs and peace research. Cooperation exists to a limited degree, and there is some transfer from academic teaching to field experience. There is, however, a certain antithesis. Typically, the Quaker program director has little time for reading and hopes to get all his guidance from observation or listening to the right people. Peace education in local meetings and the Service organizations is keyed to specific campaigns, with interest only in research that develops facts for the campaign. Operating programs are always understaffed and underfinanced, so that if dollars are avail-

---

15. Lewis F. Richardson, *Arms and Insecurity* (London: Stevens and Sons, 1960); and *Statistics of Deadly Quarrels* (London: Stevens and Sons, 1960). Both books were published posthumously.

able for either research or action, they will inevitably go for action. Moreover, in operating programs with many nationalities involved it is difficult to build in a research factor without imposing interviews, questionnaires, or other techniques on suspicious or unwilling subjects and thus disrupting the program. It is significant that certain East German participants in Quaker diplomats conferences were warned not to participate in any role playing or simulation techniques. The one or two times when this had been tried previously had evidently been reported through official channels in the East European network.

Added to the usual gap between the practitioner and the theoretician is a special Quaker element. While one element of the Quaker religious background has, it is true, led many persons into science as the place to search for truth, another aspect, that of bearing witness as the spirit leads, inclines Quakers to be suspicious of a theoretical approach, which depends mainly on logic and reason rather than on immediacy of experience. These two strands of thought coexist in some tension. Fortunately, in the case studies we have reviewed, Quaker organizations were in touch with able advisors on their committees and even recruited as their emissaries persons like Roland Warren and Adam Curle, who were interested in peace research.

Assistance from peace research could, however, be greatly strengthened. Quaker peacemakers should know something of the different forms of conflict, the phases through which a crisis goes, the psychological mechanisms operating to increase antagonisms, with their antidotes, the different techniques of conciliation, such as listening, message carrying, and proposing solutions, and their proper timing. A Quaker conciliator could benefit from a training program such as that pioneered by the International Peace Academy with its seminars on conflict analysis and peacekeeping or the peace training advocated by Paul Wehr, former executive director of

COPRED, the North American federation of peace researchers.[16]

Careful analysis of conflict situations with all the help that historians and peace researchers can give is valuable for any intelligent intervention, but it is even more important as an aid in distinguishing the types of conflict where conciliatory intervention may be a mistake.

Conciliation or Confrontation

Our thesis that unofficial, third-party conciliation can be valuable in certain situations requires us to consider when such activity is appropriate and when it is not. The typical liberal Quaker believes in an innate goodness or divine element in all humans and is predisposed toward solving all problems by better communication, more persuasion, and changing of perspectives. This conviction has been strongly challenged on several scores, but particularly by Marxists and others who say that conciliation is not valid for conflicts in which there is a glaring inequity between the parties. In such conflicts, the challengers say, conciliation will only play into the hands of the party with the greatest power, ensuring the submission of the weaker party. Rhodesia (Zimbabwe) is cited as a prime example where power is predominately on one side and justice on the other. In such cases the challengers to the status quo say that conciliation will only consolidate injustice and what is needed is a raising of consciousness on the part of the weak and oppressed people and confrontation—violent or nonviolent—against the ruling group.

The international programs undertaken by the Quaker organizations in the postwar years all had a common element

16. Paul Wehr, "Some Thoughts on Conflict Education," International Peace Research Association, Fifth General Conference Proceedings, 1974.

of attempting to improve communication across various gaps: cultural, political, ideological. The student seminars were built on the thesis that people of diverse interests brought together in a favorable setting would learn how to create a better climate for peace from each other and from the consultants. This pattern was transposed to government officials, diplomats, and leaders in newly established African and Asian countries. For many years the directory of members of diplomats conferences stated in the introduction: "The two Quaker service organizations, believing that sound human relations are essential to sound international relations, sponsor a series of annual private and unofficial conferences." As an observer of the American Friends Service Committee wrote, the Quakers "have an almost mystical faith in the healing powers of communication between contending groups."[17]

In a polarized situation, when channels of communication between opposing parties broke down, the Quakers sent their international representatives (QIARs) to establish indirect communication by going back and forth from one party to another. The chief function of the third-party intermediary was to improve communication in order to correct misperceptions and explore common advantages in the resolution of conflict.

This Quaker point of view, based on an interpretation of biblical, historical, and religious premises, found strong reinforcement from the newly flourishing sociopsychological study of conflict. Thus, the following quotation from a discussion of "third-party consultation" by a social scientist could well be part of the Quaker manual on conciliation:

> Improving communication is perhaps the most pervasive third-party function, since it is required to clear up initial misunderstanding, to make accurate diagnosis possible, to

17. Elliot Carlson, "Focus on Friends," *Wall Street Journal*, 11 vember 1966.

explore alternative means, goals, and areas of commonality and so on. Thus it is essential at all stages of the process, and is basic to the success of other functions.[18]

A number of other social psychologists and international systems scholars could be quoted in a similar vein. John W. Burton, with his plan of controlled communication, emphasizes bringing people together in an atmosphere that enables participants to treat conflict not as a battle to be won, but as a problem to be solved.[19] Many of these same social scientists were used as consultants by the Quakers in their conference programs, so that the congruity is amply verified.

Roland Fisher and other students of human behavior recognized the limitations in the use of third-party communication techniques. Fisher, for example, says that such techniques are less applicable to economic and power conflicts than to ideological or value conflicts, but these same scholars are more intent on expanding communication by various methods than they are on exploring its limits or studying the alternative situation, where the parties communicate and understand well enough, but are still at sword's point.

If I had written this study of conciliation twelve years ago, I would not have worried about the limitations of Quaker efforts to improve communication and whether such efforts had been appropriately applied in the three cases studied. In the late sixties, however, a sharp and dramatic challenge to the inequities of the status quo reverberated around the world like thunderclaps in the mountains. Students took

18. Ronald J. Fisher, "Third-Party Consultation: A Method for the Study and Resolution of Conflicts," *Journal of Conflict Resolution* 16, no. 1 (March 1972): 85.

19. John W. Burton, *Conflict and Communication: The Use of Controlled Communication in International Relations* (London: Macmillan, 1969).

over university buildings in Tokyo, Paris, Berkeley, and Addis Ababa. Underprivileged minorities demonstrated, and riots ensued from Memphis, Tennessee, to Derry, Northern Ireland. In the miniworld of conflict analysis there occurred the dramatic confrontation between researchers of different schools at the Conference of the Peace Research Society, International, in 1968, and the International Peace Research Association in 1969.

The challenge to peace researchers came from several sources and on several grounds. The theorists of deterrence strategies were accused of preoccupation with the super-power conflicts of the 1950s and early 1960s in which the actors were nation-states, games theories were relevant, and peace was a superordinate goal of all parties, since doomsday was the likely result of war. The social-psychological researchers were attacked for assuming that conflicts arose from differences in attitudes and behavior and all that was needed was to change the perception of goals so that compatibilities could be seen and more basic difficulties resolved. The most disturbing accusation was that the whole apparatus of peace research was supported by governments of nation-states and was thus inevitably tied in to support of the status quo for the benefit of elites while every year inequities within and between nations grew worse.

The position was ably summarized by the Nordic scholar Herman Schmid in his essay on "Peace Research and Politics."[20] While acknowledging that the emphasis of peace research in the fifties was justifiably conditioned by the necessities of the cold war, he pointed out that many conflicts are a matter of objective structure rather than attitudes or behavior and hence are not resolved by changing attitudes. In these situations conciliatory efforts to harmonize attitudes and bring conformity of behavior through a different per-

20. *Journal of Peace Research*, no. 3 (1968), pp. 217–32.

ception of goals may lead to peace, said Schmid, but it may be the peace of the master-slave relation. In situations where there is asymmetry of power between the parties and gross inequity in terms of humanistic values, conciliation or integration does not solve the conflict, but only reinforces the unjust situation. Such basic conflict can only be solved by structural change. For this, says Schmid, polarization is necessary, confrontation inevitable. He thus proposed a new emphasis in research.

> It [peace research] should formulate its problems not in terms meaningful to international and supranational institutions, but in terms meaningful to suppressed and exploited groups and nations. It should explain not how manifest conflicts are brought under control, but how latent conflicts are manifested. It should explain not how integration is brought about but how conflicts are polarized to a degree where the present international system is seriously challenged or even broken down.[21]

Even more pointed are the words of Andrew Mack:

> The so-called "third-party approach" to conflict resolution was rooted in the belief that there were common or transcendent interests which the protagonists shared but did not perceive as a result of the good/bad stereotypes which are created in intense conflicts. Conciliation, mediation, "controlled communication" were all approaches designed to make these interests manifest. The task of the mediator was to assist the parties to discover the common or transcendent interests *for themselves*. However, suppose one didn't assume that there were these common interests. If, as in the case of South Africa, for example, it was assumed that interests and goals of blacks and whites were irreconcilably opposed, then the third-

21. Ibid., p. 219.

party role becomes redundant, may confuse the issues at stake, and could positively obstruct the movement of liberation from white rule.[22]

The same kind of challenge to Quaker conciliation efforts came at the same time from within the Quaker ranks. In fact, the danger of conciliation lending itself to oppression has haunted Quaker consciences many times in history. During the fifties the Friends Service bodies were aware of the injustices and inequities between classes within the affluent societies and between the Western world and the Third World, but they were preoccupied with the dangers of East-West conflict, and they shared the general optimism that betterment could be achieved by improving domestic and foreign policy within the given framework. They were aware of the use of foreign aid to support the donor's military and strategic aims, but kept lobbying vigorously in the hope that the aid would be more geared to the real needs of the underdeveloped world.

The Suez Crisis of 1956 gave support for this kind of optimism on the part of British Quakers; old-style British aggression seemed to give way before opposing public opinion in Britain. Vietnam, on the other hand, produced a rude awakening for American Quakers. The American Friends Service Committee had warned in 1954 of the danger that the United States would back into an imperialist war by taking the place of the French in Indochina, but the inevitability of this trend was not appreciated until the reality was full upon us. It was then that the whole operation of the military-industrial-university complex became evident.

Following time-honored patterns, the AFSC set to work to relieve suffering in Vietnam, trying to work on both sides, but at first only successful in the South. The collective conscience was sorely tested when a regional office of the AFSC chal-

22. In *Conflict Research Society Bulletin*, April 1973, p. 2.

lenged the medical-prosthetic work in South Vietnam as necessarily connected to the American military effort and thus in some ways implicated in the cruel "pacification" which was going on. The humanitarian, moral appeal of fitting artificial limbs for people torn apart by a war in which the United States was much involved was so intrinsic to the Quaker way of thinking that the resolution of the argument was never really in doubt. As one staff member put it: "Our business as Quakers and as a committee is to see what love can do, and we have believed that as long as we were free to work in our own way no situation is so overlaid with evil that love is rendered powerless."[23]

After thorough consideration, the AFSC board of directors decided to continue the program on the ground that one should help where one can, even if only on one side. The protest moved the AFSC to make its witness for peace clearer in three ways: by publicly proclaiming at the medical center in Quang Ngai Province that services were provided to all alike, regardless of their political position; by redoubling efforts to get Quaker medical aid into North Vietnam and into the territory of the National Liberation Front; and by increasing efforts to oppose United States participation in the war. All three of these measures were carried out, and eventually all agreed on the wisdom of a course that contained compromises but held both to the ministry of reconciliation to wartime sufferers and the witness for justice.

After 1965 more and more Quaker voices were raised generally against the violence of those social structures that involved oppression while affording the semblance of peace. In an address to the Fourth World Conference of Friends in 1967, Roland Warren said, "The role of the peaceable mediator, seeking out areas of agreement, seeking to ease tensions,

23. Stephen Cary, "Memorandum to Regional Offices," 10 November 1967, AFSC Archives.

seeking for possible steps forward is a comfortable one for Quakers." At this point he no doubt had in mind the role he had himself played in the conflict between the two Germanies. But then, he asked, "Can Friends avoid taking sides?"[24] and he pointed to the structural violence characterizing the three social evils: unequal distribution of wealth, racial and religious discrimination, and war. These require, he said, a different kind of approach. In addition to the individual testimony of living according to God's will ourselves,

> we can look for the root of social evil in a network of social institutions which involves us all and which leaves little room for effective individual choice in the total situation. If the individual is to be able to change we must concern ourselves with changing the social institutions which form him and limit him.[25]

The most cutting charge of the radical school of peace research is that the traditional school is identified by position, class, culture, and ideology with the dominant, status-quo-oriented elites of the West, and therefore the traditional claim of objectivity is suspect. The Quaker establishment could be similarly criticized as middle class and elitist, a fact only partly corrected by the wisdom of Quaker leaders in the past and present who have recognized the limitation and tried to overcome it. A. J. Muste, a hero of pacifism and Quakerism, made a strong plea to emphasize justice before peace when he said, "In a world built on violence, one must be a revolutionary before one can be a pacifist."[26]

24. "The Spiritual Basis of our Outreach," in *Report of the Fourth World Conference of Friends* (Birmingham, England: Friends World Committee for Consultation, 1967), pp. 89–90.

25. Ibid., p. 85.

26. Nat Hentoff, ed., *Essays of A. J. Muste* (Indianapolis: The Bobbs-Merrill Co., 1967), pp. 179–85.

What then is the answer to this challenge, coming as it does both from peace researchers and prophetic Quaker voices?

The first answer is to accept the fact that there are circumstances when confrontation may be more appropriate than conciliation, circumstances when conciliation, defined as harmonizing opposing perspectives, may be entirely inappropriate for goals of human betterment. The two indeed serve quite different purposes: confrontation strives to increase the awareness of latent or patent injustices; conciliation aims to compromise conflicting human goals in some median position that is bound to contain elements of injustice for one side or both. Any given situation may call for agitation and conciliation in different proportions and at different times. The third-party intervenor has to be in touch with the major contending forces at all times, alert to the actualities, and pressing conciliation when appropriate and possible.

Quaker efforts have also been directed toward confrontation, since the first days when Quakers were themselves contesting the adverse rulings of church and state. Nonviolent methods are necessary, the Quakers would claim, to maximize human compassion in the methods used and be surer of achieving the compassionate goals desired. Both experience and research along these lines has taken place in the last ten years. On the experience side community relations programs of the American Friends Service Committee, pressing for empowerment of the powerless, could be cited, as well as nonviolent direct action programs of A Quaker Action Group and, its successor, the Movement for a New Society.[27] In research the Haverford College Center for Nonviolent Conflict Resolution, unfortunately short lived, was designed to link peace action and peace research in the practice of non-

---

27. George Lakey, a spokesman for this movement, presents a rationale for nonviolent revolution in *Strategy For a Living Revolution* (San Francisco: W. H. Freeman, 1973).

violence in conflict situations. Since we are dealing in this work with conciliation, it is beyond our scope to explore these efforts further, and we turn to see whether conflict analysis can help in identifying the nature of a particular conflict.

At this point the challengers and the challenged, the practitioners and the researchers are hard put to find the clear concepts or objective judgments that show which conflicts should be approached with conciliation and which ones should be allowed by the conciliator to run a course of confrontation. The several attempts made so far to develop a classification of conflicts are too general and too vague to provide easy pigeonholes for concrete situations. Galtung's notion of "structural violence," the inequity of lack of fulfillment of human potential that is built into societal patterns, while difficult to apply, is a revealing formulation.[28] The distinction between conflicts essentially or preponderantly arising from misperception and conflicts based on real differences of interest is another imprecise, but useful, mode of thinking. A number of authors have made the distinction between symmetric conflicts where political, economic, military power of the parties is relatively equal and asymmetric conflicts where it is not. One subtype of asymmetric conflict is the situation of oppression of one group by a dominant power. Thus, the methods of conciliation would be pertinent in conflicts where structural violence is not a major factor, where misperception is an important phenomenon, where the parties are in a relatively symmetric relation of power to each other.

A valuable discussion is that of Adam Curle in *Making Peace.* He shows the factors—balanced and unbalanced power,

28. Johan Galtung, "Violence, Peace and Peace Research," *Journal of Peace Research*, no. 3 (1969), pp. 167–92; and "A Structural Theory of Imperialism," in *Journal of Peace Research*, no. 2 (1971), pp. 81–177.

degree of awareness of latent conflicts, goals of human fulfillment—which must be weighed in any situation. In the unbalanced situation, where there is preponderance of power in the hands of "top-dogs," there is no room for conciliation, says Curle, until through education, raising of awareness, and a series of confrontations, the "underdogs" are in a position of greater equality. At that time, conciliation and bargaining may be productive and necessary. Just when this balance of power is reached is of course extremely difficult to decide, nor is it the role of a third party to judge the matter, but rather to be available and sufficiently in touch to be called in by one or both parties when needed.

It will be helpful in the future if peace research can develop indices of injustice or maldistribution similar in form to the gross national product, but better designed to reveal how distribution relates to basic human needs. The World Indicator Project of the Oslo Peace Research Institute is hoping to achieve this. This is just one of the many possible projects in what Kenneth Boulding calls "justice research," a field whose complexity and vastness he outlines:

> The time is now surely ripe for a similar [to peace research] major effort in justice research. Preaching about justice and exhorting about justice, again may produce a demand but will not produce a supply; and only much greater understanding of the real processes of society which either increase or diminish those elements in society relevant to justice is likely to produce a supply in response to the demand for it.[29]

No taxonomy of conflict,[30] however sophisticated, will

---

29. Kenneth Boulding, *Bulletin of Peace Proposals*, no. 1 (1974), p. 68.

30. See Anatol Rapoport, "A Taxonomy of Conflict," in *Conflict in Man-Made Environment* (Baltimore: Penguin, 1974), chap. 16.

exactly reveal a particular situation, and the dilemmas will have to be studied in the concrete each time. With this background let us look at the three particular case studies to judge whether conciliation was appropriate.

In the case of the two Germanies, the goal of the Federal Republic was twofold: the nationalist-patriotic goal of unifying a divided people, and the libertarian goal of freeing the East Germans from what they conceived as a political-economic tyranny. The goal of the leaders of the German Democratic Republic was to retain and develop a Socialist system of production and distribution against what they conceived as the subversive lure of capitalist productivity and affluence across the border. It is debatable whether this East German goal was shared by the majority of the people or imposed by the Soviet Union for its own strategic purposes. Our analysis was that the goal was probably imposed at first but came to be accepted by the majority of East Germans after the Wall of 1961 cut off the options and after increased prosperity brought more acceptance of the Socialist order.

Charges of structural violence were leveled by each system against the other, the Socialist claiming that the capitalist system kept the poorer classes down, and the capitalists claiming that the Socialist system kept its citizens in bondage. Each side claimed basic interests as the reason for their struggle. Between the two systems in conflict, however, there was a symmetry of power and a superordinate goal of avoiding catastrophic war between the superpowers to which they were attached. Therefore, the conciliation effort was devoted first to reinforcing the reality perception of certain West German leaders that a united Germany was impossible without grave risk of war, and then interpreting back and forth across the Wall the reasons for the hostile claims and charges that arose during the precarious moves toward détente.

Many on the Western side throughout the twelve-year period said that the humanistic goal of "liberating" East Germans should not be abandoned by any deals with what they called "the regime" in East Germany, even if such "liberation" were not possible in the near future. This is an example of the subjectivity of goal analysis in any situation which makes categorical judgements difficult. The Quaker representatives did not accept this analysis, affirming on the contrary that the East German government was constantly gaining in "internal recognition" and the people would benefit more from recognition by the West than from continued ostracism.

The case study of India and Pakistan reveals two examples, one of unbalanced power where confrontation was necessary, one of balanced power. The background study of the colonial situation gives the first example, the 1965 war the second.

The efforts of the India Conciliation Group shows one response to a situation of unbalanced power or asymmetry. The more perceptive Quaker leaders saw clearly the basic injustice of the British colonial system in India. They realized that confrontation was necessary, and they espoused the Gandhian movement as one especially congruent with Quaker belief in nonviolence. Despite their name, the India Conciliation Group was assisting at first in confrontation. The effort was not aimed to blunt the thrust of the revolution for independence, which was bound to gain momentum without help or hindrance from outsiders, but rather to smooth the way for it by interpreting the strength and characteristics of the mass movement to the British people and government. When the movement was in a position to enter into a bargaining relation with a weakened British government, the Conciliation Group was then available to carry messages across official barriers of noncommunication.

The India Conciliation Group directed its major efforts to the conflict between the Indian people, as represented by the

Congress Party, and the British rule. Only in a minor way did it undertake conciliation between the Congress Party and the Muslim League, bodies which came into increasing conflict during the independence movement, leading to partition, the Kashmir War of 1948, and the War of 1965.

In the 1965 India-Pakistan War over Kashmir there were claims of injustice from each side. Pakistan, particularly, espoused the welfare of the inhabitants of the province who, they claimed, were oppressed by the Indian government. The Quaker team counted these issues as less important than the conflict of national goals: Pakistan needed Kashmir as part of its Muslim-state concept; Indian leaders thought that any concession of this kind would be a danger to the heterogeneous composition of the secular state The goals were thus completely incompatible, and what was called for was a cost accounting to show how much more disastrous all-out war would be to both goals. By the time the Quakers arrived on the scene, the leaders of both countries, with the help of the United Nations and the Soviets at Tashkent, had come to the conclusion that continued war was the worst solution. The job then was to help each side realize that this indeed was the view of the other, and that belligerent voices of extremists were being countered by responsible leaders. This kind of interpreting from one side to the other seemed highly appropriate for the Quaker team.

The Civil War in Pakistan in 1971, though not part of our study, provides another instructive example. When the Quakers thought to send a mission to the West and East Wings, as a follow-up to the earlier mission, Adam Curle and others were not enthusiastic. They felt that the situation was one of such rank oppression, with 70 million Bengali's being massacred and brutalized by 150,000 soldiers of the West, that any Quaker visitation would be in the position of persuading the Pakistani army to be less violent and the Bengali's to be more docile in order to restore a status quo that had created a sense of injustice and desperation over many years. The Quakers sent no conciliatory mission.

The conflict between Nigeria and Biafra was considered by many an outright case of oppression of a minority, the Ibos, by a majority, the Northern Hausa-Fulani. There was a strong tendency in the European and American worlds to espouse the cause of Biafra. Biafran leaders made the most of this. The Quaker analysis, helped by observers on the scene, found this black-white picture much too simplified. While sympathizing with the plight of the millions of Ibo refugees in Biafra, the Quakers were not at all sure that independence was a possible solution for them. They thought that secession would open up a Pandora's box of divisiveness and anarchy, within Nigeria itself and perhaps throughout the new nations of Africa. Moreover, it was questionable whether the large minorities within Biafra would find their goals of self-fulfillment in an Ibo-dominated Biafra. Thus, the Quakers sought to explore a basis of agreement between the parties that would ensure security for the Ibos within a federated state. The goal of the Federal Military Government to retain the unity of Nigeria was clear enough; their goal of bringing the Ibos back into the union with equal status and security, while stated as an official policy, was not so clear to the Biafrans or to observers. The Ojukwu forces on the other side emphasized two goals, security of Biafran peoples and independence. The first goal was clearly the more important, since independence was usually argued only as a way to security. The job of the conciliator was then to show to the Ibos that their stereotype of the Lagos government as dominated by northerners bent on genocide was wrong and to help General Gowon in his task of moderating the zeal of his generals and hard-line politicians, who at times gave some semblance of truth to the charge of genocide.

In the three main cases here presented our analysis shows the conciliatory appraoch to be appropriate. They were not clear cases of unbalanced or asymmetric power coupled with gross injustice, in which one party needed to develop a greater parity before bargaining could take place. While vital interests were involved in each case, the negative payoffs from continued conflict were far greater than the possible positive results. In the one case of revolutionary process in India the effort at conciliation in which Quakers led was aimed at assisting the confrontation that was taking place, not displacing it.

Before leaving the subject, I must record a caution deriving from recent experience. Confrontation, especially if it is violent, carries with it grave dangers of leading to a situation of such chaotic, uncontrolled violence that any aim of equalizing the potentials of different groups of human beings is lost in the general suffering afflicting all, the oppressed more than any. In Northern Ireland, I would say, from my own experience, that the laudable 1968 demonstrations for human rights and political equality for the Catholic minority unfortunately loosed the hounds of violence from private and official armies and opened up the ancient wounds of strife between incompatible national allegiances. Thus, the status quo remains largely in effect, although the unified control of a Unionist (Protestant) elite has been fractured and replaced by direct rule from Westminster. There seems no practical alternative in sight after ten years during which the amenities of life have been eroded, particularly for the poorest people, and all are condemned to live in a climate of fear, hatred, and strife. In such a plight, where a parity of despair has been achieved on all sides, the third-party conciliator may help by pointing to alternatives more acceptable than the complete ruin that might come from outright civil war, but the problem of armed minorities who stick to their "no compromise, this is our last chance" position remains.

Evaluation

Evaluation of the effectiveness of one element—Quaker efforts—in a complicated series of historical processes is difficult if not impossible. It is like asking for the effectiveness of one thread in a mainsail halyard of many filaments. Quakers tend to avoid the issue of objective measurement by affirming that a person is led to an action because of its intrinsic value; the concerned person does what he does because it is right, whether his work is crowned with external success or not. The emphasis is on intention behind the act and the means used rather than on a calculation of likely consequences. To those who would say that this is substituting subjective evaluation for objective or scientific evaluation, the Quakers would answer that the judgment comes from a higher source, a divine reference above human objectivities and subjectivities.

Thus, the Quaker mission to the czar at the time of the Crimean War, though it did not stop the war, was not considered futile by Friends. The biographer of Joseph Sturge says, "Humanity does not progress to greater perfection merely or chiefly by achieved success, but rather by moral effort put forth and repeated again and again in the midst of apparent failure."[31]

This appeal from current failure to eternal justification has a ring of fundamental truth, but it may also contain an element of irresponsibility. At times Quakers need to be reminded that success in stopping wars and improving the human condition is important, and it is not enough to say, "We were led to do this, no matter what the result." Such an attitude may become an excuse for muddled thinking, poor planning, sketchy performance, and wasted resources.

31. Stephen Hobhouse, *Joseph Sturge: His Life and Work* (London: J. M. Dent, 1919), p. 146.

The three cases studied show a serious attempt to play a useful role in three highly complex situations, using a mixture of resources and techniques. In looking back one can see flaws and inadequacies but, on the whole, a valuable effort. In general, a greater in-put from the intellectual disciplines of conflict analysis would have helped. There is no basic incompatibility between expressing Quaker faith through conciliation and using scientific procedure and methods to do the job better, but there are practical problems and a difference of emphasis.

At the end of each case study we have tried to evaluate the methods used and ask the question of results obtained. In the case of the two Germanies, an emerging détente was influenced by a host of factors. The process would have gone on without any Quaker intervention. All one can say is that the Quakers assisted at certain key points. In the case of India and Pakistan just after the war over Kashmir, the heads of each government used the Quakers to communicate with each other opinions and intentions that could not be publicly stated, particularly with a view to testing the strength of moderate forces working to continue the truce. In the Nigerian war, the Quaker aim of a negotiated peace was not achieved, but peace by military victory resulted in an amazing degree of magnanimity toward the defeated side. The Quakers may have had a small part in this result, because their efforts were welcomed by certain Nigerian leaders.

The one objective index of effectiveness available was the fact that the persons involved retained continuing access to top leadership over a considerable period of time rather than being sent away as importunate meddlers. It is perhaps safe to conclude from this that the Quakers were carrying on an operation which others found useful and not just fooling themselves. Heinrich Albertz, former deputy mayor of Berlin, testified to this. Continued usefulness to the parties in conflict is still not an adequate gauge of influence and a long way from any measurement of "success." So we must end with a restatement of the Quaker faith that a concern, carried out in the right spirit and with a mustering of all resources available, mental and physical, has its justification in the light of eternity; whether it commands respect in the councils of man is important, but secondary.

Index

DATE DUE